Florida Cow Hunter's Handbook
A Glossary of Terms and Phrases

Howard S Jones, Jr

Copyright © 2013 Howard S Jones, Jr
All rights reserved.
ISBN: 0982483023
ISBN 13: 9780982483022

Thanks to the Crackers of Florida,

including Partner, Hubert, Junior, Finis, Solon, Frank, Gary, Steve, Ralph, Fred, Bill, Wessel, Jerome, Gator, Martin, Clarence, Baby, Rudy, Jack, Russell and particularly Dr. Frank Handley, all those who worked on the cattle ranches in the heart of Florida; and others too numerous to mention for their help in my education and imagination, and especially to my ever-present companion, Embellishment.

A Cracker glossary will include many Southern ideas, but some are unique to Cracker cowboys.

In this collection I in no way intend to ridicule any of my family or friends.

Someone may think I am teasing, mocking or criticizing Cracker culture.

No. On the contrary, I use some of these terms daily.

They are a part of my heritage and fill the fond memories living in the back hallways of my mind.

For those who might be offended: "Lighten up, folks."

By Way of a Half-hearted Apology
To the people I have cited both living and dead:
I have borrowed your words, but they are being read.
And if I have misquoted, or mis-spelt a name:
Accept my regrets, my errors—my shame.

ELIAKIM KATZ

Contents

Introduction   Beginnings ix

Part One   What is A Florida Cracker? 1

Part Two   The Crackers I Know 7

Part Three   Cracker Terms, Phrases And
               Definitions 11

Acknowledgements

It would be wise to acknowledge my appreciation to my tireless, obsessive wife, Hunter, for her encouragement and proofreading skills and to my stepbrother, Frank W. Williamson, Jr. (known herein as Sonny), for his insights. Without their encouragement I probably would have been content to write the *Handbook* only for my family and close friends. Many of the stories, explanations, terms and phrases are found in my other books, *The Green Jeep, Fireside Tales as Told by Florida Cracker Cowboys* and (soon to be published) *All Creatures Mean and Tough.* I must also acknowledge Kentucky's Dr. Carl Hurley, whom I never met though he often visited Okeechobee, humorous Southern speakers, Jeanne Robertson, Robert Henry, and Joe Griffith for their insights and styles of humor. I knew Robert Henry in the early days in Auburn, AL, but I didn't realize his influence on the national humor scene at the time. The others don't know me from Adam's house cat but we are kindred spirits. Unknowingly, they have greatly influenced my already twisted sense of humor.

> *"Kissimmee Basin area ...that's one of the areas of Florida that you can still go to and, if you look for it, it's there, you can see Florida just like it was seventy-five, a hundred, or more years ago."*
>
> A LAND REMEMBERED, PATRICK SMITH

Introduction

MY CRACKER life began at the old Caloosa Ranch in Okeechobee, Florida, in 1960. Ten years later, as a practicing veterinarian, I was immersed in the Cracker culture for over twenty-five years. I not only learned a new vocabulary from the ranches there, but brought some additions of my own.

Some of these *Glossary* entries might be confusing to those unfamiliar with the culture. While various words or phrases were locally originated, mostly from Cracker cow hunters, others came from other areas of the country, especially the South.

In order to clarify these terms, I must begin with some kind of definition, for it is in their attitudes, eccentricities and language that Florida Crackers are distinguished. One cannot appreciate the terms and sayings until one understands the culture that spawns them. Therefore, I begin at the beginning with my definition of Cracker.

PART ONE

What is A Florida Cracker?

THE IMMEDIATE problem in defining the Florida Cracker is that the term means different things in different regions of the country. It is a pejorative term in some areas, while in Florida's cow country it's a badge of distinction. One approach toward a definition is by Dana Ste. Claire, the former curator of an exhibit, *The Cracker Culture in Florida History* at the Daytona Beach Museum of Arts. Ste. Claire proposed in an article printed in the September issue of the *Halifax Magazine* (1997) that there are three main theories of the origin of the term Crackers, though he admits that none of them is a precise definition. He wrote, "Not every pioneer in Florida could justifiably be called a Cracker. Pioneers move into a new territory and develop it. They bring in churches, schools, railroads and various other trappings of civilization. Crackers might settle into a new territory, but they are too self-reliant and independent to need everything that development brings." My question is what happens when the pioneer does adopt the character traits of the Florida cracker? Can they then be called Cracker?

To my way of thinking, the explanation, "*They are too self-reliant and independent to need everything that development brings,*" is not to be ignored. That particular expression has been addressed many years ago by descriptions of pioneers on the wild frontier when Kentucky was the desolate fringe wilderness of the colonies. I must admit a little bias here in that, in contrast to Ste. Claire, I do think the pioneer mentality is a good basis for the definition of Cracker—certainly not to be completely excluded from consideration.

In developing his theories of the origin of Crackers, Ste. Claire firstly concludes that one theory is Celtic in origin, citing a Shakespearian reference to Cracker, meaning braggart or loudmouth, in reference to King John. Secondly, he lists another theory which relates to the grinding or cracking of corn for grits or meal. It is somewhat pejorative in that respect, meaning that it refers to poor, rural southerners of South Georgia and Florida, though it wasn't always used in that context. The third theory is probably the most popular and refers to the crack! of whips used in working cattle in deep woods and rough country. Most people seem to think this is the true origin of the term.

Other references state that *Florida Cracker* is synonymous with Florida cowboys or cow hunters. For example, in 1998, Martin Metzer of the Miami Herald wrote:

What is A Florida Cracker?

Hands gnarled, skin leathered by year-round sun and a few too many plugs of chewing tobacco, these rough-hewn outdoorsmen resonate in harmony with Florida's natural rhythms. They know the tranquility of solitude in a state growing by nearly a thousand people a day. They savor the exhausted delight, the sore satisfaction yielded by rugged physical labor.

They are unpretentious, colorful, and sometimes earthy to a fault. They are a link to a little-known past, a warning of what Florida could forfeit as it gallops headlong into the future.

The few outsiders who know of their presence call them cowboys. They call themselves Florida cow hunters, or, with pride, Crackers.

Preface by Martin Metzer,
in Cracker-Florida's Enduring Cowboys by Jon Kral

This being said, I think I may have found another basis for the term Cracker–or at least some of it. I knew but didn't know why I knew it. The roots of Florida Crackers may lie in a common origin with western frontiersmen. As a boy reared in Kentucky I well knew people of similar character and attitudes as Florida Crackers. This may be the reason I find it so easy to adapt to them.

Two authors come to mind regarding the similarities. From a book entitled *Westward Ho!* James Kirke Paulding wrote about Kentuckians, when the state was considered the western frontier:

> The result of their peculiar situation, habits, and modes of thinking has been a race of men uniting in a fearlessness of danger, a hardy spirit of enterprise, a power of supporting fatigues and privations, and an independence of thought which perhaps were never associated with the pursuits and acquirements of civilized life in any other country than the United States.

In a quote of Fredrick Jackson Turner, in *Frontier Mind: A Cultural Analysis of the Kentucky Frontiersman*, by Arthur Moore, another possible beginning of the Cracker mind-set is found:

> Reckless, exuberant, lawless, violent, brave, the frontiersman of Kentucky acted the part of the utterly free agent and by word or gesture expressed a lively contempt for artificial ethical prescriptions. Admittedly, the cords, which bind the individual to a given cultural frame, may be snapped by prolonged danger and isolation, but such a consequence is by no means inevitable, at least not to an extreme degree...

> Most of those who trudged over the Wilderness Road, while not officially rebellious against society, probably intended to achieve in the Garden of Kentucky a way of life conspicuously free of impediments familiar to the East. Such an exception of unalloyed freedom, intensified by and involved in myth, inevitably precipitated irresponsible acts ranging from gross to foolish and eventuated in an unusual state of mind – *The Frontier Mind.*

What is A Florida Cracker?

Turner continues

The result is that to the frontier the American Intellect owes its striking characteristics. That coarseness and strength combined with acuteness and inquisitiveness: that practical, inventive turn of mind, quick to find expedients; that masterful grasp of material things, lacking in the artistic but powerful to effect great ends; that restless, nervous energy; that dominant individualism, working for good or for evil, and withal that buoyancy and exuberance which comes from freedom—these are traits of the frontier.

Elizabeth Gilbert, in *The Last American Man*, has also written of this subject:

Think of the many articles one can find every year in the *Wall Street Journal* describing some entrepreneur or businessman as being a pioneer or a maverick or a cowboy. Think of the many times these ambitious modern men are described as staking their claim or boldly pushing themselves beyond the frontier or even riding into the sunset. We still use this nineteenth-century lexicon to describe our boldest pioneers; they are talented computer programmers, biogenetic researchers, politicians, or media moguls making a big splash in a fast modern economy.

In this context, the word, pioneer, is romantically trite. But notice the similarities of the Ste. Claire phrase, "They (i.e., Crackers) are too self-reliant and independent to need everything that development brings," when compared to Pauling's "a race of men uniting in a fearlessness of danger, a hardy spirit of enterprise, a power of supporting fatigues and privations, and an independence of thought which perhaps were never associated with the pursuits and acquirements of civilized life." and Turner's "reckless, exuberant, lawless, violent, brave, the frontiersman... acted the part of the utterly free agent and by word or gesture expressed a lively contempt for artificial ethical prescriptions."

I see a link between the Western pioneers and Florida Crackers: "...a way of life conspicuously free of impediments familiar to the East. Such an exception of unalloyed freedom intensified by and involved in myth, inevitably precipitated irresponsible acts ranging from gross to foolish and eventuated in an unusual state of mind." –*The Frontier Mind* (Turner).

At first, I was more than slightly impressed that there seemed to be a connection between pioneer Kentuckians and Florida Crackers–at least by basic definitions. But, there is another subjective factor in the attempt to define Crackers. It depends on one's experiences and the locality. Here again, bias enters my characterizations. Being only exposed to Cracker culture in the Florida counties of Okeechobee, Glades, Hardee, Desoto, Sarasota, Polk, St Lucie and Highlands, I openly admit my personal experiences are limited to the hard-working ranchers and cowboys of these areas.

Nonetheless, here go some of my thoughts:

PART TWO

The Crackers I Know

IN THE FINAL analysis, subjective as it is, the only way I can define them is to recall the ones I know. The Florida Cracker cowboys (or cow hunters) familiar to me are mostly uninterested in the latest fads. They don't particularly care what their dog, horse, saddle, whip, hat, boots, britches, truck or home looks like. They don't go in for really fancy things; they'll choose things that work, rather than look good.

Many will carry three-bladed pocketknives made from a softer metal that sharpen better than modern steel ones. The blades are honed so often and wear down a bit every time that they will trap a dime or two between the closed blades when knife and change are carried in the same pocket.

Working cow pens are built to be efficient, not pretty. The cowboys have to be hard working people and usually smell of honest sweat. Crackers admire folks who tend carefully to their jobs–whether cowboy, woman or veterinarian.

They're God-fearing (or at least moral), don't always go to church, but are loyal and generous. Crackers who know and like you can be called upon for help, literally day or night, when you're in a tight. They tend to be like Scots; if you make one of them mad, you've made his whole family and his friends mad, as well. Like pioneer Westerners: free spirits that *ride for the brand.* They will work from before daylight until the job is finished, sometimes putting in a fourteen- to sixteen- hour day, and repeating this for weeks at a time–of course, followed by wild times in town, at parties, socials or a juke joint.

I've known Crackers to do crazy things, like ride an ostrich or take their wives down to the closed Okeechobee Livestock Market, running them through the ring, bidding on them, commenting on their assets, or climbing to the top of a cabbage palm, demanding, "Cut 'er down boys. I'll ride 'er down to the ground." In this regard, some are like the man I know who went back to riding bulls shortly after one threw and fell on him so hard that his front teeth scraped the zipper of his jeans. If they don't know you, they are a little stand-off-ish, sizing you up. They might be loners, keeping to themselves, making no big deal out of work or isolation.

Most enjoy good Blue Grass and Western music, parties, dancing, roast wild pork and grass-fed beef, swamp cabbage, rice and gravy, guava pies, beans and peas, grits, cat-head biscuits and sweet iced tea. Also, they have been known to consume considerable amounts of whisky during social affairs – shortly before the fights begin.

My Crackers appreciate folks that keep their word, cheap veterinary fees, honest medical doctors and bankers, but they hate a liar. They pay their bills, albeit a little slow at times, and often settle their disagreements before they get out of hand. But some disputes do end in inflammatory words, skinned knuckles and sore lips. I've heard of some who've traded the same horse back and forth several times, each thinking that he made a good deal in the trade.

A gun is a given – mostly considered simply as a tool with accompanying responsibility, but they rarely clean them. An amazing amount of trouble is avoided because everyone is aware that most others also have guns. One told me that he named his rifle, Security System, so he could deduct it from his shop's income taxes.

They have short memories when it comes to past wrongs. Quick to forgive, tolerant and non-prejudicial, they are loyal and gregarious, will kid you in a heartbeat, and love stories (liable to tell tall tales), practical jokes and tricks.

There doesn't seem to be a firm retirement age. Old men are esteemed, and mostly old-fashioned; many still carry pocket watches. They know how to respect people, judging them only by their honesty and abilities regardless of idiosyncrasies, race, age or wealth. The older women are revered, as well.

Their courage extends to helping a fellow who gets in a tight with a raging bull in the cow pens. That quick thinking and spontaneous action has saved many a life–although their dogs might bite you during the rescue. They love their dogs but rarely pet them, though one told me once that the reason he came to me was that I was the only veterinarian who ever talked to his bird dog like he did. (This particular man was otherwise meaner than a snake.) Usually only a glance will reassure the dog of his master's approval. Crackers work hard, love to hunt in the woods, guard your back in the cow pens, take an inordinate amount of risk for little pay, work even when in pain, enjoy life in general, and appreciate a complement.

I agree with Ste. Claire in that getting a precise definition of the encompassing term, Crackers, is like trying to keep ants in a pile, but I have about resolved this issue in my mind that the term is related to the frontiersman or, at least, the pioneer mind-set, adapted to cow hunting in Florida.

You can tell by the amount of words and time I have spent on clarifying this particular category of folks that I think it is important. They are disappearing, being replaced by generations that lack the flare, tradition, spice, fire, flavor and lovability of their cultural heritage and the Cracker mind-set. I hate to see them go from the Florida scene. I hope Crackers always survive somewhere in time and space, just as do the only Celts in the western hemisphere, now living in Nova Scotia.

Now, with context, here are some phrases and words I've heard Florida Cracker cowboys use:

PART THREE

Cracker Terms, Phrases And Definitions

A

Act ugly: indicates that someone, something or some action has turned sour, untoward, or is showing bad conduct. Examples include: "Ol' Bulldog acted ugly whin Doc stuck him in the behind with the needle–he like to have hung a tooth in his hand." "Boy, sit up and quit actin' ugly." "Everthin' wuz goin' fine til the black bull started actin' ugly. It was downhill frum then on. He really showed hisself." And, "I wuz almost home whin the motor started actin' ugly." (Also see "Showed his country behind," "Ain't it purty", etc.)

Adam's house cat: used to denote unfamiliarity or lack of recognition. It is a rather common phrase in some areas. For example, "I went in there to buy a pocket-knife on credit and the salesman didn't know me from Adam's house cat."

After all... if ya own a dog you don't hav ta bark: comes from England, where a principle was expressed in a backdoor fashion. It is used to illustrate that the something or someone had things under control, the issue had been settled beforehand, or there was no need to spend any effort on solving a particular problem or situation. For example, "A man named Webster has already prepared a comprehensive list of word definitions in a Dictionary, so why bother? After all... if you own a dog, you don't have to bark." Right? (Biba, my stepsister, responded to my mother's chicken and dumplings in this way. And this is why I never needed to develop roping skill with all the good cowboys around me.)

I had the opportunity to teach my Michigander friend Southern dialect. I started with something simple. I told him, "Try to pronounce scissors the way they do in Sale-mha (Selma), Alah-bamah (Alabama). Try this... say, 'shu-suss'." After several tries he couldn't do it, probably because we were laughing so hard. After we regained our composure, I said, "How would y'all say it up north wher' you cum frum?" He loudly said, in crisp words, "Gimme sumthin' to cut with."

I tried the phrase above, "After all, if you own ah dog ya don't hav tah bark." It didn't register well because he wanted to use the phrase in the same context but it came out, "Well, after all you don't have to slap the dog if you're going to the barn anyway..." (I'm still working with him but I think I'm whippin' a dead horse.)

Ah Buck-an-June place: a descriptive phrase that indicates a café or small restaurant that is laid back, informal or quaint. "Do I hav' ta put on a clean shirt whin we go there?" "Naw, itsah Buck-an-June place–wear whut you got on." To paraphrase Wes, my nephew, "Some things are difficult to decide whether they are quaint or just eye sores."

Crackers usually don't ask what they should wear. They don't care, except for a buck out (See term) or church. But a story circulated for a time in Highlands County where a fella

Cracker Terms, Phrases And Definitions

had had enough of civilization and stress. He contacted a real estate broker and asked if he could locate some isolated property out West somewhere. He told him, "Look, all I want is about forty acres and plenty of water where I can keep some chickens and few head of cattle."

Several weeks later the broker said he thought he'd found the perfect isolated property. The man went to Wyoming to look it over. Sure enough it was a fine piece of property with a little cabin, plenty of acreage, a good spring and rich pasture. It was about fifty miles from a small town with a passable road. He put down a deposit and returned to Florida to sell out everything and then moved to the splendid isolation. No phone, no TV, no stress, no irritating neighbors or noise...

Things went well for about a year. He'd go to town once a month for supplies and mail and was content. One morning he was sitting on his front porch, drinking coffee and patting his dogs. Way off, he could see an old beat-up truck coming and stirring up a cloud of dust. The truck pulled in the yard, pulled to a stop and the driver got out and said, "Hidy, neighbor."

The man said, "Neighbor? I didn't know I had any neighbors."

The neighbor replied, "Yeah, I'm just thirty miles from you. See that little ridge of mountains over there? My place is just at the base of them... I come to invite you to a party."

"A party? I ain't been around people for nearly a year... I might be interested in a little socializing..."

Neighbor said, "Well, there's gonna be a bar-be-que. There'll be all kinds of fixin's. We're gonna have some dancin' an' a little drinkin'. Now, I hope you don't mind a little drink or two."

"Naw, I don't mind... as long as it don't get rowdy."

Neighbor replied, "Well, you know where ther's dancin' and drinkin', there's a good chance ther'll be some fightin', too. You alrite with that?"

"I might get outta the way... but I don't mind... It might be fun to watch."

Neighbor said, "Alrite. Be there about dark; you cain't miss my place... Head straight for that mountain. I'll have fire out front so you can see tha house. I'll see you Saturday night."

As Neighbor headed for his truck, the man asked him, "Hey... whut should I wear?"

Neighbor turned around and said, "It don't matter... it's just gonna be me and you."

Ahgoodun: a good one. "Sumtimes a fella has to go through two or three women before he finds ahgoodun," is an example of usage. A horse, bull, cow, calf, dog, truck, sermon, lawyer, banker, vet, day-worker, mama, sister, paycheck, lariat, a pair of boots, belt, shirt, new baby or a reliable truck can be ahgoodun.

Ah good suitah clothes: used to indicate the over-conditioning or excessive fatness of a bull. When purchasing bulls many defects in conformation could be covered or hidden by overly fattened bulls (or cows for that matter). This was the situation where I heard the phrase first used. After inspecting a group of bulls presented for sale, a potential buyer turned away and said, "Ah good suitah clothes'll hide many a defect."

My mother used a phrase when she was describing a well-dressed man; she'd say, "Why, he showed up dressed like a Philadelphia lawyer." I met a Philadelphia lawyer at a theater one time. He grinned when I told him what my mother used to say.

Ah handful of quarters: an uncommon but humorous phrase that describes what happens when a divorced young man whose wife and two children come by to give him what is left over from his paycheck. This phrase came about when a newly married young man was talking with an older married man. The newly wed fella said his old girlfriend come by the family business when everyone but him was at lunch and indicated that she was interested in continuing their relationship —even though he was now married. The offer was somewhat of an ego booster for the young fella but the older man gave this sage advice: "Son, I wanna tell ya, if you git hooked up with that gal, the next thing you know yer wife will divorce you and all you'll see is her arm out tha window of her new car as she drives by your trailer out back an' throws out ah handful of quarters once a month… that's all that'll be left out of your paycheck…" (See Split tha blanket.)

Ah termite inna yo-yo: as in, "Man, I'm as confused as ah termite inna yo-yo…" Think about it. A synonym is bumfuzzled.

Ah thank: a dialectically altered response to a statement or question that means, "Yes! That's obvious." This term is used frequently to affirm or to voice an implication. It is also used to understate the obvious or to respond to an understated observation. For example: If one man dryly comments on the fact that his male dog, Brownie, has bred his friend's female nine or twelve times, he might say, "Well, ol' Brownie's sure takin' care of bidness…" His friend might reply, "Ah thank!" Or, if someone made a comment about the obvious, such as, "It looks lik' after his wife leaves him the fifth time, he'd figure out the problum mite be his drinkin'." The proper response could be, "Ah thank!" Also, "That little bulldog just ate up his bruther durin' the fight! I believe they hate each other's guts!" Followed, while looking at the poor defeated dog, by, "Ah thank!!!" My stepbrother Sonny reminded me that the term has also been heard in a different form, "Ya thank?" In this context, it confirms the obvious. It could be used in response to statements like, "I 'spect that cow'd eat your sack lunch!" Since it is obvious in this context, the appropriate reply would be, "Ya thank?"

Ain't it always tha way: People frequently ask me what breed I would recommend for their family. Crackers preferred "business dogs," but also had pets for the kids.

During one such exchange at a social function, a man asked me this question. I asked if they liked indoor or outdoor dogs, frisky or laid back types, that shed or not, how active the kids were, who would take care of the dog and several other things to try to determine what breeds might be best for that family. After a long discussion amidst several couples who were interested in the conversation, it became apparent that this family should probably have a small breed, one that was child-friendly, easy to maintain and loving. The man appeared to be satisfied with the conclusions and, as a parting comment I offered, "Remember, a spayed female makes the best companion and tends to stay home more." Dr. Davis, a sex therapy counselor, spoke up, saying, "Ain't it always tha way?" as she raised her drink in salute. (I am not making this up.)

Speaking of listening in on conversations:

My partner in practice came there as a green young man and developed into a weathered practitioner very quickly. When a veterinarian hires a young partner, he/she is often uncertain about that junior's table-side manner. They have a lot to learn.

I was in the adjoining exam room on one occasion and listened in on a conversation between a client and this new doctor. (As Yogi Berra said, "You can learn a lot by listening.") An elderly couple in their eighties had lost their beloved pet to old age. It was a difficult time in their lives and they said they would never get another pet as she was irreplaceable.

A month later they came back to discuss their decision to get another pet—to fill the void of the deceased beloved one. The conversation went somewhat like this:

"Well, I hear you all are thinking about getting a new puppy."

"Yes, Doctor Young. We thought about getting a small one. We have our eye on a Jack Russell Terrier. What do you think about them?"

A small alarm bell sounded in me. I was curious to see how he would field the question without discouraging this sweet elderly couple. The Jack Russell is a high-octane dog bred to chase and kill rodents. They get bored easily and don't seem to tire. Sort of like the "EverReady bunny. They require daily wide-open exercise for the first 6-9 years, and then they slow down a bit. Definitely not an appropriate pet for these folks.

He replied, "Well, I think you all have made a fine choice. I think the first thing you should do is buy a thousand-acre ranch with about 200 head of cattle. I'd look for one that had about 150 acres of citrus trees, with all the maintenance equipment, then hire five or six full time hands to run it."

They gaped fishy-eyed and speechless at him for a full ten seconds. When they recovered, the husband asked, "Dr. Young? Why in the world would we want to do all that?"

He smiled gently and replied, "Well, if you get a Jack Russell, he's gonna need something to do."

They laughed, "Well, maybe that's too much dog for us." I laughed, too, and relaxed about this new associate. He would do.

Ain't you ah site? Ain't that ah site? Wadn't that ah site? or That'd be a site: Euphemistic Cracker term for the present, past and future tenses of: "Now that is/was/would be interesting." The common use of the phrase was as an exclamation rather than a question. (See next term for the same kind of humor.)

Ain't it purty or Ain't you purty: used to express disgust in response to an action that is just the opposite of pleasing, as a bull running over your tied horse, breaking the reins and terrifying the horse. Someone would say, "Well, ain't that purty... He sure showed hisself, didn' he?" A rusted bolt could elicit this same angry comment, followed by a severe beating with a hammer, "Ain't you purty!" (Bam, Bam, BAM!) Sonny could add an element of sarcasm when I approached in clean jeans and shirt, "Well, ain't you purty!" Another variation sometimes heard in the same vein is, "Ain't you ugly!" or "Well, ain't it ugly!" Same idea. It was used as a suitable substitute for an outburst of angry profanity.

Ain't much of a driver either: This comes from a story in a local headskin (See below) where a Cracker truck driver was minding his own business, having some lunch and dessert. Three nasty-looking motorcycle riders walked in, took a brief glance around and, as if aiming at him sat at the counter flanking him. One helped himself to his iced tea; another pulled his plate over and purposefully gobbled down the meat loaf and mashed potatoes, while the last one reached over, forked his pie, tasted it, then smashed it flat. The Cracker didn't say a word, got up, went to the cashier, paid his bill and left. One motorcycle rider said maliciously to the waitress who was cleaning up the mess, "Ain't much of ah man is he?" She replied, "Ain't much of a driver either… he's just drove his truck over three motorcycles."

Air hungry: a severe depletion of air reserves. For illustration: Mr. Hill, one of our clients, came in the clinic and had several strips of bed sheet material wrapped around three fingers of his right hand.

Of course, I asked, "Mr. Hill, whut in the world happen to yer fingers?" Mr. Hill was a fine individual, but had a severe vision problem. He could see shadows and movement, but that was about all, even with the help of his coke-bottle thick glasses.

He explained, "Well, ya know my pit bulldog, Mama Boots?" Heads nodded. "We got a bunch of chickens around the house and Mama Boots is bad to catch one ever now and then. She caught one of my best hens yesterday. I tried to git it outten her mouth but she wouldn' let go. So I jobbed her head down in a bucket of water 'til she got air hungry and let go the chicken. Whin she come up, I grabbed the chicken an' Boots grabbed me!" What a picture that elicited!

Cracker Terms, Phrases And Definitions

All that's cummin' are here: although the phrase was not ordinarily used by a Cracker, indulge me a bit with a rabbit trail. A young man I know joined the Marines and progressed well in training, due to his physical skills and good attitude toward team work. Though still a little rough around the edges, he was made platoon leader. The first day during assembly he was called to give the attendance report. The proper response is to shout, "All present or accounted for, SIR!" When asked for the response, he panicked a little, saying, "All that's cummin' are here!" (He told me that he knew everyone was accounted for but it didn't come out right.)

The Lt. Col. invited him to meet in his office afterwards. He asked him, "Where in the h - - - did you come up with that?"

The platoon leader told him he didn't mean disrespect, saying, "Sir, I... I wuz nervous..."

The Lt. Col. had him repeat the proper report a few times, smiled and told him, "Don't do that again. That will be all, Corporal." (Yes, Mildred, that's a true story.)

Alleyway: a passageway for the movement of cattle to specified pens. These can be short or long, narrow or wide. The wide alleys are for movement of large herds, but for individuals they should always be narrow enough to prevent cattle from turning around and jamming up the flow of other cattle. They also had to be high enough to prevent cattle from jumping over the sides.

The worst days of my life were spent at pens with wide alleyways. Cattle would start down the four foot wide alleyway toward the chute, then stop, hesitate a moment and turn around, intending to get back with the other cattle. We'd have to open the back gate, let them all run out, and then start over. The worst wrecks were when a cow reared up and fell over on her back. We used halters or lariats on horns to control the head. It would take several men pushing and pulling her back to her feet. Some cows would get their feet and legs through holes or under the fences. They'd sometimes get cast or trapped in odd positions. It was always handy to have a saw, hammer, nails and spare boards to repair the fence after the extrication of these animals. The best way to design alleyways for cattle is without dead ends or sharp turns; they move along smoothly. (See "touchus.")

Ant rassle: an obvious waste of time. Rarely used but indicative of a useless occupation, as in, "Boy? Why don't you quit watchin' them ants rasslin' and pay attention to the cows?" Or "Oh, he stopped way back ther, watchin' sum ants rasslin', I 'spect." It could be used to indicate where one plans to go when it is regarded by the speaker an obvious waste of time: "Yeah, me and the wife are goin' to ah ant rasslin' over to her mom's house." It is related to a statement about an insignificant town, as in, "He's frum Ant Rassle, Georgia," similar to Bug Tussle in that respect. (See "Bug Tussle.")

Arch welders: substitution for hot shots or better known as cattle prods. Hot shots are battery-powered tools that apply an intense, but by no means harmful, localized electrical shock; they're used to persuade (prod) cattle to move down an alleyway, to break up fights among cur dogs and as a plaything for rowdy kids. It was great sport and common for someone to walk up behind a resting cowboy, pinch him in the butt while mashing the button of a hot shot harmlessly in the proximity of the pinch. The "buzz-zz-zz-zz" sound of the hot shot and the pain of the pinch made the man jump by reflex and always created comical reactions. (This reflex could also be elicited by jobbing a thumb into a man's posterior with a simultaneous snort-blow sound that a bull calf would make.) I have been hit by hot shots (and thumbs) on several occasions. It ain't that much fun, but not near as painful as childbirth (or so I'm told).

There is some controversy about the use of hot shots among animal activists but almost all cowboys agree that that there can be incidences for judicious use of the tool. (It works well during prison riots, too.) I have known foremen who've insisted on very limited use of hot shots or have banned them altogether. Excessive hot shot use can cause cattle to become belligerent or frantic in the pens. (Can't say as I blame them much...) One of the worst days in my life was when I worked a herd of wild Brahman cattle with only the owner and three watermelon pickers as a crew. The men were scared of the cattle and tried to use the hot shots as protection. The cattle became wilder as the day went on. It was a long day with lots of pen re-building.

But returning to the arch welder term, one day in the pens in Okeechobee, I heard a foreman tell the men, "Y'all take yer arch welders back with ya and bring tha cows to the hopper." To interpret, he was using a humorous descriptive metaphor to indicate the sound of the hot shots. Arch welding makes a hard sizzling sound as welds are made on metal. A good example of Cracker dry humor.

Arountoit: as in, "Aw, we'll finish whin we git aroundtoit." I don't think this term is limited to Cracker country.

At air: refers to a particular item of interest. I first heard it after being finger-printed in the Florida Highlands County Sheriff's Office on a false *en masse* arrest of nine men hunting over a dove field. One man had run from the Officer on a request for license verification, so, in logical Federal and State protocol, and to save face, they arrested everyone in sight. (The case was thrown out.) As I left the cell, wiping ink off my hands, the deputy casually commented about me to an associate, saying, "At air docter takes a good picture, don't he?" (Somewhere in the bowels of the Highlands County Court House is a section where dismissed case records are stored. As if he knew all along it would be so, there's a good picture of a smiling veterinarian.)

At-it awewite: a summary phrase (very closely related to "At air") used by many of the crew, meaning, "That's it alright." It was characteristically used by Okeechobee's Robert Arnold, a fine man whom everyone loved. Robert had a slight speech impediment, though it was ignored by all that knew him.

When Robert and the men finished a task such as working a load of calves at the end of a hard day, he'd say the concluding phrase. It caught on and spread among the cowboys who seemed to grin when they said it, though Robert didn't. (See "Dat wuz dood ta me, un-huh.")

Awe-ite: a term of agreement, ending a matter. "Come on in here if y'all want to look at yer x-rays?" a vet would ask a cowboy if he wanted to see the radiographs on his horse's leg. The answer might be, "Awe-ite", "Shurnuff", "Shurdo" or "How much is this gonna cost me?"

Aw'rite: Same as above, but difference in pronunciation; a positive response to a question. The best example which comes to mind was my first flying lesson while on active duty in the Air Force stationed in Texas. (And, before you ask, yes, there must be some with a Cracker mentality in Texas, too.) I enrolled for flying lessons, completed the ground school instruction and met my first instructor–he was Dutch. He spoke his broken English with a strong accent. I spoke in a cross dialect–somewhere between Kentuckian and Florida Cracker. I could barely understand *him* if I concentrated, but he was totally lost. I took my first flight at an active Air Force base, flying between F-102 jet pilot training missions and being careful to stay out of their way.

He asked me if I'd ever flown before. I said that I had flown with my stepbrother a little. I made a big mistake there for he had me wear blinders–so I could see only the instruments. (This was disorienting, to say the least.) He instructed me to fly at a low altitude in the thermal layer of unstable air in northern Texas, in summer, in the middle of the tornado belt. The wind tossed the small plane up and down, this way and that and I grew more and more nauseated.

In order to retain some semblance of dignity, I was forced to tell him, "I need to git on the ground–I'm getting sick."

I guess he understood <u>ground</u> and <u>sick</u> because he quickly responded in barely discernible Dutch-English, "Thish is

Cracker Terms, Phrases And Definitions

guud idea. Vee've had enuff for today." He continued, "See that vater tower? Fly for it. Vin you get over it, call the Control Tower and say, 'Perrin Air Force Base, Thish is Cessna Nora Alpha Niner Fiver Four. I am five miles east of the runway. I am approaching the vater tower, requesting landing instructions.'" I understood most of this directive.

Bracing against the nausea, I looked out toward the north and saw the landing lights of three F-102's approaching. They procedurally turned on their lights about 15-20 miles out so I knew that I had only minutes to land. I had to do it right the first try, scoot down to the first diagonal turnoff and get out of the way–they were coming fast! I was sweating and chilled as I called the tower, struggling to hold down my lunch and repeated what the instructor had told me to say.

The Control Tower came back with aeronautical exactitude, rapidly giving runway number, direction for approach, wind speed in knots, wind direction, barometric pressure, the Dallas Cowboys score, the latest quote on Texas Instruments stock and several other things I couldn't understand. Now, not only holding down nausea, but also panic, I remembered from somewhere that a novice could get a control tower's attention if they announced that they were a student pilot. I spoke in the clearest Cracker dialect I could, saying, "Perrin Air Force Base, this is Nora Alpha Niner Fiver Four; I'm a student pilot requestin' landin' instructions."

There was a long pause; I guess the occupants of the tower were trying to recover from their laughter. The controller came back to the microphone, "Aw'rite... You see that li'l ol' water tire down ther aways? Fly rite at it. Whin you git ther, make a hard left. See that little strip of concrete with tha big ol' numbers 180 on it? Aim fer that. Whin you git ther, hang a hard left and set 'er down as clos' to tha numbers as ya can. Git outtha way as soon as you git to the cross lane. There's some big boys want to come in behin' ya. Okay? Perrin Tower out."

I replied, "Roger, Perrin." I've often wondered if the F-102 pilots could hear our conversation. This ended my first lesson in small aircraft pilot training. It went aw'rite, I guess.

In another circumstance, I have fittingly used the term: recently several men in our church were selected as deacons. Among our duties was the responsibility for the upkeep of the building and the functioning of all therein. The men's room urinal wouldn't flush properly, so I and another deacon went in the room to adjust the flow rate. As we were standing there watching the adjusted water flow, a man walked in and came around the corner. There we were, two big men standing at the same urinal. I said, "It's aw'rite, we're deacons." For several seconds, he was unmoving as he processed the statement. Then he saw the wrenches and laughed.

B

Backerds: the opposite of frunterds "I believe you got 'er in backerds."

Backhanded humor: a humorous response with a double meaning or unexpected ending. Crackers are noted for dry-witted humor and comments. When a fella got hurt working in the pens, he called out to his wife in the adjacent house, "Honey, call 911!" She hollered back, "How do ya spell 911?"

Justin Wilson, the Cajun chef, told of cooking for an isolated duck hunting camp many years ago when telephone numbers were made up of letters for the first two numbers. (For example, Evergreen 5-1515 meant 385-1515.) One of the men at the hunting camp was ill. Justin said they told him to go to the nearest phone and contact the sick man's personal physician. So Justin asked the operator for the number of the doctor's office.

She said, "The number is Capital 2-3892." He didn't respond.

She repeated, "Capital 2-3892... Sir, did you get that?"

Cracker Terms, Phrases And Definitions

Justin said, "Jus' how doah fella make ah capital 2?"

Another story is told of some Cracker cowboys taking a break in the pens. One had a stick of dynamite in his shirt pocket. The boys were curious, so one asked, "Leroy, Whut'er you doin' with a stick of dynamite in yer pocket?" He responded, "Well, y'all know how ol' Gator keeps slappin' me in the chest and breakin' my cigars? Yeah, well now I"m gonna blow his d - - - hand off!"

On one occasion I had a cowboy use this artful type of humor with me after we delivered an abnormal developed dead calf. He asked me, "Whut you reckon caused that?" I said, "Somewhere along the early stage of development a cell didn't divide correctly; the deformities are the result of the abnormal cell growth." He replied with a wry smile, "I don't unnerstand all I know about that."

A story that has been told that is an example of backhanded humor is the one about the fella drinking his morning coffee on his front porch before work. He noticed a county truck stop across the road from his house. It stopped and one man got out, got a shovel. He then dug a hole, some two-foot deep hole by three-foot in diameter. The man returned to the truck and got in it. In about ten minutes, another man got out, shoveled in the dirt into the hole and returned to the truck. They then moved the truck down the road about twenty yards and repeated the event. Curious, the fella went over to the truck and asked, "Whut are y'all doin'?" One man replied, "Oh, tha' man who plants tha' trees is off sick today.

Banana-horned: a rudimentary floppy bow-shaped deformed horn that may or may not be attached at the base of the skull.

Barah soap: refers to either a literal or figurative size. "My new granbaby ain't bigger'n ah barah soap." is an example. Another, "Whin she come out tha kitchen, she was totin' a steak that wadn't bigger'n a barah soap." A synonym is "Big as ma' fist", as in, "Tha knot on my horse's leg wuz as big as ma' fist."

Beady-eyed: to squint, stare with quiet attention or to inspect suspiciously. When a man is handed an official looking document, he'll examine it with a beady-eyed look.

Beat an' frammed 'round: a phrase inserted as qualifiers when something tears up or comes loose. An example would be: "Tha drive shaft come off an' beat an' frammed tha truck 'til I got'er stopped." Also, "Mama left my pocket knife in my britches whin she warshed... it beat an' frammed lik'ah hammer inna drum."

My brother-in-law, Terry, told of a coon hunting trip he went on many years ago. He said they rode in an old model four-door car. Their dogs loaded in the trunk, supplies loaded up front and off they went. When they reached around 35 mph, the dogs began to fight and scramble in the worst way imaginable. They stopped; the fighting stopped, too. They opened the trunk and the three dogs were hunkered in the corners, wild-eyed with heads held low. No problem. After closing the trunk and loading up, they drove on. At about 35 mph, the dogs again broke into vicious fighting. Terry said, "We knew something was wrong but couldn't figure what it was." They stopped again, shut off the engine, went back to the trunk and found the same cowed, wild-eyed dogs huddling there. This time they inspected the trunk closely. They moved the pile of hemp feed sacks, which served for bedding, aside and found a rusted-out hole in the floor. Apparently the feed sacks would get tangled in the universal of the drive shaft and every time they reached thirty-five mph the centrifugal force caused the sacks to beat and fram the floor of the trunk and the dogs. The panicked creatures couldn't take it and commenced to fighting among themselves–but only when they reached thirty-five mph.

Beech Nut wormin': an old time method of de-worming horses. It was not uncommon in the forties for Florida ranchers to buy a case of Beech Nut Chewing Tobacco for their horses. They would add a pack to the horse's feed once a month to help control intestinal parasites. The active

Cracker Terms, Phrases And Definitions

ingredient was nicotine, and nicotine sulfate does in fact have some anti-parasite properties. In elevated doses it could kill. Nicotine will also make kids green in the face and throw up. (See Callin' Roy and Buick) For some reason I have discovered that goats will follow you for tobacco. Apparently they crave it. I watched a cowboy give a goat some snuff and the goat chewed and licked vigorously, and soon followed the man around the pens. I do not know if this goat was from Hollywood, California, or if all goats will do this,

Bellied up: to enthusiastically indulge in eating and drinking; the word is often used in phrases like, bellied up to the bar. It is also used to describe a form of gluttony, such as, "I wanna tell ya, them calves just bellied up in that new grass" or "Is your horse eatin' this mornin'?" "Yeah, he bellied up on oats tha first thing."

Bicycle-horned or Harley-horned: though rare, describes the shape of horns which resemble handlebars of a bicycle or motorcycle turned forward. For instance: "We need to cut out the ol' yeller cow with the bicycle horns whin she comes through."

I can't help but remember a story told by Dr. Carl Hurley some years ago about a high school classmate of his. Carl said the boy was tough. Every afternoon he'd walk home and cross a man's cow pasture to save some walking distance. Coming home after a late football practice, it was about dark when the boy, as usual, cut through the pasture. He didn't know that the farmer had recently purchased a Jersey bull and released him in the field. Well, Jersey bulls are notoriously aggressive and apparently a boy walking through his domain irritated him.

In the dark the bull came up behind the boy, knocked him down and began to maul him. The boy got his footing at last and grabbed the bull by his horns, wrestled him down and beat the stuffings out of him.

The next day he came to school all stiff and bruised. The kids asked, "Whut in the world happened to you?"

He replied, "Well, as I wuz walkin' home late last nite; I cut across the pasture lik' I always do and a fella cum up behind me in the dark and knocked me down. And, by golly, whin I got up I beat the tar out of 'im... but I lik' to hav' never got 'im off his bycicle."

Bidness: The word can be used in many contexts: A dog can do his bidness, someone can have a bidness deal or get down tah bidness, and Whut kind of bidness do y'all have? There's cow bidness, rodeo bidness, citrus bidness, monkey bidness, or a bidness which is up to no good.

Most people know the use of the word and all the variations. But I am reminded of the young Cracker whose family was in the furniture bidness. He was sent to a wholesale outlet to buy new stock. While there he ran into a young woman from Sweden who was visiting an exchange student at a nearby college. She didn't speak English (and he didn't speak Swedish), but she was smiling at him, so he thought he'd try to communicate. He took some paper and drew a truck and pointed to himself. She smiled and nodded. So he escorted her to his truck. There he drew another picture of a café with a table and food in it. She grinned and nodded affirmatively. So they went to dinner. He then drew on a napkin a couple dancing. She took the napkin and drew a bed on it. When he got home he told his daddy what happened and then concluded, "Daddy, I don't reckon I'll ever know how she figured I wuz in the furniture bidness?"

Another tale circulated when the carnival came through Okeechobee. The sideshows included a strongman demonstration. Several Crackers went in to watch. As a final trick, the strongman squeezed a lemon dry and told the audience, "Anyone in here that can squeeze another drop out of this lemon, I'll give $50. A lean muscled little man stood up, walked to the stage, took the lemon and squeezed it, releasing a drop of juice. As the strongman gave over the $50, he asked, "What is the secret of your strength? How'd you do that?" The Cracker said, "I bin in tha cattle bidness fer forty years.

Big-footed: a somewhat complimentary term used to describe a healthy, teen-age growing boy, but doesn't necessarily refer to his foot size. "Them big-footed boys like to hav' eaten all the cobbler," and "Y'all see all them big-footed boys stir out tha house like a pack of cur dogs?"

Big wood frum kindlin': a descriptive phrase to denote contrast. The first time I heard the phrase was when we had a visitor from Miami: a middle-aged doctor who owned a local orange grove my stepfather managed. With typical hospitality, my parents invited him to visit the ranch if he ever wanted to inspect his grove. Pa would show him around.

Well, some weeks later, they got a call from him. He said he needed to get out of Miami for the weekend, wanted to see how his fruit crop was fairing and would be in the area on the next Saturday.

He showed up with a companion–an overly-neat young man, hair salon-styled, tight slacks, loafers and a golf shirt. The doctor was in shirt and tie with a light weight blue blazer. During the conversation, I couldn't help but note the contrast between Cracker lifestyle and the effeminate behavior of our two visitors. I have to admit I was somewhat wary, but my parents were as gracious as ever.

After the tour they came back to the ranch house and we had a nice visit, enjoying a cup of coffee and my mother's famous pecan pie. We said our goodbyes and Doctor Blazer and Salon Boy drove off.

As they cleared the driveway, my mother said, "Frank, what would you do if the doctor made a pass at you?"

He rolled his cigar, took a puff, and replied, "Humph... he knows big wood frum kindlin'."

Blind-sided: to be caught, hooked, butted, hit, knocked over, or run over from behind or from an angle out of the peripheral vision, totally unprepared. It is used mostly to describe an assault by a bull or cow. Of course, it also was used at juke joints when a fella was caught cold by a fist blow. In the cowpens we often requested, "Y'all watch behind me so I won't git blind-sided." Fortunately, most bulls and cows will snort just before they hit. This was great sport for the boys at times with goosey men. They would catch someone standing fairly relaxed, another would sneak up behind him, blow like a cow and job him with a thumb. The reaction was sometimes not humorous to the job-ee.

We also had a saying: "One-eyed bulls are always timid and afraid of being blind-sided." Bulls that have had one eye removed for treatment of cancer-eye tend to hold back from the competition to mate. In very small herds, though one-eyed bulls seem to do as well as herd sires. Many a bull has been blind-sided while having all his weight on his hind legs and rammed by another aggressive bull.

A fella can also be blind-sided with divorce papers.

Blind staggers: describes the condition of an animal with a neurological disease, such as encephalitis. The affected beast will literally be blind with severely impaired coordination. These animals will aimlessly walk in random circles. Circling to one direction is usually a lesion or abnormality on one side of the brain while general brain problems cause more general signs. To the cowboys it meant sleepin' sickness, which is horse viral encephalitis (viral brain inflammation). The term is often used in jest when describing the characteristics of a hangover, recovering from an illness or just returning from a honeymoon, as in, "Well, lookie her' boys... ya reckon he's got tha blind staggers?" It could be used as a term for illness when the cowboy had no idea what was wrong—all he knew was the horse or cow was acting uncoordinated.

Cracker Terms, Phrases And Definitions

Blue-bottle flies: referring to a species of insect that is larger than the common housefly and characterized by shiny blue-green markings on the body. The term is often used to describe a large number of individuals, as in: "They wuz thicker'n blue-bottle flies ona dead gator."

Biscit: a small oven-baked cake made of flour, milk, grease and baking powder. Also, the name of a girl in South Florida, where she was named Biscit, because her sister said it sounded like a can of biscuits opening when she unbuttoned her jeans. A cat-head biscuit is one made very large, equivalent to two canned ones. It was not unusual to use canned biscuits in some kind of illustration, as in, "I heard you shoot over ther', it sounded like my mama openin' a can of biscuits."

Bitin' (*fill in the blank with a descriptive noun*): a ubiquitous phrase describing the bad habits of a cur dog. There was a young man named Henry Lanier who had some Florida cur dogs that were half Chow. They were peculiar, in that they were usually rather phlegmatic, rarely if ever barking. They'd just be there when the action began. Unlike other dogs, they never growled before they bit a stranger—they just bit the fire out of him. Cow whips were effective in discouraging this activity and over time they settled down. They were truly bitin' (*expletives deleted*). Funny, Henry was a quiet fella, but he could get into more trouble with the least noise of anyone I remember. They say (i.e., *they* being some drunks under a bridge somewhere, I figure), ah dog will take on the characteristics of its owner. Could be.

Boar's nest: a place where cowboys frequent, hang out, rest or live, such as a bunk house, where women usually are not present. It would have made a great juke joint name but I have not seen any headskin named that. "Wher' y'all gonna be about dark?" one might ask. Another replies, "Whin we finish here, we're goin' to the boar's nest." Other similar phrases using porcine terminology include sow's nest (See "You sound like a sow makin' a nest."), meaning a critical remark about the condition of one's living quarters, as in, "Boy, you better clean up yer room—it looks like a sow's nest!"

Boar quail: a male quail used as a metaphor for a frisky man; as in, "Yeah... whin he saw her he fluffed his feathers, dropped one wing and run at her lik' a boar quail..." This really is the way the male quail behaves in the presence of a female.

Bobbertail or bobistail: slang for cut the hair off the end of the tail of a cow (or bull) for marking purposes. For example, when pregnancy testing, an open (non-pregnant) cow had to be marked so she could be sorted out of the herd. Any herd member that had a bobbed tail was destined for some purpose, usually for sale at the local livestock market. It was quick, lasted as an identification mark until the hair grew out and dulled many a pocketknife. Sometimes, a fella could fill a bucket with cowtail hair. We'd also mark open cows and reject bulls with a bright sticky Crayon-like livestock marker, often called a grease pencil. The cattle could move through a chute while a man applied a stipe of a bright colored chalk high on the body so it could easily be seen by a man that parted out marked (selected) animals into a separate pen. But, when no chalk was available, bobbin' 'er tail worked well. The cowboy in charge of bobbin' would let the tail slide through his hand until the end of the tail slipped passed the fingers, then he'd slice off the hair just below the tip. This left a neat squared-off tail.

I was able one time to make good use of that discarded hair for a Young Life skit: I took a mixed sample of the long hair, washed it thoroughly and glued it inside a cowboy hat. With a cow-tail wig of long ratty-looking hair, flowing in rhythm, a pair of Hank Williams, Jr., sunglasses, a purple cowboy shirt, with the two top buttons open, and a gaudy gold-plated medallion around my neck, I was Johnny Clash. The kids were amazed (and delighted) when I played the guitar Johnny Cash style and sang "Understand Your Man" in a monotone, "Don't holler my name out tha window as I'm leavin', I won't even turn my head...."

Cracker Terms, Phrases And Definitions

Needless to say, I was not asked to repeat my performance, though the kids were breathless from laughter and I enjoyed it, too. (No, all the pictures were destroyed.) See Check 'er fer lice.

Bog, bogged, or boggin': a place of soft, deep organic matter into which one might get stuck; also the act, of getting stuck in a place of soft, deep organic matter. "Man, he drove in there like a house afire an' bogged 'er down to the axles." Or, "Y'all better stay out of that end of the swamp—you'll bog your horse in ther'." Or, "Boy, did ya bog 'er down or whut?" (Answer, "Ya thank?")

The word is also used to indicate that all the work had shut down from an equipment failure.

Bog it to tha hub or bogged 'er to tha hubs: to insert fully. When one of the younger cowboys was learning the art of administering vaccinations, this phrase was part of an instruction for placing the needle in the muscle. "Don't be shy, boy, take the needle an' bog it to tha hub before you mash the plunger." The original use no doubt referred to a vehicle that has been stuck in a mud hole: "We tried to make it through the swamp, but we bogged 'er to tha hubs."

Boogerin', boogery, boogered: prodding or startling slow or stopped cattle, getting them to move on. A synonym is spookin', spooky and spooked. This takes advantage of the animals' wariness of humans. Crackers would say, "Boy, the thunderhead came up quick on us. It sure was boogery." Or, "Son, that man is boogery," referred to one who was nervous. A boogery horse could kill you getting away from a startling sound or sight. I have seen herds or individual animals that were extremely anxious and would booger at the slightest movement. The cow crew knew it to be true, too, since heifers and steers could go into open panic at the slightest thing. You didn't have to booger them much. Old tame cattle, like dairy cows, would take a lot of boogerin'. I guess you could conjugate this term to the extreme: the boogeror was the one making the noise and actions, the boogeree was the one boogered and a boogerette would be a small girl on horseback, boogering cattle.

Bot nits or bots: the larvae of a parasitic fly that lays eggs (nits) on the legs of horses. The eggs look like tiny grains of yellow rice. They hatch and migrate to the stomach where they develop into pupae. The pupae hatch and come out in the manure to begin the life-cycle again. They look like fat, hard and inactive maggots and cause problems with colic and unthriftiness (poor quality). The old time treatment was carbon disulfide given by stomach tube. There are many less toxic drugs now. A botty horse was one that was thought to have masses of bot pupae in the stomach. Many times an owner would ask this question about his puny-looking horse, "Doc… you reckon he's loaded with bots?"

Bow up or bowed up: to get angry, resistant, stubborn, fractious, uncooperative or ready to fight; as in, "Whin he seen her with her old boy friend, he jus' bowed up." Or, "Don't go back ther'; that speckled bull jus' bowed up an' lik' to hav gutted my horse." A daddy might say to a stubborn son, "Boy! Don't you bow up at me; suck that bottom lip in or I'll knock a knot on yer head."

Breakeven: usually means only meeting expenses with no profit on a business endeavor. It implies that one has recovered cost and did not make money on the deal, trade or activity. However, I heard a Cracker use the term in a different manner. He was working on a broken-down tractor, and as he was finishing the repair with squinting eyes from the smoke of a drooping cigarette in the corner of his mouth, he said, "Doc… this is a breakeven deal." I didn't see the connection and asked, "Whut do you mean?" He grinned and said, "It's gonna break even if we fix it."

Buck-egger: colloquial pronunciation of buck ague; a synonym for buck fever. The word, ague refers to a fit of shivering or successive stages of chills and fever experienced in the early

Cracker Terms, Phrases And Definitions

stages of illness. The term is obviously used in the context of deer hunting. The onset of signs is simply the aftermath of an adrenaline surge. (See Peein' ah drop at ah time.) When hunting, especially after an intense excitement, one could get shaky or excited. Many times, a buck-egger occurred <u>after</u> a buck was shot. I've seen a man touch a downed buck with a shaking foot to check for life signs. (Shot bucks, thought to be dead, can rise and attack the hunter. It is not a pretty sight. They can inflict serious injury; the front hooves can cut the clothes off a man.) A buck-egger can occur after watching a buck for thirty minutes before he gets close enough to shoot. I remember watching a buck for over an hour as he warily grazed toward me. He'd lift his head every now and then; the antlers seemed to get bigger and bigger as he approached. Snuggled down in a little clump of small maples on the edge of a marsh, I had little fits of chills throughout the long episode

The same thing happened to me, off and on for three hours in Montana, as I watched a herd of elk. The bull only came out last in the herd. He was the most cautious of them all.

I know there are some who get all upset on the subject of hunting large game. They forget that every hamburger, pork chop, chicken, etc. comes from a harvested animal. I am reminded of the seventies when there was a severe drought in the Everglades. There was an outrage from the animal rights crowd, forcing the State of Florida to compromise an agreement between them and hunters. The anti-hunting crowd said harvesting deer by hunters was unconscionable. The hunters maintained that the drought would kill more than they ever could. So, in a political solution, the State opened hunting below one of the main highways in the southern Everglades while allowing animal rights people to trap and transport captured deer on the north side of the highway. This, of course, made the news. But the rest of the story was never revealed. There was a tremendous death rate in the captured and transported deer area. In fact most died due to trapping and loading into trailers from broken necks and various injuries, and many died due to severe stress. The hunted (harvested) portion of the Glades had just enough deer removed to promote a healthy, vigorous population with plenty of food sources. In other words, the harvesting allowed enough food for the survivors to prosper and reproduce healthy offspring.

Buckout: a synonym for a party, a square dance, a get-together, a social or some such affair. Many times when the county Cattlemen's Association's annual affair was coming up, one of the men would ask, "Y'all goin' to the buckout tonite?" The term arose from the breaking of horses. An unbroken colt might violently buck when first ridden, but when finally tired, he settles down. He has bucked out. Good trainers, ones that really know horses, can break colts or fillies without letting them buck or buck out.

With all the drinking, joke-telling and dancing, I suppose the cowboys felt like they would get all they could from the party, thus resembling a wild horse's antics.

Bucksnort: the sound that a deer makes when startled. It is more of a rapid blow of air and carries well on a cold morning and especially on a quiet night. By the time one locates the source of the sound, the buck (or doe) is flagging away. I attended a meeting in Nashville, Tennessee one year. The restaurant was called Bucksnort Bar-be-que and Beanery. On the menu was an item called, Bucksnort Beans. This leads to an indelicate explanation that I'll leave to your imagination. ("Did y'all hear that bucksnort?" And the reply "You stepped on a frog, didden you?")

Budjit: Wes O'Berry approached me one spring day with his dog, a Blue Heeler, tougher than a bus station steak. Wes had nearly cut her left rear leg off with a side-bar hay mower, the kind that cut wide swaths of grass. The unfortunate dog was perfectly content with the leg that had healed at an outward 45-degree angle, unaware that anything was out of the ordinary.

Cracker Terms, Phrases And Definitions

Wes said, "Doc, we wrapped it up and gobbed (See gobbed) some salve on it and she done awrite. The ol' lady don't like her to run around with it all cockeyed as it is. Tige don't seem to mind tho'. She still cow hunts with us."

The leg had actually healed nicely, though crooked. Well, I began to discuss all the options open for the dog. Somehow I always felt like a fish hooked on a line with Wes. He had a way of cutting to the bottom line and ending up with all the advantages on his side. After discussing all the possible practical solutions we got down to money. I started at the top. It went something like this: "Wes, we ought to check the dog into the hospital, x-ray the leg, clean the wound and attempt to straighten it and save the leg. I don't know if that is possible but we could try. I'll need to keep her for several days and change bandages daily. You'll have x-rays, anesthesia, surgery, hospital care and so forth."

"How much would something like that cost, Doc?"

"Oh, about $250 to $300." (This was back when money was money.)

"Now, couldn't you jus' whack it off?"

"Wes, don't you want to try to save the leg?"

"To tell ya the truth, Doc, I got a sackful of cow dogs at tha house and I ain't goin' to spend much on her. What is the cheapest thing you could do for her?"

Figuring that he was now in full control, I asked, "What kind of budget are you allowing for the dog?"

"Budjit? Whut's that?"

"You know, how much money have you budgeted for the dog? How much have you set aside for her?"

"I don't know anythin' about ah budjit."

Cutting to the very bottom line, I said, "Wes, I could take her in right now, put her under anesthesia, try to put the leg back in line if she has a good blood supply to it. If it doesn't work, I'll amputate it and you bring her back every day for 5-7 days for wound checks. I can do that for $50—no frills, no extras... you pick her up in 45 minutes."

Wes smiled, saying, "Doc, if I had a budjit, $50 would be on it."

Bug tusslin" or bug tussle: similar to ant rasslin', indicating insignificance, meaninglessness or in wasting time: "We wuz just sittin' there watchin two bugs tusslin' whin she come up to the pens." And the mythical town as used in illustration for Ant Rassle, Georgia, could be replaced by, "He's from up aroun' Bug Tussle."

Build: to assemble, as in, "Well, we're gettin ready to build a pot of coffee. Y'all want some?" As a good illustration, on a one-lane bridge near Chiefland, Florida, Paw, my stepfather, and his hunting friend were about one-third the way across a narrow bridge in a swamp, when a carload of Yankees pulled in at the other end. The vehicles met nose to nose about two-thirds of the way, toward the Yankee end. They blew the horn repeatedly, hollering out, "Youse need to move your vehicle and let us by!" After two or three times of this, Paw shut off the motor, got out, went around back, and rummaged around in the camping gear. The Yankees got out to see what he was doing. They approached cautiously, not sure if they were inciting an incident. As they approached, they saw that he was getting out a coffee pot. He turned and walked down to the water, and dipped the pot in the water. One of them asked, "What are you doing?" He mildly replied, "It looks like we're gonna be here awhile; I thought I'd build a pot of coffee." They talked it over, got in their car, and backed up. Paw put the pot back and went on to the huntin' camp. He smiled sweetly as he drove by.

One can also build a fire, build camp, build a cake etc.

Build ah fire under 'er: a tongue-in-cheek phrase, referring to a means of making a sullen cow get up and move on. Brahmans were notorious about lying down on their sternum

Cracker Terms, Phrases And Definitions

and refusing to rise. This pretty much stopped the flow of cattle through a chute and reminds me of a story about Boy McGown at a ranch north of Parrish and Ft. Greene. We had such a cow decide to lie down in the alleyway and sull. She'd not respond to any prodding or any kind of encouraging her to leave the narrow alleyway. If approached, she'd just lower her head and bawl.

Boy turned off the hydraulic chute and we took a breather. Dr. Handley said, "I guess we'll hav' to build a fire under her." Boy responded, "Yeah, we'll hav' to go git some Cabbage fans." We sat awhile, drank some cool water and visited, giving the cow some time to consider her options. Then, with no warning, Boy jumped off the fence and ran at the cow, yelling, "Whou-ou-ou-ou-ou-ou-ou!!" She bawled, rose and ran out of the chute to the pasture. This was a perfect example of "boogerin'." (See term)

Old and weak cows were notorious about sulling in the pens. Many just couldn't take the stress and gave up. We'd have to "tail them up." (See term) Sometimes we'd move the herd out toward the pasture and leave a cow alone, leaving the gates open so she'd eventually get up and catch up to the herd.

Bull hole: a depression where a bull has pawed out the dirt or sand. It can be as large as three feet deep and seven feet wide. The behavior is instinctive among bovine and related animals, like American Bison. Bulls will often get on either side of a fence, lower their heads, snort, low and bellow at each other and throw up dirt behind them six feet in the air or job their horns in the earth They'll often return to the same hole and belligerently proceed to enlarge it. The dirt falls on their backs on occasion, scattering the resident flies. Butt-headed bulls, hornless ones, will rub their heads in a manner to mimics this behavior.

A bull hole is also a great place to wallow, thus it is sometimes called a bull wallow. Apparently the wallowing alleviates itching and it's like a good back scratching. But predominantly a bull hole is where a bull displays how bad he is—to the other bulls but especially to the on-looking ladies. Bulls will often bellow at other bulls or cows. Most of the time, bull holes are dug near places where a bull is separated from the cows or when he sees another bull. They are generally not dug in wet places, but rather in drier earth or elevated places. In the case where two bulls get together for a bull session, they brag on themselves back and forth. If not separated by a barrier, such as a fence or gate, a bull fight can occur. Sometimes there are serious altercations but most are concluded quickly. These fights are over when one quits. The same instinctive behavior is seen in herding animals where the dominant bull gets to mate with the majority of the available females (Deer, elk, sheep, Mountain Goats, Musk Oxen, bison, moose) and at places like The Speckled Perch Bar and Grill in Okeechobee, The Watering Hole in Highlands County, The Buck Snort Bar-b-que House, and at several establishments called, Bubba's).

Bull holes can sure ruin your day when you accidentally hit one in a truck or tractor. Dropping a front tire into a bull hole at night is an easy way to get a knot on your head. They make good places to lie down when hunting if dug on an elevated site like a dike. Pioneer Westerners used them as defensive places in their gun fights.

A story is told about two bulls walking down a fence looking for a way into a pasture full of heifers. The young bull said, "Hey! Lookie here! Let's jump the fence and breed us a heifer!"

The old bull said, "Naw... let's walk on down to the gate, tear it down and breed 'em all..."

On cold nights in the cow country of Florida, in December or January, when the air is crisp and still, some bulls will bellow out a mournful, lonesome call. Brahmans snort-grunt while English and other breeds will low, often answered by another, but sometimes they are calling into the night to no one in particular. It is almost as comfortable a sound as Bob White Quail calling at dusk.

Bull-headed: stubborn.

Burnt holes in a blanket: a phrase used to describe the dark, sunken eyes of a sick (or hungover) cowboy. The observer said, "Man, yer eyes look like two burnt holes innah blanket." Pretty descriptive.

Butt over teakettle: I never understood why we used that descriptive phrase. We never made tea in the woods. It was used in the context, "Well, her' he come through the palmetto patch, wide open on his horse! 'Bout half way through, the horse steps in a armadilla hole and pitches butt over teakettle!" (Of course, in all honestly, many Crackers substituted another descriptive word for butt.)

By hob: an expletive used to add emphasis, as in, "I headed for the barn, by hob—that thunder cloud was plum boogery." Or "By hob, I'll teach you to run rabbits!" to a dog that is distracted from the hunt by a passing rabbit. (See Meat stick for description and use.) Another use is, "Boy, he played hob whin he roped that crazy horse" or "Whin he married that woman he played hob…" (I never really knew where it came from, but assumed the speaker or listener could make it mean anything he wanted. Everyone knew what it meant, as in, "By hob, she reminds me of an ol' gal I usta know…")

C

Cain't 'til cain't: "From before daylight until after dark, or from the time when we can't see, through the day, until the time we can't see again. This might be used when a new day-working cowboy asked a fulltime crew member, "How long are tha days her'?" meaning "How long are the usual working hours?" The answer, "Cain't 'til cain't," meant the hours were uncertain or that work always continued until completed—whatever it took in time to finish the day's activities.

One of my friends told me that he used to work summers for Wes O'Berry in Highlands County. He said Wes got a full day's work out of the boys, working them hard loading bales of hay long hours as described by the term. He said, "I asked Wes one time, 'Why do we have to sneak up on the bales of hay before daylight?—they ain't goin' inywhere.'"

Call his mama: used in dealing with an irresponsible individual. It's indicative of the supreme court of Cracker behavior. I understand it to mean that the individual about whom this is used has in some way offended or failed in some responsibility, like: "Somebody ought to call his mama about this." I have found that this technique works well with some but not all Cracker men. I would recommend that the user actually know the man's mama and that she be a strong God-fearing woman. Otherwise, you're wasting your time.

Callin' Roy or callin' Buick: though not a pleasant subject the phrase is used to describe someone in the throes of emptying their gastric contents from illness, after gettin' "gassed" (See term), during a hangover or from the flu. It could be heard as, "Wher's Ronnie?" "Aw, he's over behind tha trailer, callin' Roy..." (In the background you might hear Ol' Ronnie heaving, Bu-u-u-ick...

Cans ya sees ma finances: translation of, "Are you able to see my money?" Suzie Glass was the cook and housekeeper for my stepfather and mother in the sixties. She was a loyal sweetheart, but she talked funny–it sounded like a quacking duck. She had Paw hold her money each week and only take a little for necessities like Sue Bee snuff and the like.

So when vacation time came, she had two weeks coming and lots of money saved for her vacation trip to Georgia. He warned her once, "Suzie, don't you let anybody see that you have this money; they'll knock you in the head and take it away from you."

She said, "Naw, Mr. Frank, I won' let nobody sees it."

The next morning she appeared, ready for the ride to the bus station, in a clean, heavily starched white dress. She walked up to him, lifted her skirts and said, "Mr. Frank, cans ya sees mah finances?"

He said she had on white bloomers, her little skinny legs sticking out of the ballooned underwear. She had pinned her finances inside the bloomers. He said, "No Suzie, I can't see your finances." We laughed about that for years. He'd ask my mother occasionally, "Cans ya sees my finances?"

Can ya pass a football? a story opens with a young man just starting his career in high school coaching. He had heard about a prospective football player in the county and took his assistant with him to see the boy. After traveling on sand roads for a prolonged time, they were just about to give up on ever finding the boy. Just then, in the distance, they saw a big, gangling, raw-boned boy in the road. He was wearing bib overalls, no shirt, bare-footed and draggin a small bear behind him. As they approached him, they saw he held a live rabbit by the ears and had a dead dove in his pocket. They stopped by him and the assistant asked, "Boy, how far Is it to tha little school house out here?"

Pointing down the road the boy said, "It's jus' down tha road apiece."

Curiosity got the better of the coach; he told the assistant, "Ask 'im wher' he got that bear."

The assistant coach said, "Boy, wher' in the world did you git that bear?"

The boy said, "Well, he come outta the woods and attacked me—I jus' run 'im down an' crushed tha life outta im... I'm takin' it home to make a rug."

The coach was intrigued. "Wher'd you git that rabbit?

The boy continued, "Aw, he run acrost the road and I run 'im down... takin' 'im home for supper."

The coach couldn't avoid asking, "Wher' you git the dove in yer pocket?"

The boy replied, "Wellsir, he flew over me down ther' an' I picked up a literd knot and knocked him out tha air."

The coaches were really interested at this point, with one asking, "Boy, you think you could pass a football?"

The boy studied a few seconds and replied, "Wellsir, I think I can pass nir 'bout anythin' I can eat."

Carry tha mail: to accomplish a task with haste. It refers to carrying on, keeping on or hurrying. It could apply to a race horse, as "Look at that colt! He's carrying tha mail, ain't he?" Or, as a descriptive phrase: "Her' he cum, carryin' tha mail all tha way to tha barn."

Cash: A term which means different things to different people. For example, we had a check-in sheet for the veterinary hospital. It had record-keeping information for our receptionist to prepare a medical record for whatever animal came into the hospital. It documented important things like owner's name, address, telephone number, animal's name, breed, sex, color, and a place for the Primary Complaint or Requested Services, etc. At the bottom was a list of payment methods with little boxes by each option: Cash, Check, VISA, Master Card and Savings Check. (Credit among some people is bad for commerce—especially among owners who aren't sure their cur or hog dog will be alive tomorrow.)

One day a pure Cracker came in leading his hog dog on a hay baling string. Bow-legged, sweat-stained, sun-burned jaws with a three-day beard, he walked to the desk and said, "Hey, Ol' Pistol needs somethin' done for his ear canker." The old dog did have a bad ear infection (one that the feed store couldn't cure). He filled out the information sheet, handed it to Gail and sat down for a short wait. The exam and treatment was routine and without incident. As I cleaned the exam table I over-heard him say, "Y'all send me the bill."

Cracker Terms, Phrases And Definitions

Gail said, "But Sir, you checked the 'Cash' box... We don't extend credit until you've been with us for a year."

He said, "I will pay cash... whin I git it..."

(We changed the sheet to "CASH NOW.")

Another incident illustrates a similar scenario. A nicely dressed man came in for routine vaccinations for his fine-looking German shepherd. The vaccinations were administered and he walked to the receptionist's desk and said, "Send me the bill?" (He too had not indicated there would be a problem in payment.) Gail was consistent in trying to obtain payment at the time of the visit because billing was time-consuming and expensive. So, in her sweet voice, she mentioned the other payment options. He denied them all. So Gail knew she was whipping a dead horse with this fella and she relented. He then asked if he could borrow the telephone to make a local call. He dialed Pizza Hut and ordered five Pizza Supremes with everything, dipping sauce and bread sticks and four big bottles of Coke. He asked what was the total cost and repeated the amount for clarification, "That'll be $78.55?" Then, "Okay, I'll be there in twenty minutes..." (Oh, he <u>had</u> the money for pizza but not for his dog's services...)

Yogi Berra once said, "Cash is almost as good as money."

Carryin' capacity: a term used to indicate an estimation of how many acres would provide enough forage for a cow for some length of time. Another term was stockin' rate, i.e., how many cows to put (or stock) on a pasture). A twenty-to-one carryin' capacity meant that it would take approximately twenty acres to keep one cow for the year. This example of low carryin' capacity was typical of a ranch containing a lot of scrub areas. In the Everglades there are ranches with tremendous capacity to grow grass. It is said that some of these pastures, with intensive management and care, can carry cattle at a one-to-one or two-to-one carrying capacity. The reason many old-time Crackers did well on poor pasture land was because they owned pasture land debt-free and tough hearty cattle. For that reason, they could stock the cattle on poor land at a very low carrying capacity and do well. They had no loan re-payments to cut down their profits, having inherited the property from the family pioneer of many generations ago.

The skilled Cracker cattleman could inspect a property and predict about how many cows could be stocked on it. Truth is, however, they usually over-stocked it. This would sort itself out when they culled the poor doers or under-performing cattle. In effect, they were selecting the cattle that had adapted to the conditions. The true Cracker ranches were often rode-hard-and-put-up-wet family operations. These no-frills ranches had rough pastures, coarse cross-bred cattle and raggedy pens (but the pens worked well). They had a term that expressed the situation: A poor man has poor ways. These ranches incurred limited expenses, kept all costs low and did well at a return from about seventy- to eighty-percent of the cows having calves. Out of the calf crop would come some replacement heifers and steers destined for sale at the market.

As land appreciated, taxes increased and operational costs climbed, it became harder to make money on these old style ranches. There are tales told where sons inherited vast properties from prominent Cracker pioneers and within a short time the ranch was in serious debt. The boys just had to have the latest trucks, good cow horses, rodeo equipment, tractors, new homes, etc. (It was as if they were tired of Daddy's way of doin' things...) Many of these young men rather quickly put sections of pasture up for sale to folk who dragged trailers into what was once dotted with cows and calves. The story is summarized in the adage: They got too big too quick. But many of these young men adapted, having modified the operation somewhat, and learned that some of Daddy's ways were really good–all they needed was tweaking a little. (It doesn't sound any different from other businesses and families in other situations, does it? Poverty is more a state of mind than a condition.)

The purchased and mortgaged ranch was under the gun, so to speak. Under these conditions a calf crop of eighty-percent or lower wouldn't service the loan payments and provide a profit for everything else, including all living expenses. All of a sudden the push was on to increase the pregnancy rates and to manipulate the timing of calf births to optimize the higher calf prices for big calves. In other words, they had to increase the pounds of beef at weaning. This can only be done a few ways: obtaining better bulls for increased hybrid vigor, selective culling of inferior cattle, early pregnancy testing and culling open cows, proper nutrition by grass management, and by increasing the herd's fertility and the numbers of quality calves. Management became more intense and the old style didn't seem to work for the mortgaged ranch.

Today there are innumerable resources available to the cattleman. The University of Florida, the Extension Service, the Florida Cattlemen Association, various breeder's associations, internet resources and word of mouth serve much of the cattle producer's needs. Much technology is available, but like the fella told me, "Wait a minute… We don't use five-percent of whut we know now and yer're givin' us more?" ("The biggest hurdle to progress is change" is a saying of forty years ago by a past President and CEO of the A & P Food Store chain.)

Cattlemen would ask me, "We're thinkin' of getting some crackerjack bulls. Do you think that'll help us? Whut do you think we need to do to improve production?" I'd reply, "It's ah three-legged stool: You'll need to increase fertility in tha bulls _and_ cows, develop improved nutrition and jack-up your management… workin' on only one leg won't work." One replied, "Whut if ya don't hav' a stool?"

Speaking of how many cattle to put in a pasture, Steve Bronson of Lorida once told me of a rancher talking with a banking loan officer. The rancher needed to borrow some money. The banker was ponderin' the situation, i.e., trying to determine how many cattle the pastures would carry so he could estimate return and whether the loan could be paid back. In other words, could the ranch have enough carrying capacity to make loan payments? (This was way before ACORN was in existence.) There was an old Cracker named Mr. Prescott nearby who happened to hear the conversation. Pushing his hat back on his head he offered, "Boys, I can tell ya ezzactly how many cows that pasture can carry; put three hundred head in ther' now an' come back in the spring an' see how many is left alive."

Catch dog: refers to dogs bred or selected for working cattle, catching the aggressive ones by the nose or other appendage and restraining them until they could get their owners to help. Also, hog dog, cow dog or any type of bull dog. The words are often pronounced, Ketchdawg.

Catywampus: Spelled kata-wampas by Greek scholars, it refers to a large item that is out of level or plumb. The difference in sygoggled and catawampus is highly subjective, but generally used interchangeably. One must take the age and cultural attitude into consideration when classifying another person's usage of the words. In a general illustration, a sygoggled screw will cause the picture to hang catawampus. Severe sygoggling will result in a catastrophic catawhamic failure of something at a later time.

Catwalk: a long, elevated walkway beside and parallel to a crowding pen or narrow alleyway in a cow pens. This allows a man (or woman) to lean over from above the long chute and goose up cattle that have stalled. Catwalks afford a little protection for the cowboys as cattle can jump or climb onto them when trying to escape. Catwalks come in all varieties and are often located around a parting pen to save climbing the fence every time cattle or individuals have to be boogered to go toward the restraint chute.

Cracker Terms, Phrases And Definitions

Chainsaw convenchun: refers to the sound made by copious buzzing. I first heard this used in Florida to describe the snoring of several men while on a fishing trip in the Ten Thousand Islands area. The description by the haggard sleep-deprived fella went something like this: "Well, if that wadn't bad enough, about midnight Dan cut in with his Poulon. Then the Homelite came on and alternated between Dan's Poulon, Hiard's Husqvarna and Jack's Stihl... It was 'HE-e-e-e-e-ah HE-e-e-e-e-ah', follered by 'HUN-da-dah-h-h-h HUN-da-dah-h-h-h'; ever now an then there'd be ah 'Buzz-z-z-z-z-z'... Then you'd hear sumbody gasp for air like they'd been choked for a minute... It sounded like a chainsaw convenchun. I lik to hav never got any sleep..." (See Dirt dauber inah beer can.)

Check 'er fer lice: The tail is a great place for cattle lice to congregate for conventions or committee meetings. Old timers would dip the tail in kerosene or turpentine to eradicate the lice. It worked well until the stuff is slung into your eyes by an irritated cow. (See Ringin' 'er tail and bobbinertail.)

Check 'er or 'is eyes: Examine the eye(s) for injury, infection or cancer. One-eyed cows could generally continue a productive life in the herd, but one-eyed bulls in commercial herds were usually culled (sent to market) because of their fear of being blind-sided by other bulls. They tended to not breed and became shy of other bulls.

Trying to turn a startled one-eyed horse reacting to a fright is risky because the horse turns his head so the good eye is looking back, the blind eye forward and, therefore, he can't see well directly in front as he runs. (I got the scars to prove it.)

Check 'er or 'is teeth: the dental wear of a cow (or bull) should be evaluated. Old cattle often were thin and had worn teeth to the point of being useless for cutting grass. Careful observation of the way cattle (and horses) take in grass often gives a hint as to their dental condition. Cattle grasp the grass with lips and a coarse dental pad on the upper mouth and sharp incisor (cutter) teeth on the bottom. Horses grasp grass with the lips and jerk-cut with upper and lower incisors. When a Cracker is concerned about the body condition of cattle or the purchase of cattle, he'd want to check 'er teeth.

The age of cattle (and horses) can be estimated by examining the incisor teeth and knowing when the individual pairs of adult incisors erupt from the gums. Checkin' 'er teeth is used for preliminary information about the age and disease status of a cow. For example, a thin cow with poor or no teeth is old and wore out and is usually destined for sale. On the other hand, excellent dental condition indicated some other problem than age.

Chin strap: a chain or band of leather which sits loosely in the chin groove on the back of the horse's lower lip and fastens to the bit on either side to add extra pressure to the bit. The ordinary cowboy uses the western bridle. The entire headpiece used on a horse, headstall, bit, chin strap and reins, is called the bridle. When in a tight, and the horse is especially "cold-jawed" (prone to grip the bit between his teeth and run away with the rider; see term), I've seen fence wire made into a chin strap. It worked well. Occasionally, these additions to a bridle are incorrectly positioned too high or are too tight. This causes the bits to rotate forward and the rider has a less effective response from the horse. Incorrectly applied bridles and bits can make a horse fight the bits and toss its head. Many add a nose band to give even more control to the bridle. This nose band is attached by a strap from the bridle to the girth band under the horse's belly. This stops the head tossing.

Gentle and easily handled horses can be used with what is called a bosal. This is an elongated loop which fits over the animal's nose and has reins attached. Rigging a western saddle has some art to it as well as science. (See Got the bit in his (or her) teeth and cold-jawed.)

Choke 'im down: to actually choke, strangle, stifle, asphyxiate, or render unconscious–either actually or metaphorically.

Cracker Terms, Phrases And Definitions

It could be used in the context of "jerked a knot in his tail" (See term) or in the past tense for the description of a fight when one fella ends it up pretty quickly. An engine can choke down or stall when under certain conditions. I had a Cracker tell me, "It's a little known medical fact that choked-down sneezes cause poochie bellies." In this context choked-down means stifled. (He may be right.)

One cowboy told me he witnessed a choked-down horse incident. He said the horse was tied to the fence inside the cow pens. Whoever tied the horse had used a slip knot. This is dangerous since the knot can slip down tight on a horse's neck pulling back to escape a threat. A mean bull was "cleaning house" (See term) and the horse pulled the rope down so that it was chokin' him. One of the men saw what was happening, pulled his pocket knife, and slashed the rope off the horse's neck, cutting the skin but giving the horse breath. The cowboy that owned the horse questioned, "Man, why did you cut my horse like that?"

He replied, "We can heal a cut but we damshur cain't a dead horse." (Made sense to me.)

Chute or catch chute: a device for restraining cattle for treatments. There are many types: some are rudimentary mechanical monsters with man-killing levers and handles requiring the muscle, coordination and weight of two or three men. Others are exceptionally complex with hydraulic levers and pistons to control the panels (sides), head catch and tail gate, but all parts are controlled by one man at the levers.

Civey (civit) cat: a skunk, or its cousins; i.e., wild cats and raccoons. One tale went this way: a man lived near Lake Okeechobee in a little Cracker house on pilings. Often the water would flood the area and it helped to have your house up a bit above the potential summer water levels or after those from hurricanes. The house was built with the chimney's foundation on the ground. This left about a 2 ½ to 3 foot crawl space.

In the winter, dogs and wild hogs would crowd in under the house for shelter and nestle near the warm fireplace bricks. As the story was told, the man of the house lived alone, cooking and tending to himself. On occasion, the pigs would fuss among themselves, squealing and banging around, shuffling for the warmest position

The man would sometimes be awakened in the dead of night by the pigs' loud fussing and shuffling. He said he'd had enough of it one cold night, so he removed a floor board near the fireplace and dumped a pan of hot water down the space—right on top of a family of skunks! (They had been the reason the pigs were fussing.) The skunks reacted as skunks are inclined to do and sprayed musk on everything, including each other. He advised, "D - - - man! Don't never throw hot water on civey cats—they'll run you out frum the musk-stink! I had to sleep in the truck fer nigh onto a week. Tha stink'll take away yer breath."

Clean house: a term having nothing to do with housekeeping. It means to empty the premises by whatever means, usually pugilistic methods. "Whoever turned tha pig out at tha dance sure cleaned house, didden he?" A mean bull, dog, horse, or man can clean house. Whatever the circumstances, the idea is that what or whoever is striking fear in the hearts of the bystanders causes them to leave. An irritated cow can clean house when she bows up about something she perceives as a threat. (It could be as simple as the sight of a man in the pens–especially if she has a calf at her side.) A rattlesnake, mean catch dog, hornets, wasps or bees can clean house, too.

Colder'n kraut: a phrase indicating something is actually cold or knocked silly or unconscious. "Son... that bull knocked him out colder'n kraut." Colder'n ah pickled pig's foot or colder'n a deviled egg are related phrases.

I recall a time I went to the local library. They were having a sale of old books, making room for new editions and I found a few on Southern humor. When I went to the desk to pay

Cracker Terms, Phrases And Definitions

for them, a sweet gray-headed lady was sitting at the table and looked them over. As she put them in a sack, she said, "I see you got books on Southerners."

"Yes'm, I enjoy humor from anywhere."

She casually said, "You know... my daughter and I have always thought you can tell a true Southern lady by the number of deviled egg plates she owns."

"Is that right?" I said.

"Yes..." she said; "My daughter and I have twenty-seven between us." (I ain't making this up either.)

Cold-jawed: a term usually describing a horse that becomes insensitive to control by the bit. It could be used of people when they became reticent, stubborn or strongly determined, as in, "I tried to tell him how to do it, but he went cold-jawed on me..." or "Whut are you so cold-jawed about?" Often the term is linked to "took the bit in his teeth," a phrase referring to a horse that clamped the bit in its teeth and wouldn't turn loose. We had a mare like that. She'd clamp down on the bit and you couldn't get it away from her for nothing. We named her Sailboat. When you tried to cut cattle with her, she'd sail on passed the turn point, swinging way out in the pasture before you could get back to business at hand.

Cool yer jets: settle down, get quiet, calm, relaxed, restrained or under control. Men would comment to a vet, "Yer gonna hav' to give him a shot to cool his jets. He's a little rank." Also, "After I explained to her that I wuz with her daddy in town when the gal showed up at the house; that cooled her jets..." I've heard it used by a nervous young woman after a stressful day at work. She said, "I think I'll go by the Watering Hole and hav' a beer–that ought to cool my jets."

Cooter: a term of unknown origin, perhaps from coot, a diving pond bird or a snapping turtle. One extension of the word is Cooter Brown, a mythical figure that could be referred to in a variety of ways, such as, "That ther' dog is uglier'n Cooter

Brown's mule." Another use is in reference to a snapping turtle. They are common in the United States and considered a delicacy in some quarters—if you can keep all your fingers while catching them. There is also the fabled, cootagator. I have no idea what that is, but from the name alone I don't want to meet one. It is used to denote an elderly man, as in, "That ol' coot slipped up on us and caught us flat-footed." There may be other uses of the word with which I am not familiar.

Couden kill it (or him) witha crowbar: describes someone or something that is tough. It is used with wry humor about something that had survived despite the odds. For example, if a female dog had puppies and one got separated from the nest, when found alive, cold and near-starved, the owner could say with pride, "You couden kill that little fella with a crowbar." (See Tougher'n ah bus station steak)

Couden slap the smile offen his face: describes the observed joy of one when something turns out better than expected, for example, a newly acquired horse that is superior in its abilities: "Son! Whin he roped off that horse the first time, I don't think you coudda slapped the smile off his face."

Coughs-per-minute: a technical term used to evaluate cattle pneumonia. I first heard about coughs-per-minute from western feedlot cowboys. Feedlot cattle often have a twenty-four hour truck ride to reach the feedlot. They are stressed from handling, mixing into large groups, as well as stress from the travel. They often break with respiratory diseases within a day or two of arrival. These problems can be as mild as runny noses or as serious as pneumonias. In the feedlots a foreman directs the cowboys to go out to a suspect group, sit on the fence and count the coughs-per-minute. It sounds odd, but it is an effective way to diagnose the extent of the disease. Coughs can range from harsh and dry in mild respiratory disease, to rattling and wet, suggesting serious pneumonia.

Cracker Terms, Phrases And Definitions

There was a dairy where a mild respiratory disease was going around. The manager asked me what he should tell the men observing the herd. I said, "Tell the boys to watch for cows that refuse to eat and for dehydrated cows with sunken-in eyes," and added, "They should listen to the herds for cough-per-minute," explaining that this was an objective means to measure the increase or decrease of the severity of the disease. He understood.

The next time I saw him I asked how things were going with the herd. He said, "Well, I told tha boys whut you said about countin' tha coughs-per-minute... One of them came in an' said "Tha cows seem awrite but I think ole Emmett is comin' down with pneumonia... he's coughin' two or three times a minute.'" (Emmett was one of the herdsmen.)

Cow caught: to be butted or hooked by an aggressive cow. Close calls happen frequently and on occasion someone is caught and tossed or knocked down which could lead to a serious injury. All the other men and one (or four cow dogs) will take to the angry beast before the man is hurt. Sometimes this happens in other parts of the cow pens. I remember seeing a cow chasing a fella around and around for several intense minutes before she left the pens. One of the men stood by me at the fence. He glanced over at me, grinned and said, "Kinda like watchin' *National Geographic*, ain't it?" (See Acted ugly)

One time in Texas I noticed an unusual set of cow pens. They were made from oil well sucker rods from old oil wells. These were used metal rods welded to form a fence pane and painted. The whole pen was sturdy and durable. But I noticed that the bottom rod on each section was a little high off the ground. I wondered about this until I saw a Mexican cowboy being chased by a cow. He ran for the fence, fell and rolled under the bottom rod. The cow hooked the rod while the cowboy brushed off his clothes. Just another day at the office.

Cowed down: retreat, become sheepish, meek, ashamed or beaten. "Man, he thought he wuz ah bronc rider 'till he got throwed off the second horse; he cowed down quick."

Cow huntin' and Cow hunters: obviously referring to the search for stray cows out in the Florida woods and prairies. The term is common among cowboys, whether Florida or Western. Florida Crackers were originally considered cow hunters, but Georgia Crackers are a "whole nuther bunch ah dogs" (See term).

The term Cracker is assumed to have originally come from the characteristic cracking of whips in attempts to drive cattle out of the thick woods. You could hear them coming out of the woods a long ways off. It sounds like a twenty-two caliber rifle firing. Tah-POW and Whack are some of the sounds of a braded leather whip. Just as you wind up your whip overhead, you'll hear a softer ch—wohup sound, ending in a loud crack. It sounds like a fishing rod, swooshed through the air with a slight pause, then a twenty-two caliber pistol firing at the end of the initial sound. It is an art form that has largely been lost in modern times, but you still can see whips at some Florida ranches. You could lightly snap a cow in the behind as she was hanging up in a gate–to encourage her to move along. It is an excellent means of getting a mean dog's attention, too. When a bad bull would bow up in the pens, sometimes a whip strike on the nose would get him to leave so work could continue. (Although, I have seen some foremen call a water break, accomplishing the same thing.) Your face would smart for hours when you got a backlash.

Men good with a whip could just about knock the fly off a cow's ear and not touch the cow. The whips were a part of the Cracker cowboy's gear.

Someone came into the clinic one day with a new handmade whip. I couldn't stand it–I had to try it out. I went out in the yard and Kha-tow'-ed it several times. The next thing I knew, the whole clinic emptied to watch the demonstration.

I guess they had never seen a fella in a white shirt and tie, cracking a whip. I received considerably more respect for the rest of the day.

Cow hunters think differently than the rest of us. Once, a couple of Crackers were discussing the unexpected demise of a neighbor rancher. The one said, "Well, I guess you heard that Ol' Joe passed away." The second one said, "Yeah… whut'd he have?" The first said, "Oh, 'bout 300 brood cows an' 700 acres."

Cow pie: surely you all know to what the term refers. It's a round flat pile of bovine manure, sun-dried or wet. In under-developed countries where wood is scarce, dry cow pies (also called cow chips) are used for fuel. Interestingly, fresh cow manure is only 20-25% moisture and the rest is partially processed fibrous material. Other uses of dried cow pies include chunking at brothers and sisters in the pens, placing on the chest or in the hat of sleeping cowboys at a noon nap, kicking when discussing serious issues in the pens, etc. Wet manure pies are useful for watching the reactions of tourist visitors in the pens when they step in them. Wet manure is often stuck to palpation gloves and serves as a means of getting some room to work when flung in various directions. By-standers give you plenty of room when it is spattered in their direction. (See Dingle berry and It cain't be dirty.)

Cracker-jack: excellent, good, fine, great, ideal or perfect. "Boy, those bulls are cracker-jacks, ain't they?"

Cracker pony, Florida cow horse or Indian pony: a somewhat smaller horse or pony, than the 1200-pound Quarterhorse. They are lean, well-muscled, tough and reliable in the woods and marshes. Most weigh in the neighborhood of 900 pounds. Many historians say they descended from the Spanish horses and were adopted by the Seminoles. Few people realize that Florida has been a cattle state since 1530 when the Spanish established St. Augustine. The somewhat smaller body mass gives an obvious advantage to these Cracker horses. A big, heavy, well-muscled horse can easily overheat—especially if too fat for working. Notice that animals in the colder (Northern) areas of the continents naturally have bigger, thicker bodies and longer coat hair, while the closer to the equator, animals tend to be thinner. Elephants, Brahman Cattle and Water Buffalo are the exceptions. Interestingly, Brahman cattle out west and left in the high country grew longer hair coats. Heat stress in animals brought into Florida is a problem at times and requires some adaptation to the heat and humidity.

Crazier'n ah bulldog atta clown college: Can you picture big-footed and paint-faced clowns dressed up in funny clothes and wigs, honking horns and shooting off fire extinguishers? Believe me that would drive a bull dog insane—he'd catch every one of them. One time I heard a Yankee say, "He's crazier than a pit bull at a postman's convention." (Same idea) I also heard a cowboy ask, "You know whut the difference between my wife and my pit bull dog is?" The reply was, "No, whut?" "The pit bull quits barkin' whin I turn the lights off..." he retorted. (His wife was not present during this exchange.)

A sheriff's deputy told this story of a young Cracker woman named Charlotte. Living by herself in a small isolated house, she returned home late one afternoon and began to check her computer for email. Dark came as she studied various things on her screen. So intent was she that she did not turn on any lights in the house and a thief, assuming that the house was empty broke the small bathroom window and started sliding his legs through the frame. The scoundrel was half way through the opening when Charlotte jumped him. She beat him with a hair dryer, broke one of his legs, bruising him so badly she had time to go get her phone to call 911. By the time the deputy and emergency services got there, the man was begging to be arrested. The deputy said, "That hair dryer was nothing but guts and wires hangin' on a cord—she'd tore it completely to pieces."

Cracker Terms, Phrases And Definitions

I happened to see Charlotte a few days later and asked, "Well, Charlotte, break any legs last night?"

She replied, with a straight face, "Naw, it wuz purty quiet last nite."

(To my thinking, this is not the best example of crazier than a bull dog at a clown college, though it is close. I do think "She's tougher than a bus station steak" fits.

Crazier'n ah blind gun-fighter: no explanation needed. Crazier'n ah blind javelin thrower has the same idea.

Crazier'n ah outhouse rat: describes any violent and aggressive animal. This term was often used by one of our cow crew, Hubert–only he used a German slang word for outhouse. Crazier'n ah runover dog and crazier'n a sprayed on roach or crazier'n ah mailbox spider or crazier'n ah coon innah garbage can are similar phrases.

Croker sack: a burlap or hemp bag, sometimes called a potato sack or feed sack; or a poke, meaning a sack for carrying essentials. Croker sacks in Florida often served in place of the Western saddlebag. And, then, there were colorfully designed cotton sacks containing ground wheat flour which could be used for dresses or shirts.

Cumon upher: implies that help is needed, as in, "Y'all need to comeon upher–tha fence is busted all to h - - -", or "Cumon upher... this guava tree is loaded."

A classic illustration of the phrase occurred in the desert of Arizona when my cousin was driving from California to home in Kentucky with a friend. The car did not have a working air conditioner, it was about 4:00 pm and the car was intolerably hot. The model of auto had the little triangular vent-windows at the front of the side windows. They could be turned inward and direct a stream of outside air into the driver's seat. The big old Ford was on cruise control, both vent windows turned fully inward. Her friend said, "I am so sleepy, I think I'll lie down in the seat and hang a foot out the window."

She then told the rest of the story: "I was gittin' sleepy, too– and it was hot... so I hung my left foot out the driver's side window and let the vent blow air on me. The cruise control had us steady at about 80 mph. We had the CB radio cranked up, listenin' to the occasional chatter. I began to get sleepier and didn't see the trucker easing up behind us."

All of a sudden, the CB cut on and the trucker said, (Squawk) "Hey, Charlie–cumon upher... I want you to see a big woman!"

It finally dawned on Cousin all the trucker could see was one woman's head and a foot out each side of the car. (I guess that would be ah site...)

Curlew: a spoonbill pond bird.

Cussinum: Dr Frank Platt, an Okeechobee veterinarian, told me of a Cracker that worked at the Mormon-owned and -operated Deseret Ranch near Kenansville. There was a man day-workin' there whose name I think was Lightsey. (See Day-workin'.) There were several distinct properties at that time; each had a set of cow pens, and each was run by a Mormon foreman and a regular cow crew. Day-workers were hired when there was need for extra help, none of which were of the Mormon religion.

Well, Mr. Lightsey, in the heat of work, reverted to the common cowboy language. His job was to bring the cattle down the narrow alley ways to a restraint chute. They were quite often uncooperative and would back up or turn around, which caused considerable delay. Often frustrated, he'd curse the cattle calling them by various colorful but profane words and descriptions: "Step up, you pig-eyed (*expletive deleted*);" "Go ahead, you silly son of a (*expletive deleted*);" "Get on outta here, you snotty nosed (*compound expletive deleted*);" "You puzzle-gutted, wall-eyed (*expletive deleted*);" and other diverse and common variations.

After a bit the foreman came over and politely informed him, "Mr. Lightsey, we don't curse on this place; I'd appreciate it if

Cracker Terms, Phrases And Definitions

you'd cut it out." This made Mr. Lightsey a little tight-jawed, but he cooled his language.

After the day's work, as the men were packing their gear to leave the ranch, loading trailers and personal affects, Mr. Lightsey paused, got a faraway look in his eyes and reflected, "Ya know... I worked cattle all my life and I dent know ya could workum without cussinum."

Cut a cabbage: to chop off a cabbage palm around the bud to obtain the heart. Yankees call this heart of palm, and it is considered a delicacy in some places. Crackers took the heart and trimmed off the tender portions, put it in a pot, added fried bacon, onions and tomatoes to make a vegetable dish. The cabbage palm is a common and readily available food source. It goes well with beans, rice, biscuits, fried meat and tomato gravy. Ooooeeeeee!

Cut a colt or cut a bull: castration of the male equine or bovine, one of the oldest veterinary surgeries known. Funny, we cut a bull calf to get rid of the testosterone, replacing it with short-lived implants of anabolic steroids to obtain lean mean and rapid growth. The practice is done to improve efficiency, to alleviate the bad secondary traits of masculinity and fighting in cattle management.

On occasion one would hear "cut on 'er" in reference to dogs. In referring to the male it meant emasculation; in females it was an ovario-hysterectomy.

They say baldness in men is related to testosterone levels. I heard a woman psychologist one time say she'd rather have a bald virile man than an average one with all his hair. This observation reminds me of a song I wrote a few years ago:

Well us males do some very funny things,
like take a family trip in a truck.
A ten-minute rest stop is all we'll allow
to let the family rest up.
Now it's plain to see that the name of the
game is, "Man must conquer the road."
So if you think you'll need to pee my friend,
better carry your own commode.

There are some good things to consider
when you think about this hormone -
Like men bringing home their paychecks
and protectin' wives, kids and homes.
But can you imagine what it'd be like upon the battlefield,
If a General stood in front of the troops and said,
"Excuse me, but how do y'all feel?"

Cut some slack: to be more tolerant of, give the benefit of the doubt, or to do some action that stops pain or gives support. If a young man was having trouble moving cattle and someone criticized him, another might say, "Y'all cut that boy some slack…"

Cut out, cutter out, cutim out or cutter in: sort, single-out, separate or isolate a group or individual. The term was so common it was just part of daily cowpens usage. "I want y'all to go git tha marsh cattle and cut out tha bulls," is an example. Or, "See that white-face cow? Cutter in tha loadin' pen."

Cut the cheese: to cut hoop cheese, wrapped in brown butcher's paper that has been stored on the dash board of the truck. The sun usually heats it so that the grease oozes from the cheese and saturates the paper. This usually indicates that the soft cheese is just right to cut. The term is often used to indicate that you would also cut the smoked sausages that were in the greasy brown butcher's paper next to the cheese.

Most of the time, when hunting with Okeechobee's Jack Coker, the cutting of the cheese occurred after a successful deer hunt, after near misses or a terrible day of hunting or when you hadn't seen a deer all morning. It almost always occurred after someone's shirttail was cut off for <u>missing</u> a shot at a deer.

D

Damshur: to be firmly positive; Lorida's Rudy Ashton was a fine Cracker pioneer who lived on the banks of Lake Istopoka. He'd go down to the nearby grocery in his brogans, bib overalls and floppy cowboy hat, sit on the porch and read the paper. He'd sold a small piece of property not far from the grocery where it looked like a RV and trailer park were going in. The neighbors knew something was up, so one of them asked him what was happening, "Rudy, I see you sold some of yer land to some Yankees…"

Rudy, shook out the wrinkle in the paper and grumbled, "Yeah and they damshur know they bin to a sale, too."

He then went back to reading the paper. Rudy had probably paid $30 an acre many years ago and sold it for $400 an acre; to him it was a regular sack full of money—especially pleasing since it was Yankee money.

The term is used in a story about a Cracker cowboy who brought a fine looking gal to a Western wear store and had her try on some outfits. He kept telling the salesman, "Man… I want you to git the finest boots in here… an' tha best clothes you got. Money ain't no problem. Git her a hat, jeans, an' ever' thin' she needs." The gal spoke up, "Yeah… he just told a man he'd pick up a barrel horse for me next Monday, too." So the clerk loaded them up with everything she wanted. At the end of the shopping, the Cracker said, "Tell you whut. I got good credit, here's my credit card. I'll be back here Monday to pick ever' thing up." With that he left.

On the following Monday, as he walked in, the clerk and owner stopped him at the entrance, saying, "Son! That credit card wadden worth anything." The cowboy smiled and said, "I know, I jus' come by to say thank ya... I damshur had a good weekend."

Danged if ah didden forgit: The best example of this phrase is from Tom Powe's describing his Master's Thesis. He said he took his thesis in to his major professor who read it over two days. The professor said, "It's too long; I want you to reduce the page count from 498 pages to about half that amount." Tom said he worked for months and did in fact reduce it to 253 pages. He then said the professor told him it was still too long and to reduce it to half the pages. Tom said he worked another six months and had the thesis down to 121 pages. The professor then told him, "Tom, your work is good but I want you to reduce the whole thing down to one word–just one word that is the pure essence of your research!" Tom said he worked another year and finally had it down to one word. I was curious so I said, "What was the word?" He said, "Danged if ah didden forgit it."

Dark-thirty: somewhere around or after sunset. The term is not precise but indicates a general time when one would finish a job or when to meet someone. "Whin do y'all think ya will be through workin' the calves?" "Oh, sommers 'round dark-thirty." (See "Cain't 'til cain't.")

Dash: one might commonly hear, "Boy? Dash in the barn and git me a halter." The word is usually used to hurry things along. Also it is used in descriptions of an event, as someone might say, "Well, we had ever'thing surrounded whin one of tha hogs dashed out tha palmetters an run between Junior's legs... then all hell broke loose." Also, "Son, dash to tha house an' tell Mama we'll be there for dinner in about thirty minutes."

Cracker Terms, Phrases And Definitions

Dat wuz dood ta me, unh-huh: "That pleased me very well." Robert Arnold had a slight lisp and indicated his pleasure by saying, for instance, about a pan of guava cobbler, "Thun, dat wuz dood ta me, unh-huh..." Sonny modified it to refer to other things: one time he observed a herd of yearlings run into a lush pasture, bury their heads in the new grass and immediately start eating. He remarked, "Dat's dood to 'em, unh-huh..." For another example, "Writin' these definitions is dood to me, unh-huh."

I've never met Robert but I have liked him for years. One of his relatives, DeRoy Arnold, saved me from getting crushed by a mare after a nasty fall in the isolated mountains of Montana. (See At-it awehwite.)

Dawddlin': working on a task very slowly and unconsciously. Dawddlin; is more common among southerners, Crackers, and older individuals. It is a very slow, ambling effort at a minor task (that could be completed by a northerner in a very short time). The consummate dawddler is an aged southerner who likes to stop and visit with people everywhere he goes, while forgetting that others are waiting on him. Dawddlers generally have no concept of time (or space, for that matter). Dawddlers have similar characteristics to solipsists who believe that the only reality is that which they perceive in their own minds, however, like the solipsist, the dawddler cannot cross a busy street in New York without getting hit by a taxi.

Day work: a term referring to cowboys for hire on a day-to-day basis. They usually had to furnish their transportation, trailer, cow dogs, horse, feed, gear and talents for however many days it took to work a ranch's cattle. The sorry ones usually didn't work at the best ranches. Call-back day-workers usually meant they were good at their jobs. At first, I never understood why they would work so hard, take so much risk, and seemingly enjoy so much pain and torment as they did for the little pay they got. Then after a while I figured it out: They loved their jobs. I've seen them come to work with hangovers, Technicolor black-and-blue bruises, barked knuckles and obvious stiffness and lameness. The hours were often brutal, working from "Cain't to cain't." (See term) It was not unusual for them to get up at 4:00 am, feed the horses, eat breakfast, load everything up and be at the ranch by daylight. They'd be fed a big noon meal, though some ranches were too cheap to feed them, and then they'd work until dark or after, arriving home about 9:00 pm to unpack their gear, feed the horses, the dogs and themselves. How they kept this up day-in and day-out is beyond those who are unfamiliar with their lifestyle. They are the very definition of Cracker cowboys—each being unique in personality. More than one has saved another man, woman or veterinarian from getting maimed or killed in the pens. If the truth be known, they were almost always underpaid. But like the Florida cur dogs, they were in their element, loved what they did and were good at it.

Deer season: (not to be confused with deer seasoning) the term is used to indicate the long-anticipated day when deer hunting is legal.

Didden goferit: refused

Diddlin': the use of excessive and unnecessary efforts on a project or assigned activity. By implication, 'diddling' is associated with the young or very old. A diddler is one who practices this art form and is easily distracted, like a puppy with a butterfly. Older people can diddle but by the time they practice it, they have become habitual procrastinators. Not all procrastinators are diddlers, but most diddlers procrastinate.

Dido: an unexpected and violent reaction meant to interrupt or call a halt to an undesired action. Or it can describe a prank meant to pull one over on one's friends. "Boy, I want to tell ya, that horse cut a dido in the marsh. I didn't think we'd ever catch him." The word is used occasionally to indicate that some person or animal showed hisself or cut a shine. It is used sometimes when cattle sucked back inta tha swamp:

Cracker Terms, Phrases And Definitions

"Yeah, they done fine until we come aroun' the bay head, then the ol' yeller cow cut a dido."

I recall a story that is an example of pullin' a dido. My son-in-law's father, (you remember) Bruce, had to do a safety inspection of a facility on a Louisiana island, but to reach there people had to drive over a causeway. Located at the entry to the causeway, he saw a Toll Booth. The little building had a raised barrier gate with a STOP – PAY TOLL HERE sign on it. The toll booth was unattended, but there was a little sign on the outside near an open door that said, Toll $1.00, and a small Toll Box attached to a post near the road. Bruce pulled over, looked for the attendant, and seeing no one he dropped the toll charge in the box. No one appeared or looked to see if he had put the toll in the honor system box. He waited a while but decided to drive on over the causeway.

Bruce completed his business and as he made preparations to leave, the supervisor asked, "You didn't pay the toll, did you?" Bruce said, "Yes I did." The man laughed and said, "That belongs to a fella that just set up a little building and a bar on the edge of his property. Everybody around here knows it's not a real toll gate, but he catches a little cash from strangers and visitors when they come and go." They had a good laugh at the fella that pulled a dido on visitors. (This illustration has nothing whatsoever with Crackers. It only serves as an example of a dido.)

Diesel: the name of a cow dog in Florida. I asked, Why'd you name 'im Diesel?" The cowboy replied, "Well, he's hard to git started but whin he does, he's raw power."

Diggin' in his heels: to vigorously resist being pulled; to plant one's heels in the sand, as in trying to control a colt on a rope or to throw a calf (or cow). It's also used figuratively to indicate someone is being stubborn or sullen, as in, "Boy? Whut you diggin' yer heels in for? You know you got to go to court."

Dingleberry: a small ball of dried cow manure that has stuck to the hair of the cow's tail. The small collections grow in size like limestone in elongated stalactites with repeated manure exposure. However, there are places where cattle are raised and the dried mud dingleberries become so heavy that the cow can't lift her tail. In Texas, I have heard the cowboys sometimes have to take a hammer and break-up the caked, dried mud-clay accumulations. One Cracker I know named his cow dog, Dingleberry. (You were warned this book was going to be a wealth of barely essential information.)

Dip stick: the metal stick used in car engines to determine the level of oil in the engine. The term can be used as a synonym for stupid or silly. It isn't used frequently in Cracker conversation but I couldn't resist mentioning a song title I heard from Aaron Wilburn: "All the oil may be in Texas, but the dipsticks are in D.C." (I know... I know....)

Do I owe ya anything? a question implying that one does not fully appreciate a rendered service and is thinking that he shouldn't have to pay for it. There is a difference between "How much do I owe ya?" and "Do I owe ya anything?" The former expression indicates that the person expects to pay for services or products. The latter expresses reluctance to pay, "I don't owe ya anything, do I?"

The classic story was told to me by Dr. Alan Cameron, my classmate in veterinary school. As I recall, he described a man coming into his veterinary hospital with a hen chicken in a sack. The man said, "Doc, I need ya to take a look at ma chicken and tell me whut's wrong with'er." Dr. Cameron took the chicken to the back examination room and removed the chicken from the sack. The old hen had lymphoma, which is called Mereck's Disease in the industry. Alan returned to the examination room in the front and explained that it was a hopeless and incurable disease. He suggested that the hen be put to sleep. The fella agreed. Alan went back, drew a syringe of a euthanasia solution and gave it to the hen. Painlessly and quietly the old hen gave up the fight.

Cracker Terms, Phrases And Definitions

Alan said he didn't want to spend unnecessary amounts of time with a dead chicken so he put her back in the sack and returned it to the owner. (He figured he'd already spent too much time and money on the poor thing.)

As the owner accepted the departed chicken in the sack, he said, "Do I owe ya anything?"

Alan said to himself, "Well, maybe I ought to recover the cost of the euthanasia solution at least." He turned to the chicken owner and said, "Oh… $3.00 will cover the cost."

The man looked in the sack and said accusingly, "Why you haven't even cleaned 'er!"

Dob a little: a directive phrase meaning, "Put a little bit here at this site or spot." As far as I can tell the phrase is so common among Crackers that it goes unnoticed most of the time. It can be used in a variety of applications. "Dob a little of that fly dope on the cow—the flies are eatin' her up." "Honey, would you dob a little liniment on my back wher' I fell on ah literd knot?" or "Doc, put a dob of salve on my cut finger."

Sonny and I once treated his dog, Cookie, for a severe tick infestation after spotting an engorged tick on the back of her neck. We caught her and looked her over. We knew that if left untreated ticks will paralyze a dog. Sonny's gaze fell on a small can of gasoline on the worktable. "You reckon this'll kill it? Let's see." He took a little piece of rag and dipped it in the gas, "Here, let me dob a little on it."

We did. On closer inspection we found two more, which we dobbed. Rolling her over on her back we found several more ticks. We dobbed them, too. She was in fact covered by hundreds of little ticks. After about seven or six minutes of this dobbing, Cookie began to squirm a bit. "He-ah. Hold still, Cookie. Let us git these ticks gassed for ya'."

Cookie continued to fidget and became difficult to hold. Sonny said, "Turn'er loose. That must be burnin' her skin."

I let her go and she bee-lined it for a mud-pond close by the shop. She feverishly rolled, wallowed and rubbed all over to alleviate the burning. She emerged from the pond, fortunately none the worse for wear. However, from that day on, when one of us picked up a gas can or she smelled it on us, she'd pull out for the pond. We never did that again or, as said in our world, "Well, that ended that up." (See terms)

Dog cussin': a phrase that indicates a severe cursing has been applied to someone or something. In context, "Yeah, whin he found out I wrecked his truck he commenced to give me a dog cussin'." I think the term came from handling cow dogs. Florida cow dogs, often called, Cur dogs, are notoriously tough and often flat-out mean. There have been times when one or several will revert to pure, raw evil—to wolf status. Some are worse than others. When conditions get just right, one rank cur dog (or a pack of them) can strip the ears off a belligerent cow or especially calves. Things can escalate to a point where one or all become "cold-jawed" (see term). If the bull or cow gets rough, they get rougher. But sometime in the fray, one cur dog might figuratively step over the line and get too rank. This incites the others to follow suit. That's when the cowboy gets him back under control by yelling his name, a control word or gives him (or them) a regular dog cussin'. Sometimes it takes a whip popping right close to them to get the point across. Its effectiveness depends on whether the dog has ever been intentionally or accidentally popped with a whip. Apparently one time is enough to get their attention.

I witnessed Hubert Waldron, in Okeechobee, Florida, rope his dog named Jake. The dog was tough and had gone cold jawed on a calf. Hubert got off his horse and stomped the dog's head for several seconds. As he did it, he made colorful descriptive remarks about the dog's heritage, his ultimate doom, i.e., he gave him a dog cussin'. He took the rope off, told the dog, "Get behind!" And he worked perfectly the rest of the day. He explained to me that the dog had to be supervised,

Cracker Terms, Phrases And Definitions

because he had a mean streak. "He'll kill something if you don't clean out his ears ever' now an' then."

Years later, I saw Hubert with a then gray-muzzled Jake sitting in the front seat of his car. The air conditioner ducts were turned toward Jake. He was sitting there like somebody special, like one secure in his place. He was, too. Hubert said, "He deserves riding in the front seat. He's worked hard all his life. Jake is the best cow dog I ever owned… mean streak and all." They seemed to have an understanding: Hubert leader—Jake follower. (Dogs are happiest when they're tired from work and have a good leader. Jake was truly a happy dog.)

Dog-trot: So, as the crow flies, indicates linear measurement, while dog-trot refers to distance. A dog-trot is a little ways from, not far from, close to or very near, as in, "It's jus' a dog-trot past the ol' cow trail coming out of the swamp."

Don't look now: a phrase I once used out of meanness. The story is interesting… to me anyway. Hunter's mother, Lucy, came to live with us the last six years of her life. She had more activity and fun that she'd had in many years. We moved into a bigger house where we had a room and bath just for her. She was weaker'n a kitten when we moved. She'd fought cancer for over twenty years. At the time, she was frail and weak. She could not walk, though she could stand if helped up. Hunter was in town at the time on errands. Now you must understand Lucy was a real southern lady, very proper and modest.

She was mortified that she had to go to the toilet and Hunter was not available. Finally, in desperation, she said, "Howard, I hate to ask you but I need help going to the bathroom." She was obviously embarrassed. I said, "No problem. I'll lean over, let you put your hands behind my neck and I'll stand up and you hold on until we get you up and get your balance. Take little steps to the potty." (We had a portable potty for her next to her bed.) The house was located in the middle of five acres with woods all around. The room was designed to admit light, giving it a cheerful and bright appearance. Big double windows were next to her bed so she could enjoy the great outdoors.

Once she had her balance, I eased her over in front of the potty and said, "Okay, I'll step out of the room and when you're through, call me and I'll help you back to bed." After a few minutes she called. I went in, finding her sitting on the potty with baggy pajamas covering her frail body. She held her arms up for my neck, I stood up and she was raised to a standing position. Her little body was so thin, her pajama bottoms slipped down and that was upsetting to her. I kept my head up, balanced her and reached down to try to pull her pajama bottoms up. My finger tips just barely touched the elastic waistband. With patience and extreme manual dexterity, I was able to grasp enough of the elastic to pull them up. I do not know what came over me, but thinking to divert her mind from her humiliation, I said, "Don't look now, Lucy, but the Neighbor Welcome Wagon is right outside the window." She jerked her head in that direction and then laughed when she saw there was no one there. Relieved, she smiled and, under her breath, said, "You devil…"

Don't never live innah place like this: a comment made by my step-sister's husband while I was visiting them in Orlando, Florida. They lived in a condominium there and it was a pleasant place with a small stream and woods off the patio. Charles, in dead seriousness, said to me, "Don't never live innah place like this… a fella cain't pee off his own back porch." I understood him completely.

Don't say nuthin': Though so common that it usually escapes notice, the phrase means for someone to keep an act, action, event or comment secret.

One of the best examples occurred many years ago in a story told by my son-in-law's daddy, Bruce. Bruce's daddy owned and ran a bar at the time. It happened to be in a county that

Cracker Terms, Phrases And Definitions

limited all beer sold and consumed in the county to a 3.2% alcohol level. Bruce said his daddy asked him to tend the bar while he took care of some business. While managing the bar Bruce noticed a half-gassed (See Gassed) fella sitting at the bar, loudly complaining and criticizing "the county" for not allowing "regular beer", meaning he wanted the higher level of alcohol in his beer. Bruce finally had enough of the rancor as it was disturbing the customers. So he went over to the fella, reached under the counter and slipped an oversized mug up on the bar. Looking around to see if anyone was watching, he clandestinely poured two 3.2% beers into the mug. He leaned close to the man's ear and said, "Don't say nuthin'." The man was pacified, smiling at Bruce as he sipped what he perceived as 6.4% beer. (It almost makes sense.)

Don't git me started: having too much frustration or inability to explain one's disgust, exasperation or criticism. The phrase is sometimes used but a variation is more often used in the context, "Hey y'all, whin he gits here... don't git him started on what happened to him at the rodeo–he'll be talkin' till mornin'.

That reminds me of a story told some twenty or thirty years ago by Carl Hurley. He said he and his cousin went to the new country club in their county. They'd never been to one and thought it'd be fun. So they showed up, parked and walked in. The maître'd looked them up and down, saying, "Fellas, I'm sorry but a tie is required to be served in the dining room. You all will need a tie."

His cousin indicated that all they wanted to do was have a meal, but the host insisted on the club rules. So they went to the truck and searched for ties. There was one in the glove box. Dr. Hurley said he put it on. All his cousin could find was half of a jumper cable. He cut off the clamp and tied a neat but large bowtie with it. They went back in.

The maître'd frowned at it and said, "What is that?"

As if it was the latest thing in fashion, Cousin said, "Itsah jumper cable tie."

The host pondered that but said suspiciously, "Alright, y'all can go in... but don't start nuthin'."

Don't hav' a dog in this fight: an indication that one has no interest in some particular disagreement. It is also used to indicate that a man (or group of men) is not going to join in or take sides in a quarrel, because "We don't hav' ah dog in this fight." Apparently, dogs have distinction in Cracker language. Examples include, "He wuz mopin' lik' ah ol' dog off his feed," and, "That dog won't hunt." (Also, see other terms that include dogs.)

Don't talk funny: I heard this in the middle of Florida Cracker country and it struck me as funny. A fella proudly told me in an exaggerated country twang, "Ya know, I lik' livin' in this her' area 'cause tha people don't talk funny." (I taught my five year old granddaughter to say it. She really gets a laugh from the unsuspecting adults. I think I have created a monster....)

Don't that jus chap yer lips: Obviously a reference to something that irritates, exasperates, frustrates, hampers or makes angry. I first heard it from a Texan. Somehow the correct pronunciation, "Doesn't that just chap your lips?" sounds like a New York interior designer who has one hand on his hip and the other on his cheek.

I'll never forget the time I was standing with one hand on a hip, asking a question of someone in charge, regarding the next step in a very frustrating job. I said, "What do you think?" meaning, "What should I do next?" He looked me up and down, saying, "Well, I think you're either an interior designer or you've lost your watermelon." (Yeah, I laughed.)

Down went tha price of eggs: a phrase used to describe the prevention of an expected resolution. "When he missed three trailer payments, down went tha price of eggs." Or, "I got ther

Cracker Terms, Phrases And Definitions

and realized I didden hav enough money to git in... down went the price of eggs." "That ended it up," means the same thing.

Drag rider: a term rarely heard among Crackers. So you'll know I know, there is a difference between a drag rider and a rider in drag, besides we're not talking about New Orleans. The classical stereotype of the western cowboy with chaps and red bandana over the nose was essentially non-existent in South Florida. I never heard the phrase there–only in the movies. What I often heard was, "Y'all git behind an' bring 'um."

Drink coffee: a phrase that may or may not have anything to do with drinking coffee. It is often said in the context of, "Well, come on by the house and we'll drink coffee," when, in reality, the man may be out in the barn, mending a saddle, mucking out a stall, or working with a colt. It meant, "Come by my house, I'll be there." And then, they may actually drink coffee.

Crackers and southerners don't necessarily mean it literally when they say, "Y'all come by sometime." It is a way of being polite and hospitable. Northerners, however, will jump on it, "What time?" And then show up early!)

Speaking of inviting someone for coffee and a visit, my cousin Florence once said, "Come on by... I'm always here unless I'm somewhere else." (What?)

Drinkin' coffee an' smokin' cigarettes: Hubert Waldron first introduced me to this phrase when he once said he woke up about 4:00 am every day. I asked him, "What do you do for two or three hours before we gather for work?" He said, "I sit at the kitchen table, drink coffee and smoke cigarettes until daylight." But the best retort was by Dr. Frank Handley. He had an extension of the hospital phone in his home to answer after-hours calls. One particular dairyman, Walter Mandus, called at 4:30 am. Handley answered with a brusk "Hello...." The dairyman was delighted that he had awakened Frank and humorously asked, "Did I wake you up?" Frank never missing a beat said, "Naw... I been up two hours, chain smokin' and drinkin' coffee and waiting on tha (*expletive for doomed or cursed deleted*) phone to ring." The end of the story came several nights later when Walter called again. Frank loaded up and went to the dairy to treat a cow. Holding a bottle of medication, Frank looked at Walter and said, "Walter, does the sun ever shine on this (*same deletion as above*) dairy?" (That was the last time Walter called before sunrise.)

Drop ah wing an' run at 'er: a descriptive phrase originating with a rooster's action in the chicken yard; thus indicating a similar reaction of a young man to an attractive woman. "Yeah... whin she smiled at 'im, he dropped ah wing and run at 'er." (See Boar Quail for another use of the phrase.)

My partner, Frank Handley, used the expression one time. I told him someone had released several Muscovy Ducks in the lake behind our house. (You know... the multi-colored ducks with the ugly red tumors hanging off their heads.) This flock of ugly nomads tore into our quail feeders and made a general mess of the area. They hung around like vagrants at a homeless shelter. I indicated that I was really tired of their mess and he agreed, "I know whut you mean; I don't want nuthin' that'll drop one wing an' run up on yer patio to *poop*."

Dum sumb *(expletive for female canine deleted)*: an uncouth expression, not necessarily a curse phrase as it is used so often that it has become conventional. It usually refers to an animal that "acted ugly" (See term); however, on occasion it can be applied to a stupid or humorous person. Stupid is a synonym for dum. For an example, when a man came to the cow pens with a hand wrapped in bandages, the inevitable question came: "Whut happened to you, Charlie?"

"Ol' Ring and Buck wuz fightin' agin. I tried to break it up an' tha dum sum*(expletive deleted)* like to hav' bit my hand off." Or, when a prankster turned a wild hog loose at the Speckled Perch Bar and Grill in Okeechobee, the report was,

Cracker Terms, Phrases And Definitions

"It went plumb crazy whin sum dum sum *(expletive deleted)* turned a pig loose."

The classic story in my mind is about a young Highlands County Cracker who had his Pontiac motor modified to allow him to remove a screw-cap off the manifold so his exhaust would exit directly, by-passing the muffler and blasting forth a satisfying noise, emulating raw horsepower. Well, he got caught by a Florida State Trooper on the edge of town one night. He was fined and told to fix the motor to abate the noise. When he told me the story, he allowed that he planned to be real careful to put the cap on the manifold so he wouldn't get caught again. One evening he was headed back to town. He related, "I remembered I had tah put tha cap on to muffle the engine." He stopped outside of town, crawled under the car in the grass, and was screwing the cap on the pipe when a car, with the high-beams lights on, pulled up behind him. "I figured it wuz sumbody stopped to see if I wuz broke-down. The fella walked up beside my boots stickin' out from under the car an' said, 'Broke down? Need some help?'"

"I said, 'Naw... I'm just puttin' a plug on my manifold so that dum sumb*(expletive deleted)* Trooper don't write me anuther ticket.' After a minute or two I realized that there had been a long silence. Curious, I looked out an' saw a pair of shiny black shoes an' real neat gabardine britches–it wuz tha same d*(expletive deleted)* Trooper that caught me the first time.

Talking about being involved with the law, a Cracker got into a fight one time at a local "juke joint" (See term). It ended badly with the fella being hit with a bottle. The police responded and were sorting out the incident. One deputy asked him to describe his assailant. The Cracker retorted, "That's whut I wuz doin' whin he hit me with tha bottle."

Rattling around somewhere in my mind is a poem told by Dr. Baxter Black, cowboy poet and veterinarian. In the poem, which is probably a true story, he vividly describes being in a bar out west somewhere. He related how he and his friends left the den of iniquity. "I hollered out, 'Who's the meanest sum *(expletive deleted)* in here?'" He said the men at the bar backed away from a fella who slowly turned around to face him from across the room. The man was described in detail as having prison tattoos, a chain on his wallet, cold-steel eyes, scars, a thick beard and rippling muscles. Baxter yelled at him, "Take over, we're leavin'."

As a resident in Dairy Medicine and Surgery at Auburn University, I had an opportunity to speak at the Annual Alabama Dairy Meeting where most of the state's dairymen came to Montgomery for technical up-dates. I was also enrolled in the Animal Sciences Ruminant Nutrition Program. The first speaker had charts, graphs and research references that boggled the mind and I knew what he was trying to say; I understood him. The second speaker continued on with the theories and hypotheses of his research. The third speaker covered the minute technical differences in selected management specifics in kilograms and parts-per-million. Almost everyone was lost in the maze of technical terminology. There were many blank stares in the room.

My turn came. My topic was metabolic diseases of dairy cows. I began to explain the signs of diseases that all dairymen see with the explanation of what caused these signs and how to prevent them. I hadn't gotten very far when a hand shot up in the audience. I paused and said, "Yes, sir?"

The old salty dairyman said, "Doc, you must be the dumbest sum *(expletive for female canine deleted)* here 'cause we can understand you!" (The audience broke out in waves of laughter.)

Though mentioned under another explanation, I give the context here: at another speaking engagement I had just started my talk when I was interrupted by a dairyman. I paused, saying, "Yes, Sir? You have a question?"

He said, "Doc, we don't use five percent of whut we know now an' yer givin' us a lot more."

(A Dairy Specialist must learn to tell good stories and jokes or his audience will go to sleep about 7:30 pm.)

Duncey: to be enamored with, to be crazy about, to enjoy, be enthusiastic for, to relish or passionately desire. (That ought to take care of it.) The best example of this term actually occurred in South Georgia, though it quickly spread around the local the ranches. My mother and stepfather were traveling from Texas to Florida after a visit with us.

My stepfather was not much of an eater. He'd nibble all day (and night) but never ate a big meal and didn't seem to gain excessive weight either. When he had a hankering for something, my mom usually got busy.

As they were nearing southern Georgia he happened to see a sign advertising fresh oysters. Being whimsical about some foods, yellow lima beans for example, he suggested that his taster called for oysters. So they set course for the café. After they had settled in the red naugahide booth, the waitress asked them what they wanted. He replied, "I want four fried oysters, four on the half-shell, a cup of oyster stew; just a cup—one hushpuppy and six French fries. That's all."

The waitress looked at my mother and, with a straight face, said, "He's kinda duncey 'bout oysters, ain't he?"

This word penetrated our family vocabulary. One time Mother made a cherry pie that was notable aberration in her usual expertise in cooking, especially pies and cakes. But this was runny, held no shape and spread out like warm grits when cut into slices. She apologized for it, though we dove into it like pups in gravy. When we finished eating, Paw said, "That was the best cherry pie I ever sucked through a straw."

The rest of the story was that he later sent a postcard with my name only on it and University of Florida, Gainesville, Florida. It got to me somehow and read, "Things here have gone to hell—we had a cherry pie you had to eat with a fork. Paw"

E

Ear canker: an ear infection. In its broadest application, ear canker was used by the cowboys to anything causing the dog (or horse) to fret and fidget about its ears. Ear problems in dogs could range from infection from bacteria, yeast, fungi, and mites to fight wounds (where the ear flap swelled and was irritating and painful.) Horse canker was a label that applied also to skin infections though crud was used instead of canker. In the case of ear canker in horses, severe gnat- or fly-bites could cause ear inflammation and swelling. The horse would have sensitive ears and often has flaking and infection with it.

This reminds me of Green Fungus Medicine. Dr. Handley had a gallon jug of a topical medication, made in Texas and, contrary to the name, was not for green fungi. It was a brilliant green and had a distinct aromatic odor. He'd had it for years it seemed. When a fungal infection, such as ringworm or similar fungus, didn't respond to conventional treatments, he'd dig out the old jug of green fungus medicine from under the sink. The cowboys would come in occasionally and ask for it. We'd only dispense two ounces. Why? We figured that was all they'd need. The *verbal* instructions were: "Git a cotton ball, soak it with this medicine, and dob it all over the area. It'll peal tha hide in a few days. Apply a second coat on the horse, **if you can catch 'im!**"

(Interestingly, veterinary hospitals became subject to unannounced hospital inspections in the nineties. One of the common violations was out-of-date medications. Expiration dates were usually prominently placed on all medications and biologicals. The state inspectors always went through the pharmacy and searched for outdated products. Well, the old Green Fungus Medicine was so old it had no expiration date. Our reasoning for keeping it was it was outstanding for eliminating skin ringworm and other fungi. On one occasion, the inspector found the jug, which by this time looked like something you'd find in an abandoned gold mining camp. He "wrote us up" with a minor violation. The next visit he went to the same sink, looked under it and could not find the "outdated" jug. We had fun hiding the jug for years... we figured that the evaporation of the alcohol base only concentrated the active ingredients. It did seem to take less and less of it over the years and we never had to use it more than once on an individual... mainly because we couldn't catch them!)

We also had Strong Tincture of Iodine for making "Colorado Sole Paint." Foot canker in the horse was an infection of neglected feet where bacteria set up housekeeping in the crevices ("frog") of the sole. We mixed the solution ourselves by combining equal parts of the 10% tincture of iodine, phenol and full-strength formalin. It worked well on wet and infected soles. It was dispensed in dauber bottles which had a heavy cotton ball on a wire extension attached under the lid so someone could hold the horse's foot up, daub the solution on the affected sole and not get it on his hands. The *verbal* instructions were, "Now, don't git this stuff on yer skin, you'll look like a Yankee tourist that fell asleep on the beach."

Ear bitin': the reference is to the old technique of literally biting the ear of a mean or unruly horse for some purpose which requires his cooperation. It's an old technique when nothing else works in subduing a fractious horse. I have no idea how the technique was discovered, though it might have developed by the Native Americans or frustrated pioneers. Generally, in horse restraint, there are techniques that make most testy horses submit to handling. It probably has to do with pressure points or distractions. (For an explanation see, I wuz afraid he wuz gonna do that.)

I recall working on a Quarterhorse ranch in Oklahoma. We had to vaccinate all the horses—including the unbroken yearlings and two-year olds. They didn't go for being touched, much less held for vaccination. One particular two-year old racing colt was a tough customer. He whirled around, kicked at us and stirred up all kinds of dust and dirt in the stall. One little fella, a jockey, stepped in, timed his jump and pounced up on the big colt's neck, grabbed an ear and bit it! The colt "sulled" (See term). The vaccinating went without incident. Somehow, this episode was implanted in the back of my mind somewhere, in a closet, no doubt.

A few years later in Florida, we had to sedate an unbroken horse to patch-up a nasty cut on his shoulder. The men tried and tried to catch him but had little success. I knew we were reverse training this critter, which meant he'd remember how he got away with this behavior and try it again. So, the thought bubbled-up from the fermenting pool of experience, "Why don't you try the ol' Oklahoma Pounce-On-His-Neck-An-Bite-His-Ear Technique?" I did. In silent admiration, one of the men put a twich on the mean horse and we proceeded to treat his wounds... after I had finished spitting the horse hair out of my mouth. (Salty. I guess, from his sweat.) One said, "D*(expletive deleted)*, Doc!. Where'd you learn that? You reckon that'll work on my ol' lady?" I told him, "I don't know... I'll come by Saturday nite and we'll try it."

Earmarkin': has nothing to do with politics, crooked or otherwise; earmarkin' refers to the age old trimming of cattle's ears to mark ownership. An earmark is a unique cut in the ear of a livestock animal, such as cattle, pigs, goats, sheep and even camels, to identify it. The term dates to the 16th century in England.

Earmarks are typically recorded when a stock owner registers a livestock mark or brand. Also the owner's earmark is placed in a designated ear of a camel or sheep to indicate its gender. There's even an ancient Hebrew text referring to its use in marking of bond servants where the ear was pierced with an awl before witnesses to identify the recipient as a willing permanent servant.

Though still practiced in some areas, the earmark has been mostly replaced by plastic identification tags containing information about the animal, such as ID number, age, group, significant dates, pregnancy status, etc. The tags most often come in packages of various colors, sequential numbers and/or lettering.

In hogs, there are precise locations where notches are applied by a hand tool which cuts out a triangular snip. The age, sex, etc. are easily recognized by the location of the marks on the ear flap (pinna).

It does not always constitute proof of ownership since many of the marks are similar.

Descriptive names such as steeple- or swallow-fork, over- or under-slope, over- and under-bit, single or double split, crops, and many others—each having an identifying characteristic. The swallow fork was a neat triangular portion removed, resulting in a missing wedge-like shape to the ear. A sharp or sharpee' was a description used for the literal sharpening of the ear to a distal point. A foreman might tell the earmarker, "Put a swallow fork right and a crop-split left.

Brahman cattle, Brammers, as often called by the cowmen, had huge ears, making ear marking very easy to read from horseback. Also, the crop mark was often reserved for the animal destined for sale to slaughter.

Sometimes these marks are the result of a dispute between a bull and a cur dog or three; from time to time, outlaw cattle would turn and attack a horse and rider and this was the signal for the dogs to clock in. They'd grab an ear (or whatever was handy) and hold on for dear life. The bull would try to dislodge or even kill this interference and as the dogs were thrown or hooked off, their canine teeth would strip out two parallel tear-cuts in the ear. Now that sounds rough to those who've never been in the cow pens or on a cow hunt, but it is a wonderful sight for a cowboy who's been a victim of one of these killer bull outbreaks. It was instinctive for the bulls to work their way to the edge of a tightly bunched herd. Those old mangled ears trailing strips of hide meant get out or ease out of his way—he'll eat yer sack lunch. (See Ease out.)

Most ranchers know their cattle and have little problem with retrieving wanderers. Many times I have known owners to call a neighbor to pick-up cattle that have jumped the fence or strayed into his pasture. I recall one rancher that was notorious for having cows slip the fence and get on the grassy highway right-of-way–sort of free-range grazin'. Some were hit by cars or trucks in a Florida fog, doing considerable damage to the vehicle as well as killing the animal. I chanced by one such accident just after it happened early one morning. The truck was smashed, the Sheriff's Deputy was there investigating the wreck, and the truck owner was scratching his head. I stopped, rolled down my window and asked the deputy, "Is that fella hurt?" "Naw", he replied. "I'm havin' trouble figurin' out where the cow is." He looked over toward the truck and gave a little chuckle. There, in front of the truck, was a blood trail where the dead cow had been dragged to a gate some fifty-yards away. (The ranch owner had come by while the man was walking for help and removed the evidence.)

Cracker Terms, Phrases And Definitions

CROP LEFT (L):

OVER BIT RIGHT (R):

OVERSLOPE L:

OVER HALF CROP L SWALLOWFORK R:

DOUBLE UNDER HALF CROPS:

CROP SPT L CROP DOUBLE SPT R:

DOUBLE SWALLOW FORKS:

SHARPEE L UNDERSLOPE R:

DOUBLE NOTCHES:

SPLIT L STEEPLE FORK R:

OVER HALF CROP L CROP NOTCH R:

DOUBLE UNDERSLOPES:

Ears backed (tite) to his head: a warning of impending aggression. Horses, panthers, cats and dogs pull their ears back when fighting or otherwise exhibiting strong emotion; male dogs back their ears when approaching a prospective breeding female. Just before a horse kicks the taste out of your mouth, he'll usually drop his ears and blow. Thus the phrase was used to indicate anger in humans, as in: "Ol' Ray come after me with his ears backed!" Also, "Don't you cum in her' with yer ears backed at me."

Ease out: to cautiously creep or move from cover. "Well, whin I got to the edge of the bayhead, I eased out real slow-like and saw tha ol' bull slippin' through tha palmetters." Also the term could be used in images, as in, "I got to tha house about daylite. He was just easin' out of bed." Or, to describe one's stiffness from pain, "Yeah, I knew he wuz hurtin' whin he eased off tha saddle." Story tellers often use the expression to heighten tension: "So I sez to myself, 'Son, you better be real careful whin you stick yer head up with all them mosquitoes out an around.' So, I e-a-s-e-d out of tha bushes ah little at a time till I wuz sure they hadn't seen me." (The eased out in this context is drawn out and spoken softly indicating that it was critical to be unobserved. For more on tall tales, see *Fireside Tales as Told by Florida Cracker Cowboys*)

Eat yer sack lunch: hostile attack with intent to do as much bodily harm as possible. It is used to lighten the atmosphere in a potentially dangerous situation, as in, "Boy, watch that speckled bull—he'll eat yer sack lunch if ya crowd 'im!" Sometimes it is combined with many other Cracker terms and phrases. "That puzzle-gutted whelp pur't nir like to have eat my sack lunch!" (See Puzzle-gutted, Whelp, Boogery and Purt' nir.)

Egg-suckin' (_expletive deleted_): This defamatory phrase is used of dogs that have developed the habit of stealing and/or breaking eggs, usually hen eggs, and licking out the contents. Consequently, it describes persons known to be of bad reputation, ill repute, thieves and liars. For example,

Cracker Terms, Phrases And Definitions

"There ain't nuthin' lower than a dirty egg-suckin' (*fill in the noun and/or descriptive adjectives*)." Of course, it can be and has been used on anyone needin' a good cussin'.

Even ah blind hog can pick up an acorn ever' now an' then: a curious phrase referring to good fortune or dumb luck. "I'll tell ya... I never thought I'd win the bull ridin'. That goes to show ya, even a blind hog can pick up an acorn ever' now an' then."

Even ah dead dog has purty teeth: I'll give you a perfect example of the use of this phrase, concerning a country veterinarian and his new associate in a mixed animal practice. The scene opens with the young associate seated casually at the front reception counter when the distraught owners of a beautiful Sheltie rushed into the reception area, holding their beloved pet in their arms, with tears streaming down their reddened faces. The pet was obviously deceased, having been found dead some twenty minutes before. The new associate remained seated, cocked his feet up on the desk and began random speculations as to the cause of the D.O.A.

"Well, I suppose acute heart failure could be the cause... maybe heartworm infection. Course, I reckon it could be acute kidney failure... she is pretty old... I've seen tumors rupture and aneurysms that have done this..." and on and on. Meanwhile the bereaved owners stood before him dumbfounded at this dispassionate response of thinly disguised contempt. Thinking that surely there must be some forthcoming compassion in this young man, they waited a few intense minutes, then stormed out, leaving the associate clueless as to what had just happened.

The old practitioner returned from a call and, when he had heard the story, said, "Boy, you should have jumped up, put the dog on the examination table, grabbed your stethoscope, listened for a heartbeat and felt for any signs of life. Then you should have pronounced the poor thing dead. After holding their hands a while, then you can do your speculating. Find something good to say to them, leave them with something compassionate. Even a dead dog has pretty teeth."

You can find some sort of compassionate encouragement about a loss. I heard a variation of this concept when a cowboy's horse died. His sympathetic friends offered, "Boy, he sure had a shiny coat, didn' he?" And, "Son! He wuz one tough horse, wadn' he?"

Why? Because even ah dead dog has purty teeth...

Eyes-poppin': a description of someone's experiencing an extreme emotion. "Here she come, eye-poppin' mad..." Or, "Don't you pop them eyes at me!"

In the pens one often sees Brahman bulls in a state of aggression for some unknown (or known) reason. When the adrenaline kicks in and they reach a state of frenzy, they'll whirl around just looking for a handy victim. Their eyes are popping and it is common to see tears dripping from them. (See Peein' ah drop at the time.) Adrenaline sure comes in handy on occasion—especially with ah eye-poppin' bull right behind you.

Ezzactly: distinctly, precisely, correctly, or specifically. The word is often used to confirm the obvious. For example, in response to the statement, "I believe his horse will kick tha taste outta yer mouth," would be the answer, "I wuz thinkin' ezzactly tha same thing." The use of the term which came to my mind, was the time when a Cracker went to a museum of fine art. He walked from gallery to gallery, looking at all the masterpieces. He stopped in front of a nude painting, and as he stood there, a well-dressed couple walked up to admire the work. He turned to them and said, "My wife hazza outfit ezzactly like that."

Along those same lines, I heard a story about some tourists that pulled into Okeechobee, Florida. (It is a Seminole word for "big waters." By the way, Istopoka, a huge lake in Highlands County, means deadly waters;" and when the wind picks

Cracker Terms, Phrases And Definitions

up, it IS deadly on the downwind side.) But Okeechobee is often pronounced as oh-KEECH'-oh-bee, which is wrong. It is pronounced, oh-key-CHO-bee. Anyway, the man and his wife weren't sure how to pronounce it and, in precise English, said to the waitress, "Just exactly how do you pronounce where we are? Say it for us slowly so we can understand how to say it."

The Cracker gal looked them over, leaned close and slowly and deliberately said, "FAT... BOY'S... BAR... B... QUE." (This is not an original story on my part, but it's a good one nonetheless. They also had trouble with Kissimmee.)

F

Far: a conflagration, as in, "Y'all start a brandin' far—we need to git busy if we're gonna finish by dark." Speaking of far, I once lived on the highest hill in Highlands County, Florida. In actuality it was a tremendous sand dune, shoved up during prehistoric times in Florida, since all the land there was water-formed. Our house was located some sixteen miles from the Avon Park Bombing Range, where military pilots and artillery squads practiced with live ammunition. Many times night practice took place under the glare of green flares floating down on their little parachutes, dropped from planes at high altitudes. Over the roof of the house we could see these flares; it was spectacular. No aircraft sounds could be heard in general, but occasionally there would be a one or two second, rum-m-m-m-ph of Vulcan Cannons from the sides of converted military transport planes. Each muffled sound was the destruction of a football-sized area, where 50-caliber bullets ripped up the earth in spaces only twelve inches apart.

The reason I describe it is to explain a comment I once made to a friend in Atlanta. I said, "Y'all need to come down to our house in Florida — we can climb on the roof and watch the flares." I meant seeing the military flares were a spectacular sight.

Not missing a beat, she replied, "Shoot. There's no need to come to Florida to see them — we got flares all around the house."

I was a little disoriented until I realized she meant "flowers." (She knew I knew the slang and that I would catch the play on words—if given a little time to think on it.) So, if I have the phrase correct, it is possible to have a far in yer flares.

Farm: a pistol, revolver, handgun, rifle, shotgun, or other weapon, as in, "Whut kind ah farm do ya carry?"

Far pot: a propane tank and metal chamber used for holding and heating branding irons.

Fatback: cuts from the back of hogs. It was preserved by salting it heavily and was used for seasoning or rendering lard. The location on the carcass was opposite the site where bacon is made. When preparing stewed cabbage and tomatoes Crackers often cut fatback (or bacon) into tiny chunks, tossing them into the pot to boil down while they cut a cabbage palm. Fatback was used in other cooking as well. (See Hamfat.)

I knew a fella that named his horse Fatback. He said, "It was like puttin' a saddle on a pickle barrel."

Fat nap: a phrase used by Frank Handley and his son, Jim, to describe an after-meal doze. In a sense this is a perfectly logical description of what happens to the body after a big meal during a short, but deep, nap. The excess nutrients are converted to a storage form as fat. During the Cuban missle crisis in the sixties, President Kennedy would take a fat nap every three hours or so; in this way, he was able to work around the clock. Eisenhower did the same thing during the dark days of World War II. (I had a cousin once that was so fat we had to grease the door facings with butter and dangle a sausage biscuit outside to get him out of the house.)

Cracker Terms, Phrases And Definitions

Fat hit tha far: "Things got so bad from that point on that it ended." If the cattle broke the fence and departed the pens, one might say, "Whin the red cow broke down the gate, the fat hit the fire." (See That ended it up, etc.)

Fatman atta picnic: liking the groceries in a pasture so much you refuse to leave; In reference to some lazy bulls needing removing from a pasture, a foreman said, "Y'all watch the Herefords—they'll squat under a cabbage palm an' stay there like a fat man atta picnic," meaning, be careful to not miss one hiding in the shade.

Fatman was used singly on occasion, as in response to my asking a lad if he wanted a sandwich on a fishing trip: "My daddy said 'Only a fatman eats while he's fishing.'" He then realized he was on the Kissimmee River, fifteen miles from nowhere... and I was his only ride home. He quickly added, "But I never thought that wuz true..." (Yes, he finally took a sandwich.)

Fatter'nah towndog: indicating over-feeding and obesity as is common in city dogs kept under easy-living conditions. It is the opposite of a phrase used to indicate thin, skinny, or under-nourished animals, such as, "Skinnier'n ah nightcrawler with his guts slung out." (See term)

Feeder: a device suitable for feeding cattle or wildlife. There are cattle feeders, yearling feeders, hay feeders, hog feeders and deer feeders, quail feeders and turkey feeders. Sometimes a mineral box (for cattle) is called a mineral feeder. Huge mechanical feeders can be pulled behind tractors, in which case they might be called a feed wagon.

Feeding wildlife is common on many ranches. There are battery operated feeders for deer and turkeys, etc. In basic design, they are five- to ten-gallon covered bins that hold grain with some mechanism that will open for grain to fall on a fan-like device that spins when the grain falls, thus scattering the grain in a wide area. They are hung in trees, high enough for a truck to drive beneath and re-load them with fresh grain. Some are passive, gravity-fed grain dispensers. The old-style Quail feeders were modified two-gallon buckets with elliptical holes at the bottom; they had a hinged lid with a locking device for covering the grain. Squirrels, raccoons and turkey were notorious about robbing the Quail feeders. Wild hogs would tear them up to get to the grains. It is common for some ranches to carry a bag of cracked corn and travel a circuit to re-load deer or bird feeders.

We had homemade turkey feeders on the ranch in Okeechobee, rather simple in design. A sheet of heavy plywood was set level on corner posts about three-feet high so turkeys could hop up on it. This was designed to discourage other wildlife, though squirrels didn't have any problem. On one end a small covered bin was constructed to allow grain to fall down to the bottom and a crack was left so grain would continue to fall down as the turkeys pecked it from the bottom of the bin. We'd dump in fifty pounds of corn and re-fill as needed. The feeder was located near a dike where it was convenient to stop and fill the bin.

My step-father noticed a fat raccoon that often met him leaving the turkey feeder every few days, obviously with his belly full. He decided to watch and determine how the coon was getting to the grain. "Tha ol' fat thing went to the corner post, climbed it, reached up to the plywood platform, dug his claws into the wood and climbed up. He then proceeded to load up on corn. So I decided to take the plywood platform off and move the posts in about a foot or more from the edges. My thinkin' was that the coon couldn't climb tha post an' then crawl on the bottom of the platform, upside down, an' reach tha edge. That ought to shut it down."

The re-design was set up and should have worked, but he kept seeing the coon jump off the platform and run away when he approached the feeder. So one day, he decided to park the Jeep and watch for Mr. Coon. "Sure enough, in a little while, here he comes, waddling toward tha feeder. He walked down tha dike next to tha feeder, stopped an' took a fast run at the feeder an' leapt about four feet over to tha edge of tha platform. He caught hold of tha plywood lik' a circus performer, hand-walked, paw-over-paw, 'til he got close to the bin. Then, he reached up over the edge, caught hold of the side of tha bin and pulled himself up on top of the platform. I never thought he'd be that smart."

Fice dog, feist or ficedog: the name was probably a contraction of feisty. Fice as they pronounced it was more correctly feist, meaning a lively little housedog. Ficedog apparently is considered a delicacy to alligators. The men would cluck to the dog, encouraging it to bark from the bank or from a boat. The gator just couldn't stand it. The yapping was a call of sorts, like a dinner bell. The unsuspecting gator would quietly surface to investigate this potential lunch and the gator hunters could get at it. It was somewhat common for dogs to jump into water to cool off and get a drink. When an alligator caught a swimming dog, there was usually only a brief thrashing and a sudden disappearance of the victim dog. I've heard old timers tell that sometimes the caught dog will jus' go under without much of a swirl or disturbance of the water.

Figurin': to reckon, calculate, estimate, plan, analyze, etc. I recall a story told about the Parker Island Ranch near Lake Placid, Florida, owned by Mr. J. K. Stuart. On one occasion he had decided to sell a large number of cattle. Truck after truck hauled trailers full of fat cattle out the sandy road. When awaiting trucks to load, the crew would sit around talking. Someone commented on how much money would come from the sale. The men grew silent as they figured on it. Finally one man spoke up and said, "Well, I been figurin'... If J.K. was to sell ever'thing he had on this ranch it'd take twenty-seven semi-trailers of silver dollars to carry the money." I never figured it up to prove him right, but it sounded good.

Fire-hunt: night hunting old pioneer Crackers would rig up lanterns or torches to shine in the eyes of gators or deer. A skillet could be used to make a night light, utilizing some flammable material in it. The idea was to shield the eyes or perhaps hold the light high on a pole so one could see the reflections of the animal's eyes or, as they put it, shine up their eyes. Deer and cattle have brilliant green-yellow reflections, while alligators have bright red reflections against the dark water, like rubies on black velvet. The Crackers fire-hunted many, many years before it became illegal. It was a way of making a living in some cases–especially in the Everglades. Now licensed alligator hunters use spotlights or lights attached to their heads or hats. Lights or fire-light also attract fish at night. The cowboys used to refer to Cracker Hunting Season. When I asked when it started, one replied, "Oh, about dark...."

Fire the marsh, pasture or woods: intentional setting of controlled fires or burns to marshes, pastures or woods to make room for new growth. The practice has been used for thousands of years. Generations of Seminoles used this method in the Everglades until they were driven out by the Park Service in 1947. Crackers have known by experience that controlled fires are beneficial to pastures and woods. Burning also keeps ponds and waterways from clogging with mangroves, weeds, saw grass and trash organic matter. There is a delicate balance of nature. Many Crackers witness to the decline of environmental health. All burning stopped in the Everglades National Park and this along with the altered water flow from businesses, big agriculture and tourist inflow has been a serious detriment. For a time the Park Service fought to put out natural fires, but recently there have been attempts at controlled burns. Too late? I don't know.

There are several considerations when firing the marshes and woods, such as, wind direction and speed, relative humidity, degree of moisture in the soil and muck. Crackers don't understand all the technicalities; they operate on experience and good judgment–"Things just felt right." They ride the edges on the up-wind side of the marsh and drop lit matches to start a burn with back fires, and have the fire burn out where they intended. In a matter of days and weeks there is re-growth of tender new plants. Some adapted pines drop long-held seeds only after a woods fire. Dry lightning occurs when there is low humidity and lots of static electricity, as in drought seasons. Many prairie and woods fires have been started by lightning.

Muck fires are another thing entirely. Muck is comprised of decades-old or centuries-old decayed and fermented masses of layered plant material. It is black and sticky and, when wet, it's like mud. And many a vehicle has been bogged down in muck. Caterpillar tractors, draglines and other big construction equipment that require tracks (like a tank) can move across muck patches if it is semi-dry. The second a driver tries to lock one track side to turn, the muck starts to tear and start sinking the locked track below the surface. Experienced drivers feel the change in grip and attitude and immediately release the track or stop entirely. Once a track is sunken too deeply, there is no way the equipment can back out. It will just dig in deeper.

Interestingly, the first railroads in the Everglades were built with some sections of tracks on muck expanses. The old Crackers said riding the trains was like riding rolling swells on board ship in the ocean. In drought years, fire is a hazard since muck fires can burn and smolder for months. No amount of water seems to stop them. Crackers have told me that a vehicle can even fall down into burnt out areas. Muck fires have a distinct smell, one that can be detected for many miles. I was told to avoid slightly smoking muck fire areas.

Today, the ranchers are limited in this burn activity and often assisted by the Forestry Service. In fact, some ranchers, under the State of Florida restoration programs, are trying to return some of their land to a wild or wet land state, as it was many generations ago. The Seminoles were the first who understood that regular firing of the woods and marshes meant more game and a healthier range.

First cousins marryin': though difficult to explain, the context of this phrase makes a clear implication or a sort of off-handed reference to some stupid activity or bizarre behavior. For example, when a young man drove his brand new, right-out of-the-box pick-up truck into a hay field, parked it, and left it running. It subsequently burned to the ground because the cherry-red catalytic converter set fire to the dry hay field. Then one might hear, "Well, after all, that's the sort of thing that happens when first cousins keep marryin'."

I first heard this phrase many years ago, in reference to England's Charles and Diana of the Royal Family. (Incidentally, it was an Englishman who said it.) Knowing a little about their history, it makes sense to me.

Or you might hear the phrase describe a particularly inbred dog, one that was more than a little goofy.

Speaking of inbred dogs, I happen to examine a pit bulldog that was obviously in that state. The dog had one blue eye with a pink eyelid and one brown eye. The lips on the left of his muzzle were pink, otherwise the dog was black. This dog snapped sporadically at imaginary flies and was hyper-sensitive to loud noises, constantly moving around and jumping at sudden sounds.

I commented to the owner, "That dog acts a little inbred, don't he?"

The man replied, "Doc, he's so inbred he's his own uncle."

Speaking of first cousins marrying, I recall a conversation I heard. A young woman–really a girl just finishing high school–was talking to an older married woman. The girl was expressing her desire to marry as soon as possible. The married woman said, "Honey, go down to the city dog pound and git a recently whelped bird dog. Get one who has eight to ten puppies. Take her and the pups home. Tell yer mama that yer're gonna feed and clean up behind the puppies and you'll take over all the house keepin', washin' and ironin', grocery shoppin' and cookin' for the summer. When the three months are up, come back and we'll talk about gettin' married too young."

For you educated, folk, "That's the gene-pool at work," means the same thing

Fish or cut bait: to proceed with the task at hand or quit it altogether and better sooner than later. It is used to motivate someone or a group that is dawddling or diddling, often accompanied by audible sighs and toe tapping. For example, when working cows, we would take what we called a water break. It was a time-out to replenish lost water and electrolytes, (but we didn't know what electrolytes were at the time) –so we wouldn't get bear caught, i.e., develop heat stress, exhaustion or stroke. After everyone had cooled off and rehydrated, we'd hear, "Well, boys, let's fish or cut bait!" I've heard a variation of this: "We need to cut bait or go to tha' house." It is probably a mixed metaphor like, "You can lead a horse to water... but that don't make it right.")

Fixintah: preparing to, as referring to going shopping: "Wher y'all goin'?" "Weer fixintah go Wal-Martin."

Flank'um or side'um: to ride close beside a group of cattle to control them and prevent their leaving the herd for parts unknown. To flank a calf was different; it meant to grab the skin in front of its knee, hold one hand under its neck, hoist the calf with the knee and throw it to the ground for branding or surgery. (Throwing a calf is similar to hoisting a square bale of hay.)

Flat-footed: surprised by or unprepared for some crisis. When a cow cut a dido, breaking away from the herd, the men might be caught flat-footed. My friend Hubert used the term often. It seemed to be the opposite of keep on your toes or be ready. (See "Dido" and "Cut a shine.") A synonymous phrase is, "Caught with your pants down," although a little less refined.

Flite: rhymes with sit, but I am not all that familiar with it. My understanding in talking with old timers concerns a product used for mosquitoes in Florida. In the Ten Thousand Islands, south of Naples, the skeeters were so bad that tales of how rank they were (and sometimes still are) arose by those who've experienced these blood-thirsty pests. One man told me he was camping on his small cabin cruiser on a fishing trip south of Everglades City. He said the mosquitoes would never let up during the day, but it was pure hell-on-earth at night. He had a can of Flite and sprayed the portholes on the boat in an effort to clear the screens and get a little air circulation. He said, "Tha next mornin', you could take handfuls of dead mosquitoes off the screens... Ever' screen was clogged with 'um."

Now it may be hard to visualize, but there are accounts in Florida's history of masses of mosquitoes in Kissimmee Valley. They would suffocate cattle by clogging their noses. In order to escape them, the cattle would come out of the marshes and head for the hammocks and prairies where the mosquitoes weren't so thick. Of course, fencing changed this natural instinct to roam away from the torment. That may be the main reason the Seminoles went north to Ocala in the summers and down toward Lake Okeechobee in the winters.

I am not sure, but the chemical in Flite may have been carbon disulfide, also called, Hot Shot. I've heard some old Crackers talk about squirting Flite on horse's rumps to make them buck off a rider—that and burrs under the saddle or a lariat held between two riders and flipped up under the tail of a horse... any of these pranks will work on the unspecting rider, though some back-fired into a wreck.

Fluke 'um or fluked: to administer medication to remove liver flukes in cattle. Fluked, in the past tense, means the cattle were medicated with fluke medicine. Flukes are mean-looking trematode parasites that set up housekeeping in the liver and bile ducts. Some pastures used to be infamous for having cattle exposed to the liver fluke. The parasitic disease causes unthriftiness, poor doers, weight loss and in some cases death. The youngest animal I have ever seen with this ailment was a heifer less than a year of age. She looked well-conditioned, in good shape, but was unable to rise to her feet due to weakness. Thinking she might have a severe contagious disease, we sacrificed her and during the autopsy, we found a cirrhotic liver severely impaired and scarred from liver flukes and obstructed bile ducts

Foul his nest or foul yer nest: to "rip his (or yer) britches" (See term), make a mistake, make things worse, cause an incident, etc., usually referring to one's home. Examples might include, "Whin he did her wrong, he sure fouled his nest, didden he?"

Frazzled: to be tired or worn out, spent or run-down, as in, "Sister, he come to work plum frazzled."

Frog strangler: specifies a severe, copious thunderstorm. It was often used interchangeably with a gully washer. It was used frequently, as in: "Boy! It come a regler frog strangler in the marsh." Sometimes you'd hear one say, "Son! It wuz rainin' so bad it'd choke a frog." Therefore, I conclude that frog strangler and frog choker mean the same thing.

Frothin': meaning salivating, foaming, slobbering, bubbling or slimy at the mouth. It was an expression of extreme fury. "Well, I jobbed the needle in his neck, an he commenced tah git frothin' mad." Or "Whut 'er you frothin' about?" Or "Mister man... whin she seen me talkin' to my old galfriend, she got tah frothin' at the mouth."

Fur piece: indicates a relatively long distance, as in, "It's a fur piece to the pens frum the gait." I know this seems to be a common slang in Kentucky and many parts of the South.

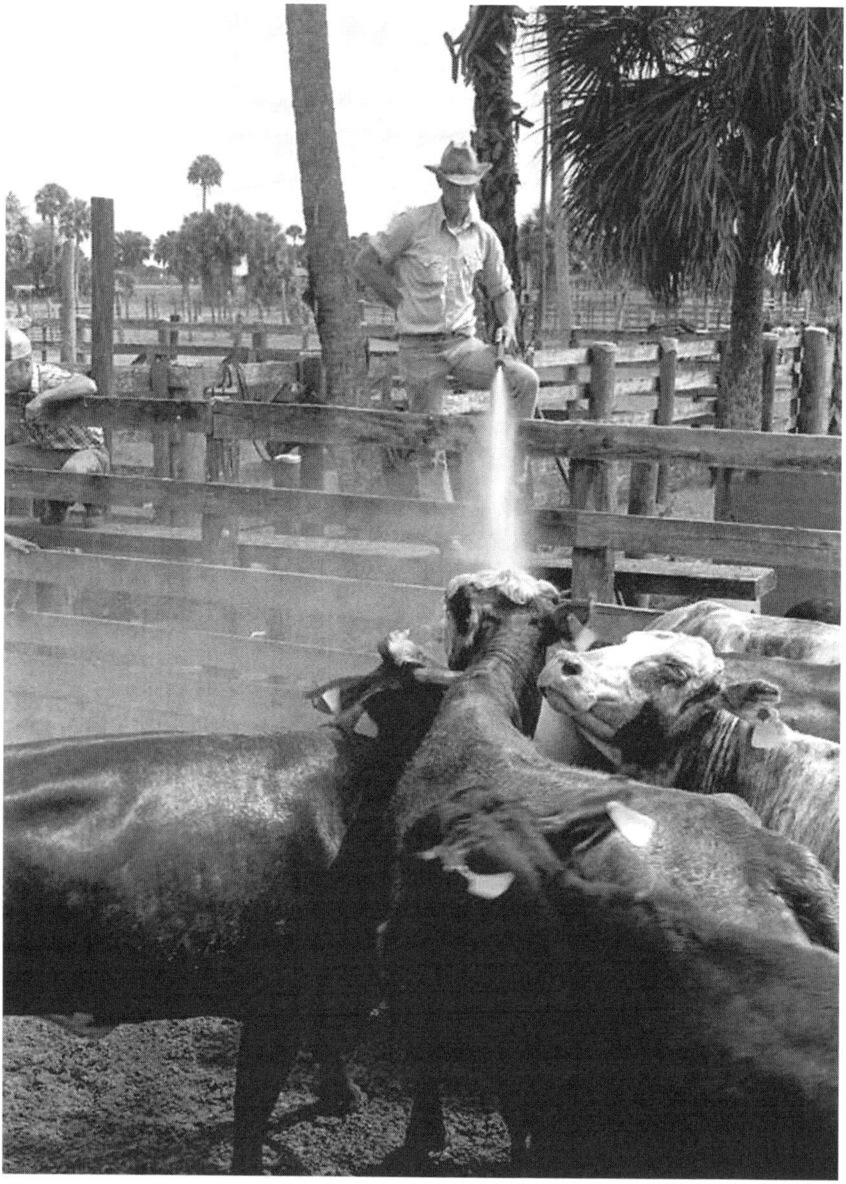

Cracker Terms, Phrases And Definitions

G

Gaggin' on gnats: reminiscent of the Biblical phrase, "You blind guides, who strain out a gnat and swallow a camel!" Focusing on too many details in making a decision. The phrase was often associated with a response like, "Don't worry 'bout tha mule–load tha wagon."

Gallanipper: a species of huge tiger-striped mosquitoes. Partner's theory was they could suck a gallon of blood each bite. He claimed that some were big enough to build a hog pen with their dried bones. Partner told me that one time he met a man coming from Osceola County just south of the county line, north of Okeechobee City. The man was flailing mosquitoes with palm fronds in frantic front and back slaps,.

Partner said, "These skeeters are bad, ain't they?"

The man replied, "Wait til you git to Osceola County, ther're hell up there."

We found a dry freshly shed rattle snake skin in the grove one time. He claimed that a gallanipper got him and that was all that was left. I discounted this as a tall tale since he also told me he saw a king snake and a rattler fighting in the grove. With a twinkle in his eye, he said, "Wellsir, the king snake grabbed the rattler's tail and the rattler grabbed the king snake's tail and they commenced to eat each other. All of a sudden, Poof... they jus' disappeared... they jus' et each other up!"

Gas offen yer stomuck: A familiar phrase of Partner whose real name was Harris Sills, a lifelong employee of the Williamson Ranch in Okeechobee. He habitually ate a can of Beanie Weanies every day for lunch. He might have other things but the Beanie Weanies were for sure. Out on the ranch, during hunting trips or just enjoying the out-of-doors, I'd get into some pretty remote places. More than once I thought I was the only white man to see such an out-of-the-way place; but there, under a shade tree, would be an empty, rusty Beanie Weanie can. We asked Partner why he had a can of Beanie Weanies every day. He pushed his hat off his forehead, rocked back on his heels and replied, "Well, it keeps the gas offen yer stomach." (See Backhanded humor)

Gassy, ain't he: a question/comment to indicate that a particular animal has expelled gas. Dogs are notorious about this occurrence, especially after certain dietary indiscretions cause a sudden change in the resident enteric or colonic bacterial population such as high-carbohydrate (i.e., cheap) dog foods. Johnny Raulerson (See Hog Hunters) and I experienced this occurrence first hand on a midnight coon chasing expedition. Raccoons were numerous and played havoc with the near-ripe citrus. We drove around the groves and let the dogs run. They loved it. Sometimes it was slow and other times it was non-stop action. Well, this night we got caught in a thunderstorm and pulled over in the woods. We shut off the engine and hunkered down until it blew over. The dogs weren't too keen on running anything during the lightening and steady rain, so they loaded up in the back of the Jeep. For those who are not familiar with the older model Jeeps, let me explain that it is rather tight quarters with two men and three big dogs. The dogs were wet and tired from running and laid down to rest. It was a windy rain storm, so the windows were cracked only inches to allow some ventilation in the sweltering vehicle. As the windows began to steam up, one of the dogs expelled an extremely noticeable odor. Johnny and I exchanged glances but said nothing, since this was a not uncommon occurrence with dogs. The windows were already as low as we could get them without getting soaked. The malodorous gas began to creep into the cracks and crevices of the vehicle. I remembered the morning's activities and told Johnny, "Somebody butchered a deer this morning—they must have feed the scraps to tha dogs…" Well, the odor was getting ranker by the minute. Finally one of the dogs rolled over to get more comfortable and expelled a loud flatus. I idly commented, "Gassy, ain't he?" Johnny said, "I don't mind the smell; it's just burnin' my eyes."

Cracker Terms, Phrases And Definitions

A Chinese man once said, "You Americans are funny people. You heat your tea to make it hot then you add ice to make cold. You add sugar to make sweet and lemon to make sour. You belch and say 'Excuse me' and you pass gas and laugh about it. Crazy people."

Git back! a strong command for a catch dog or dogs to let go and get away from the cow or bull. It is also used with hog dogs when they try to run back in and re-catch a hog. (In like fashion, it works well with kids when they are too close to danger.) "Git behind!" is also used to direct dogs to get behind you or your horse. Sometimes the close proximity of dogs can back-fire when the cow (or bull) whirls around to strike at the approaching antagonist. Under certain circumstances, dogs in the cowpens can cause unnecessary risk. There were pens where there was more danger from the dogs than the cows. The dogs would escape under the bottom fence boards and leave the men open to a charge from a provoked animal. Experienced, well trained dogs usually rested under some protective structure and only came out when a cow got rank. Most times the foreman had the boys put the dogs in a trailer or truck to avoid these misunderstandings.

I worked at a set of cowpens on one occasion where the bottom boards were about two feet off the ground. I wondered about this odd configuration until I saw a Mexican cowboy dive and roll under the bottom boards as a cow hooked the fence a second behind him. An A-Hah! moment. They also roped under-handed and sideways with the loop held down by their legs rather than overhand; as a result, the cow ran into the loop. It was a long day.

Git gassed: get drunk, inebriated or snockered. A cowboy once mentioned that he and his buddies had a game of sorts when they were partaking of adult beverages. He said, "Whut we do is go get a case of sumthin', go in ah room somewher's and start a drinkin' Then when everyone's face is blurry, one of us'll leave an' the others try to guess who left."

Git shut or git shed: to get rid of, as in, "Boys, I'll be glad whin we git shut of this job." Or, "I sure wuz happy to git shed of that woman. It tripled my take home pay."

Go-ahead or go-uppahead: It meant to the catch dog, "Get ahead of the runaways and turn them back to the herd" or to a hog dog, "Catch the hog" or "Track him to his lair." Usually, "go-uppahead", was reserved for heading cattle back to the herd. It was the opposite of, "Git behind!" Cracker cowboys use the term automatically as a part of their everyday vocabulary. I've heard one encourage another, "Go-uppahead," when a pretty girl walks by, meaning, "Go on and talk to her."

Crackers are noted for being laid back. A story circulated about a couple of men sitting on the fence at a cow pens. One was facing the pens the other was sitting faced out the other direction. A pretty girl came by. The fella facing outward saw her and spoke to her, "Hey; hower you?"

She replied, "Hey; fine. Y'all restin'?"

He replied, "Yeah." She waved and walked on by toward the barn.

His friend seated inward on the fence said, "Hey. Wuz she purty?"

"Yeah, she sure wuz."

His friend: "Son! I wish I'dah bin turned around."

Gob or gobbed: as a noun, it meant a liberal amount of something, as in: "Reach over ther' and get me a gob of grease for this bolt." Used as a verb, it referred to applying a liberal amount of fly repellent or pesticide on a cow's back: "Boys, don't forgit to gob some fly dope on the cattle."

Gobbed on the other hand often meant a disgusting excess. My mother, a bar-be-que expert, used it in this derogatory manner: "Why, they had just gobbed that old tomato paste on the bar-b-que—it wadn't fit t'eat." This comment was followed by a shutter and "We'll not eat there again. It wadn't fit for the dogs." But her absolute maximum expression for a seriously excessive amount was, "It was gobbed *all over ever'thing.*"

Go home ta see Mama: this had nothing to do with one's mother. It was in reference to one's wife. When a fella got to missing his wife, he'd indicate it by commenting, "Well, tonight, I reckon I'll go home ta see Mama." Also, "Wher's Henry?" "Aw, he had to go home ta see Mama." A variation was, "I'm gonna go see tha baby's Mama." (Same idea)

Pardon my rabbit trail: I recall a story told many years ago about the proverbial traveling salesman. The fella was making his route through the backwoods of Florida in the heart of Cracker country. He happened to be driving near a pasture when a woman in a flour-sack dress and bonnet ran across the pasture, hiked her long skirt up and jumped a four-strand barbed-wire fence. She ran across the road and disappeared in the thick brush. In a short while a big-footed boy of about fifteen or sixteen years of age came running across the pasture. As he got to the fence, the salesman jumped out of his vehicle and said, "Hey, boy! Whut's the problem? Whut happened to that woman?"

The boy stopped and sullenly replied, "That's my mama."

The salesman said, "Whut's wrong with her? Why's she runnin' like that?"

The boy sullenly said, "She's tryin' to wean me...."

(I'm sorry for this; I won't do it again.)

Goodun or goodin: an expression of high praise. "Now that's a goodun. 'Bout tha best show calf yearlin' we ever had here." Another illustration: "Boys, a fella sumtimes has to go through two or three gals to get a goodun." (I see no reason why the genders couldn't be reversed.)

Good work! or Good werk! A short praise in response to a question of whether a job was completed, as in, "Did y'all finish workin' tha calves?" Answer: "Yeah, we finished an' sprayed 'um, too." Response: "Good werk." Now, the term was often used satirically. For example, if a fella left a gate loosely latched and the penned cattle escaped, someone might say in disgust, "Good werk, Buddy. Now we got tah start over."

The phrase was often used by Dr. Frank Handley, "Did that bitin' sonofah (*expletive deleted*) hang a tooth in yer fingers?"

"Naw, we tied his mouth shut an' he quieted down."

"Good werk!"

Go git Mama: means what is says; however, it was used with anyone that was needed. When I'd stick a tractor up in a muck pond, I tell someone to go get Mama. At the barn he'd say, "One of you needs to git a tractor and go git Hiard."

The best example of the phrase was in a tale told to me by a Cracker fella about his daddy. (I doubt it actually took place but it made a good story.) He said his daddy had never been to a big city, but they talked him into going to the Florida Cattlemen's Association meeting at a fine hotel.

"Well, I took Ol' Daddy in boots an' cowboy hat an' all. As we walked toward the elevator there was an aged, somewhat wrinkled, woman standing there; the door opened and she got on the elevator. As we waited for the elevator to return, Daddy was lookin' all around tha lobby–he'd never seen anything' lik' it. Well, the elevator door opened again and out walks a fine young woman. Daddy looked 'er over, smiled with a twinkle in his eye and said, 'Boy, go git yer mama; let's run 'er through this thing.'"

Googily-eyed: to be confused, awkward, surprised, self-conscious, mildly ashamed, reluctant or embarrassed, as in: "Man! He sure is all googily-eyed about that girl. He showed us the ring he got her." Or, "Whin he jobbed his hand in tha gopher hole an' heard tha rattle snake, he come outta ther' plum googily-eyed." One could be knocked googily-eyed when sillykicked or limb hit.

Cracker Terms, Phrases And Definitions

Go onto-um, go-on toit or go toit: Example: "If we drag along her' much longer dark'll catch us—we need to go onto-um." Other phrases include, Go toit, which is interchangeable as a directive, as in, "Go toit, boys, rain's comin'." Go to'im meant "Get over there in a hurry and help—they're in a tite." The phrase was also used to get catch dogs to turn a rank bull or cow back to the herd or to catch a hog, as in, "Whup! Go to'im, Buck! Ketch'im!" (Git on with it meant to get busy and is similar to Fish or cut bait.)

Got tha bit in his teeth: a phrase describing a runaway or a "cold-jawed" horse (see term). This can be the result of poorly fitting bit or head gear or the rider will not seat the bit correctly so as to control the horse. Some horses are just difficult to control and every now and then, they will "take it away frum ya" (See term.). We had a filly named for her habit of galloping right by a cow and making a wide circle before returning to the action; we named her Sailboat because of this tendency to swing wide. Turning her was like turning a jumbo jet. The other outstanding horse at the ranch was noted for blubbering, sloshing and lip-flipping in the water trough. We named him Toothbrush.

Horses that run away with a rider bring to mind the advice: "Pull his head up in yer lap if ya want to stop 'im." This was done by pulling one of the reins so hard that the horse's neck bends and his head is facing backwards. The hoped-for result is that the horse will start slowing and turning and eventually stop.

I'll leave it to your imagination to apply this phrase to human behavior.

Greez or greezed: to salve, dob, lubricate or cover. The words can be used as a directive or explanation, as in, "Put som' greez on it." Or, "I've gotter all greezed up an' ready tah go." Lastly, "Y'all catch tha horse an' greez 'im with this medicine."

Grinnin' lik ah mule eatin' sawgrass: an exuberant grin. "Whin he told us she said, 'Yes,' he wuz grinnin' lik ah mule eatin' sawgrass." (Everglades sawgrass has little sharp teeth on the edges of the grass blades. I've never seen a mule in this activity but you get the picture.) Lik a possum... is a synonym phrase. Lik a mule eatin' briars, I guess is the way they say it in North Alabama where my wife grew up.

Groceries: Can be synonymous with food or meals; as in, "Y'all come on... let's eat these groceries." Or, as one man said to my mama once, "Y'all ain't gonna hav' no trouble getting' a cow crew with all these good groceries yer feedin' us." Synonyms include rations, feed, victuals (or vittles), grits, etc. To obtain a meal was often referred to as put on the feed sack, hang ah lip on, belly up, etc.

A tale was told many years ago about a man who ran a meat market in Okeechobee. He had modified the weigh scales with a ring attached underneath and nearly hidden from view. When he put meat on the scales, he'd sometimes hook a thumb on the ring and add a little weight. A Seminole man came to the market one day, asking for some beef. A cut was selected and placed on the scales. As the ol' thumb-in-the-ring trick was tried again, the Seminole grabbed a meat cleaver, swung at the butcher's hand. "Me no buy thumb." (The tale circulated the county for a time.)

I recall the time when a lady went to the butcher's shop to purchase a fat hen for making chicken and dumplings. The butcher only had one hen left. She said she wanted a hen of a certain weight. The butcher stirred through the crushed ice and drew out the hen. The hen weighed less than the woman desired. He placed the hen back, fumbled around with the ice and put the same hen back, adding a bit of weight to the scales with a well-placed thumb. The woman suspiciously pondered the choice, finally saying, "Tell you whut... lemme have both them hens."

Grove cow (or grove calf, steer, heifer, bull, etc.): slang for a cow (etc.) that has gained access through a weak place in the fencing and been in the citrus grove for a time. Some return to the pasture by the same break, but some remain either through preference or poor memory. A grove cow usually meant to us that one had set up camp in the grove, enjoying the fertilized grasses near the trees to excess and is "fat and sassy." One would think that it would be easy to remove a cow from a grove; however, a determined cow will dart in among and under the trees, making roping them nearly impossible. This frustrating problem is handled in a few ways: over-whelming them with man power, using good cow dogs or patience with open gates, letting the cow think she has found an escape.

Gud ferit: The best example occurred years ago when I got a call from a cowboy in need of emergency veterinary care. I arrived early at the hospital, checked the records and discovered that the fella had never paid any of his outstanding bills—most were emergency calls. I ran off a copy of his bill, figuring to present it to him as he entered the door. Well the dog was not his. It belonged to another cowboy. A bull had kicked the catch dog, popping his eye out of socket. We put it back in place under anesthesia. As the boys loaded the sleeping dog in the back of the truck, I showed the fella his overdue bills that he owed. "You know you haven't paid anything on your bill; it's always late night things, too." He studied it as if it were written in Greek, looked up, with an expression of puzzlement on his face and replied, "Doc, ya know I'm gud ferit." (Ya thank?)

Gullet: Cracker term for esophagus. Gullet and guzzle are interchangeable.

Gutshot: to be shot in the abdomen; figuratively describes a poorly, malnourished, worm infested, or sickly individual; To be shot in the abdomen was a slow, painful and emaciating way to die if there were no immediate care. It was most often used in the context, "Go out to tha double pines pasture an' bring that gutshot yearlin' back in for docterin'."

H

Had a fit or a hissy: used to indicate that someone or something had "showed his country behind" (See term). There are good fits, like when a man's wife sees her new truck and bad fits when a horse is bound and determined to get that lump off his back. (See "Gets the bit in his teeth.") Technically, a hissy is milder than fit. And a hissy fit is something awful.

I happened to be driving down I-75 one time. A big fine powder-blue Mercedes was cruising in the right lane, going about the speed limit. (Yankee tourists will run over you on that highway if you drive the limit, so I was keeping pace with traffic.) As I passed her I noticed she was talking on the phone, while her left hand was on the top of the steering wheel. On her third finger was the biggest, gaudiest diamond ring I've ever seen–sparkling in the early afternoon sun. Her hair was salon fresh and her make-up was immaculate. I didn't think much of it until she finished talking, hung up and sped on by me headed to Palm Beach. As I eased in behind her, I saw the bumper sticker: "SAW IT, HAD A FIT, GOT IT." (I have no idea whether it was referring to the Mercedes, the ring or something else. Spoiled? Ah thank...)

Hair-lip the queen: an expression of sheer exasperation and disgust, as in the case of a horse that has thrown a fit, jumped into a barbed wire fence and cut up his legs. You might hear, "I wish you'd look at that! Don' that jus' hair-lip the queen?" I heard that the expression started in Texas and moved to Florida. This phrase was used to describe a wreck. Means the same as Chap yer lips.

I would never make fun of anyone with this condition, but somehow the contrast of hair-lip and royalty struck me as funny. Perhaps that's an illustration of what happens when first cousins keep marryin'...

Cracker Terms, Phrases And Definitions

Hamfat: often used to emphasize a query or question, as in, "Wher in tha hamfat have y'all been?" or "What in the hamfat are you doin', boy?" (Perhaps a euphemistic substitute.)

Handleyism or Ah-Handley: Dr. Frank Handley, frequently mentioned herein, was noted for his quick Cracker wit. He could come up with a phrase or a quip that made a lot of folks laugh. A perfect example occurred one time when a drug salesman came to the hospital to promote a new "flea killing product." The product was a flea-toxic chemical in women's hair spray. The principle was a good one but outdoor dogs notoriously got wet and the chemical was lost quickly. Anyway, the man had me "trapped" for his presentation. I was always courteous to the salesmen, but some would take up a lot of time. During the "enthusiastic presentation," Dr. Handley walked in about the time the man was listing all the advantages of this marvelous new product. He was smoking a cigarette and had a cup of rank, left-over coffee. He listened intently for a few minutes. But then, it broke loose when he started, "Man! Do you realize whut you all have done? Why, we'll lose a lot of business... we won't be able to give cortisone shots any more... there'll be no skin infections, so we'll lose out on antibiotic dispensing... income will drop and our kids will have to come home from college... the whole veterinary profession will suffer... we'll have to raise hogs in the kennels, take in washing and ironing and sell produce out front... y'all have just destroyed us!" Frank stopped then and took a sip of coffee and eyed the man in complete seriousness. There was a long moment of silence as the man studied Handley's face and uncomfortably glanced at me. Then, I "lost it" in a burst of laughter. He had just experienced "Ah-Handley." He was never the same and never spoke to Frank again. In fact, if I was out when he came by and only Frank was there, he'd leave.

There was another trick Frank pulled on salesmen: He'd come in the room and say, "Have y'all got any free stuff for us?" It was amazing how we accumulated pens, notepads, drug samples, coffee cups, hats, belt buckles, jacketsand paper weights, etc.

Hangah tooth: to bite and/or sink teeth into, as in, "Watch that brindle dog—he'll hangah tooth in yer butt whin you ain't lookin'." "Whut happened to yer hand?" "Awe, a danged ol' pig hungah tooth in me last night."

Speaking of teeth, a story spread around Highlands County one time about the cow pens' dentist. It seems that a man was having a bad tooth ache—he came to work anyway but it was killing him. The crew knew he was suffering, but, here again, he kept on working. During a water break the man sat alone holding his jaw in deep pain. His buddy asked him, half-jokingly, if he could pull the painful thing for him.

Surprise! He said, "Yeah—I wish you'd git it outta my mouth..." So pliers were inserted and the pull began. He flinched and groaned, holding his jaw. In a few minutes, he looked up and said, "D*(expletive deleted)*, man! You pulled the wrong tooth!" So back to work the tooth doctor went, and with the repeat of the flinching and groaning, finally got the right one.

You might think that was tough, but the tooth story that impressed me more was the time a cow hooked a fella in the mouth at the front of a restraint chute, knocking out his front teeth. The man never missed a beat, occasionally spitting out some blood, finishing the day toothless as a chicken...

My partner in practice was working at a ranch owned by his long-time friend, Sanford Hartt. In the throes of operating in the pens, Sanford got his leg broken when he was caught by a big calf. Handley (as the cowboys called him) told the crew, "Cut some cabbage stalks and we'll set his leg."

They held Sanford down, out in the bald open sun, while Handley jerked the leg bones into alignment, splinting the leg with cabbage stalks and strips of cloth. The sorriest worker took Sanford on to the hospital while the crew went back to work. The attending physician said it was a piece of cake to cast since the bones were aligned and the swelling was minimal.

Obviously, this has nothing to do with teeth, but you're probably used to my rabbit trails by now.

Hang'ah spur: to spur, goose, job, or prod. In the case of riding a cow horse, spurring referred to training, discipline, an emergency situation or incidentally about a humorous episode. Examples include: "Ever'thing was fine till the bull cum at me in the palmettas. I had to hang'ah spur in ma' horse's flank to git out tha way." "Boy, whin yer horse acts ugly an' yer're in a tite, don't hesitate to hang'ah spur in his shoulder to turn 'im." Or, "That lawyer hung tha spurs to 'im whin they got to court…" And, "You tole me not to spur Bingo. I did it anyway; he cum uncorked an' throwed me a country mile."

The phrase could be used to describe a fight: "Slim said he'd had enough of 'im. He got outta his truck and commenced tah hang his spurs in 'im."

Has he (or she) ever had this problum before? a distractive question to buy time when examining a sick animal with obscure signs of disease and struggling to diagnose an obvious internal medical problem, but not knowing exactly what it was. I had a sort of standard line of questioning.

I'd say, "Lemme ask ya this. Has she ever had this problem before?" Various responses were given. "Yeah, she did tha same thing last fall." "Naw, this is tha first time we noticed she wadn't rite." Or, "We don't know anythin' about 'er."

If they said she had in fact had a similar problem in the past, my standard reply was: "Well, she's got it agin…" (It was dry humor that was not always appreciated by the listeners.)

Another standard reply was embedded in my mind. In situations where someone described a wreck or incident causing damage to their horse or dog (or themselves) always seemed to me to demand a special remark on my part. I had a man tell me, "I rode intah a little pine thicket; tha horse ran so close to the trees, I cracked both knees." He described it in grinning detail, ending with, "Son! That hurt." I looked at him very seriously and replied, "Yessir, and it's gonna hurt every time you do that ." (I learned the phrase in the Air Force from a general medical officer from Arkansas when he conducted sick call. A Sergeant came to the clinic one morning, saying, "Doc, I wuz walkin' through the livin' room last night in tha dark and I walked into the coffee table and cracked my shin. Doc, it hurt bad." Very seriously, Dr. Furlow retorted, "Yes, Sergeant, and it'll hurt every time you do that." "Okay, Doc," replied the patient. He missed the humor of the reply, but the staff thought it hilarious.

This particular doctor had another technique that the staff also appreciated. The enlisted men would pack into sick call clinic every Monday morning. Bill would look deeply into a right eye with his ophthalmoscope and say, "I see you've been watchin' a lot of TV."

The Airmen usually replied, "Yes, Sir."

Bill would switch eyes and say, "Hum-m-m-m... I see you been drinkin' a lot of beer, too. I'm gonna write you a prescription for some Tylenol and you can report back to your work station." (The Airmen marveled at his ability to determine their weekend habits by examining their eyes.)

I used this technique with older kids when I'd look in the ears or eyes of their dog; I'd say, "You been playing catch with this dog?" Or, "This dogs surely barks a lot, doesn't he?" and "You been feeding this dog after 4:00, haven't you?" (Sometimes it elicited wondrous looks.)

Have I ever told you about tha time when (*fill in the blank*)? a simple question with dramatic potential or boring repetition. I am bad to ask friends and family this question. My neighbor (as well as others) always responds, "Yes, but go ahead ... 'cause I know you will anyway."

Cracker Terms, Phrases And Definitions

Headskin: used in referring to a rowdy place where it is expected that a fight will be started and your head could be skinned, abraded, contused or lacerated; usually used to refer to a particular site where a tough crowd is assembled. It generally was used to designate a particular place, such as a bar. "Y'all goin' down to the headskin tonight?" (See juke.)

Head 'um, head 'um up, or head 'im off: a directive to "go upah head" (See term) and turn a leader of a herd in a preferred direction or away from the wrong direction. If the leaders are turned, the rest of the herd will follow.

Head up an' tail over tha dashboard: an adulterated phrase for tail up and head over the dashboard. We never knew where that came from but suspect that it was a common term used in the forties. It meant to go excitedly and purposefully. "Here he comes – head up an' tail over the dashboard!" (Think about that picture.)

He-ah: a word altered by dialect for Here, meaning, Hey, Come here, Let me show you or Stop it. I can't precisely spell it, since there seems to be a faint 'n' sound embedded into the word. If you'll call me I'll pronounce it for you. It was used in various contexts, as in, "He-ah! Grit! Pistol! You dogs back off!" or "He-ah, lemme show ya how it's done." "He-ah, I'm gonna cut me a cabbage stalk and whup y'all if you don't quit fightin'." Less commonly it would be used after, "Wher' you at?" The reply: "Over he-ah."

He ain't dun yet: a phrase meaning he hasn't completed the job, the task isn't finished, etc. I immediately think of Leo Clark, a long-time resident of Lorida, Florida. (Forgive me if I repeat a story from *The Green Jeep*.) Leo is a fine man. He's quiet, well-mannered and would do anything for you. In fact that was a characteristic of most Crackers. When they knew you, got to liking you, you could call on them in any emergency or for help when you needed it.

Leo Clark is a combat veteran; he's friendly, mild mannered and meek but he can rise to difficult situations, if there's a need. Leo had a dog named, Rowdy. Rowdy was not a good cowdog but he was a consistent one. He always seemed to get in the way in the pens. Leo would shout at him, "Git outta the way, Rowdy!" (Rowdy would stop in the middle of the alleyway, right where the cattle were to enter the chute, turn and look at Leo with what looked like a mischievous grin.) My partner, Dr. John Young, and I named the dog, "Git-outta-ther'-Rowdy" and Rowdy didn't pay any attention to us.

Leo had some health issues and was scheduled to go the the Tampa Veteran's Hospital for two days. He brought Ol' "Git-outta-ther'-Rowdy" in for us to board for the two days. That was on a Thursday afternoon. He brought him in on a string from a hay bale. We took Rowdy back to the boarding kennels and put him in a big, wide kennel. He seemed happy.

Two nights passed; Leo showed up on Saturday morning, checked in at the desk, paid his bill and we brought Rowdy to the waiting area. I happened to glance out into the room and the sight is forever welded in my memory: Leo was standing in the middle of the waiting room looking around nonchalantly as Rowdy was standing straddle-legged, slightly hunkered down and emptying his engorged bladder with the rankest smelling, greenish-yellow urine I'd ever seen. With his eyes half-closed, Rowdy actually looked like he was smiling. The odiferous pool was slowly spreading on the tile floor. We had a disconnected city fireplug out front which we put there for this very purpose and most dogs loved to sprinkle it. (Funny, the Fire Department tried to hook up a hose to it one time and it just fell over.)

I shouted, "Leo, take Ol' Rowdy out to that fireplug!"

He smiled ever so sweetly and said, "But Doc, he ain't dun yet."

(We discovered Ol' Git-outta-ther-Rowdy had never been in a building before—he'd held his urine from Thursday afternoon until Saturday morning. We marked his medical chart: "MUST BE WALKED OUTSIDE TWICE DAILY!")

Cracker Terms, Phrases And Definitions

He knows which side of tha butter his bread is on: a twisted axiom. Technically, this is a spoonerism (words or phrases in which letters or syllables get swapped). A perfect example is: It's kisstomary to cuss the bride, or, the prince tried to slip the glass slipper on her foot but it fidden dit.

He knows Mama: though often said, there is a context that really gets the gist of the phrase and was told around Highlands County years ago. In order to grasp the full import of the phrase I need to explain a bit. In Sebring, Florida an Army-Air Force base was established in the dark days of WW II. Britain was in serious condition. America had been sending war materials. The problem was Britain needed pilots for their interceptors and to accompany bombers in the effort against Hitler's machine. Thus, Hendricks Field was established about six or seven miles from the then tiny town of Sebring. (The whole county was sparsely populated in the early forties, no doubt before Yankees and air conditioning.)

This was a time when American fighter pilots took great sport in shooting up the cattle mineral boxes on route from their Avon Park bombing practice to Homestead Air Base. The German U-Boats torpedoed Britain-bound tanker ships right off the coast of Ft. Pierce. The smoke from these dying ships could be seen thirty to forty miles inland. In those desperate times, the Royal Air Force selected British men for fighter training. They were brought to Highlands County to train for combat. These ninety-day wonders went directly from Hendricks Field into combat off the cliffs of Dover without much fanfare—many died their first time in combat against the expert and seasoned German pilots.

The story is told about a surviving British pilot who returned to Sebring to reminisce his days in the training. Neatly dressed in suit and Derby and carrying an umbrella, he went to The Circle to sit on a park bench. The Circle is a little round park in the center of downtown Sebring at the junction of five streets. It is beautiful and a pleasant place.

As the Brit sat and recalled his training days, two locals happened to notice the man sitting alone on the bench. One said, "Hey, wher' you frum?"

The Brit responded, "Oh, I'm from England. I'm visiting America and thought I'd visit Sebring for a time."

In a loud voice, with hand cupped to his ear, one of the men asked, "Whut'd he say, Johnny?"

Johnny looked straight at him and shouted, "He's frum England, George!"

John turned to the Brit and said, "My name's John an' this her' is mah bruther, George... he's kinda hard of hearing. How cum you cum to Sebrun?"

The Brit said, "Well, I was stationed at Hendricks Field during the war. I was trained here for fighter escort."

George said, "Whut'd he say, Johnny?"

John raised his voice and says, "He wuz at Hendricks Field durin' tha war!"

"Oh?" said George.

The conversation continued with the Brit recounting his memories. He said, "Yes, I have fond memories of my last night here in Sebring—just before I was shipped back to England. That night I was in the company of a local woman, a red-haired beauty as I recall. She was a lovely lady but a bit on the wild side... we'd over-indulged in some adult beverages, I'm afraid. One of my fellows dared her to do a strip-tease around this circle.... She, indeed, did create quite a spectular performance... it was a wild night!"

"Whut'd he say, Johnny?"

John cupped his hand and shouted at George, "He knows Mama!"

Cracker Terms, Phrases And Definitions

He's called on you to pray: There was a tale told about an old retired deacon in the First Baptist Church in Okeechobee. He still worked on the property but had relinquished his duties in the church. He had a reputation for falling asleep during the sermons. During one of his naps, in the midst of the pastor's vigorous remarks, one of the young men tapped him on the shoulder and said softly, "Hey. He's called on you to pray." The old deacon arose immediately and began to offer up prayer in the middle of the sermon.

Hep: help, as in, Kin I hep ya? There are two or three stories that illustrate the use of the word.

A Cracker gal moved to Dallas, Texas, after obtaining a job with Air France Airlines. Her job was at the reservations desk. She'd answer the phone, in a nasal twang, "Air France, kin I hep ya?" A supervisor overheard her say it and came to her to make a suggestion. He said, in a decidedly strong French accent, "Whan yew ans-ser yew must sae 'Ahr Frawnce'." He had her repeat it a few times.

Shortly afterwards the telephone rang. She answered, "Ahr Frawence, kin I hep ya?"

Eastern Kentucky's Dr. Carl Hurley told two classic stories that I have enjoyed for years. Where he heard them I don't know.

A man was driving through the backwoods. He happened to pass a little saw mill. He noticed a man holding a rag to his left ear while he was hastily rooting around in the saw dust. The driver pulled over and asked, "Whut you lookin' for?"

The sawmill man said, "Oh, I cut my ear off with tha bandsaw and I'm tryin' ta find it."

The driver said "Can I hep ya look?"

"Much appreciated," he replied.

After a bit, the driver found the ear, held it up and said, "This it?"

The sawmill man said, "Naw, mine hadda pencil behind it."

The second Hurley story was told to me by a Cracker. It starts with an angry man knocking on the door of his neighbor's house. The neighbor's youngest son answered the door and said, "Kin I hep ya?" The angry man said, "I want to talk to yer daddy about your brother gettin' my daughter pregnant." The son was really trying to be helpful and said, "Well, he gets $300 for the stallion and $50 for the bull but I don't know whut he gets for Brother."

Another colorful tale with the word hep has circulated in South Florida. A man on a Harley motorcycle was slowing down to stop for the last red light in town. He had all the trimmings: a Nazi helmet, beard, tattoos, heavy leather gang-emblemed jacket, with thick boots and a chain on his wallet. As he revved the deep-throated engine of the Harley, an old man on a Moped ring-a-ding-dinged up beside him "Sounding lik' a dirt dauber in a beer can" (See term). The old fella wore thick Coke-bottle glasses and seersucker britches. He looked the big motorcycle over and said, "Wou-ou-ou E-e-e! Man, what a motorcycle. Mind if I look it over?"

"Naw, hep yerself," said the Harley driver.

So the old man leaned close, looked closely at the motor, the emblems, the chrome headers and fine wheels and then commented, "Boy, I bet that thing is fast."

"Yeah, it's fast," said Harley Man. About that time the light changed to green, Harley Man dropped it into low gear and sped away to the open highway to demonstrate the power. He reached 100 mph in several seconds and glanced back to see the Moped gaining on him. He opened the throttle even more but the Moped whizzed by him like he was standing still. It went almost out of sight but he noticed it coming back at an unbelievable speed. The Moped ripped by and disappeared on the highway behind the Harley. In a little while he noticed the Moped gaining on him again. He slowed down to avoid a wreck but the Moped kept coming and crashed into the back of the Harley and disintegrated upon contact. The old

Cracker Terms, Phrases And Definitions

man was slung thirty yards into a ditch. The Harley driver, pulled over, got off and ran to the old fella. He said, "Man! Are you alrite? I ain't never seen anythin' like that. You hurt? Can I hep ya?"

The old fella groaned, but finally, was able to mouth weak words, "Yeah... would you unhook my suspender from your handlebar?"

Hey: a word used in many applications and situations. Hey can be used as a soft greeting, an attempt to get someone's or something's attention, an exclamation, a directive to stop doing something, a cry of astonishment or a "boogerin'" assist in the pens (See term).

Speaking of hey, there was a man named Joe Peeples whose ranch was on the north side of Glades County. Joe was about six-foot six-inches tall, was broad in the chest and had shoulders like a television wrestler. He must have weighed 260 pounds or more. Joe always started with, "HEY! HEY! Let me tell you about Buck. He's the meanest catch dog we got." After your response he'd reply, "HEY! HEY! I mean to tell ya..." It was distracting because it always sounded like he was calling attention to something extremely important. Joe loved people and would put his forearm on your shoulder, leaning all his 260 pounds on you. It felt like a load of literd logs. He never changed the volume of the Hey! even if he spoke to you six inches from your ear. Every time he showed his pen full of catch dogs, he'd always point out one, saying, "HEY! HEY! That's tha best dog we got... a real crackerjack." (There was a pen plum full and every one the best-dog-we-got.) HEY! I miss him.

There is a tale about a Cracker that was led into an adventure called sky diving. How he was convinced to try it either involved whiskey or a pretty woman (or both). As the story goes, he expressed his hesitation as the airplane reached altitude. He was assured by the instructor (and/or the whiskey and/or the woman) that is was safe and more fun than bull riding. Well, he screwed up his courage and jumped. He pulled the cord on his main chute–nothing happened. He panicked a little but remembered he had an emergency chute. He jerked that handle and nothing happened. Now he was in a fix while falling rapidly toward a cabbage hammock. He happened to look down and saw a fella coming upwards as fast as he was traveling downwards. He yelled, "Hey! You know anythin' 'bout parachutes?"

The fella replied as he flew up passed him, "Naw. You know anythin' 'bout gas stoves?"

He's frum summers up north or -else: a summary phrase for a Yankee tourist, city fella or foreigner. "He ain't frum around here" is a similar phrase. "Dodge tha Yankees" referred to driving among the winter tourists that invaded the towns in Cracker Florida. It wasn't necessarily disparaging or derogatory. My step-father told of a time he had a fella from somewhere outside the United States on a coon hunting expedition. The man had an English accent so he really was frum sommers else. They built a fire and were listening to the dogs run the coons. On the cold, clear night the noises were easily heard and you could tell the dogs by their distinctive barks and howls. They were looking idly into the camp fire as my step-daddy said, "Boy, ain't that perty music," referring to the dogs on a hot trail.

The Englishman said, "If those (*expletive deleted*) dogs would shut up, perhaps I could hear it."

I am reminded of a story of some fox hunters in the woods. They were not far from a little country church. The dogs came back, lay down and rested. The night sounds were permeating the woods—crickets and katydids in loud choruses. As the hunters poured coffee on the camp fire, making preparations to leave, the little church congregation struck up a fine old hymn. One of the men commented, "Isn't that fine music?" Another said, "Yeah, I hear they make that sound by rubbin' their back legs together."

Cracker Terms, Phrases And Definitions

Higher'n ah cat's back: a phrase used most of the time to indicate that a price is high, more than expected or outrageous. "Man, tha prices at the fair wuz higher'n ah cat's back!" "That's a fancy restaurant, but, look out 'cause the prices are higher'n ah cat's back!"

His butter dun slipped off his biscit: mentally slow, not all there, a dumb decision, etc. (See "Limb hit") It is used the same as, "He's two cans short of a six-pack" or "His porch lites are on but nobody's home." "He ain't wound real tight."

The perfect example was told by Carl Hurley thirty years ago. He said a local town council considered hiring a kinda slow fella for some menial task to give him something to do and allow him to make some spending money. They voted to hire the boy to polish the cannon on the town square for a small monthly wage. The boy took the job, but in four months, he quit. The chairman of the council asked him, "Son? Why are you quittin'?"

Smiling proudly, the boy said, "Well, I'm goin' intah bidness for myself! I bought my own cannon."

Hog dog: a dog of mixed heritage, usually a Florida Cur or cow dog with some Bull Dog or Pit Bull blood in there somewhere. (See Inbred and Crazier'n ah outhouse rat.)

Hog huntin': the hunting of feral hogs. Some hog hunters are professionals, selling their catches, while some do it for fun. As in all sports, one must absolutely understand the dangers, love living on the edge, have physical endurance and some trustworthy hog dogs, always carry some fishing line for suture material, needle-nosed pliers and suture needles, have a truck and dog cages and a means to carry captured adult hogs, some of which can weigh upwards to 300 pounds. And, most importantly, one must have it in his blood. (That is a nice way of saying, "Hog hunters are half-crazy.")

Many hog hunters have airboats, which are flat-bottomed, propeller-driven boats with either an airplane or automobile engine. These forbidding boats can run over water or land, or both together. (I have heard that camp fires and beer-drinking are required as well.)

Feral hogs are growing in epidemic numbers throughout the South. Some Russian Boars were released or escaped from a private hunting property. (There are counties in Georgia where the hog population is a serious problem. It is likely to get worse throughout the whole of the United States.) The crossbred hogs are generally alert, elusive, adaptable, prolific, smart and mean and can grow huge in size.

Things happen quickly on a hog hunt. We'd drive around near hog sign where they'd rooted up pasture, the dogs would jump the herd or an individual and the race was on. You'd hear running, the cracking of dry cabbage fans, dogs barking, pigs squealing, whoops, whistles and hollers of "Ketch 'im, Buck..." or "Over here!" etc. Sometimes there'd be fifteen piglets. The dogs would catch one, somebody would tie its feet while the dogs ran down another one. It was wild fun with an air of danger–you never knew when you'd come upon a bad hog. By the time you'd run a few hundred yards wide open, caught up to a held pig and tied it down, you'd be quivering from the excitement and exhaustion. Then it'd be "Here we go again."

The boars are nasty with their sharp tusk-teeth, but sows can wreak havoc with just their teeth, as well. They all tend to assume a defensive position in the rankest places you could imagine. Dense bays, swamps, palmetto patches and dark tangled under-growth are typical places for them to go to ground when the dogs catch up with them. Usually these places are so dense that only the dogs can penetrate them. Hog hunters will wade in sometimes–amid the intense clamor of baying dogs. Many hunters and dogs get viciously cut in the close quarters. (And ya dang sure better stay on yer feet...) Some hunters shoot the hogs in these thick patches and spend considerable time dragging them out. (Hubert Waldron told me about easing into a thick palmetto patch

Cracker Terms, Phrases And Definitions

after a huge, battle-scarred boar. The dogs had enough sense to hold back. The killer boar was smart and patient, waiting for the victim. All Hubert saw was an alert eye watching through a tangled mass of roots and palmetto fans. He shot it in the eye. It took three hearty fellas to drag the thing out. I had it mounted for display. The razor-sharp tusks were about three inches long. He was an ugly and mean-looking beast.) Other hog hunters wait until the dogs immobilize the hog by holding its ears.

The dogs work as a pack, hazing, circling, and watching for an opening, then catching and holding and all the while barking at feverish levels. Some dogs hang back while others plunge into the fracas without hesitation. The young dogs learn by watching the older dogs. Most survive. Some male pigs are castrated, marked and released so the hunters can identify them for harvesting later.

A sow can have a litter of six to ten piglets a few times each year. Every "three months, three weeks and three days" is the rule of thumb for the gestation period for swine. The hog population explodes rather quickly, especially if there are plenty of food sources. Some people trap them with baited traps; it works well until the hogs figure it out.

Hogs are smarter than dogs; in fact, they are fairly intelligent. A friend gave me a tiny ten-day old piglet. I thought it would be an experience for my daughters. Hunter, my wife, wore a long plaid robe on the cold mornings and that little thing was instinctively drawn to going under the robe's edge. She was really comfortable under the protection of a mama-shadow, trying to follow wherever it went; Hunter discovered this behavior one morning when she couldn't find her. After several hunts throughout the house, she found Rosie peeking out from under the edge of that robe. She would stay anywhere Hunter put the robe.

When she got a little age on her, the dang thing would try to root our dog off the heating pad in the dog house at night.

(I know, go ahead and laugh.) You'd hear them fussing at each other at 2:00 in the morning as they shuffled around trying to take possession of it. It took only three or four weeks for the pig to outweigh the dog and win the competition every time. She thought she was a dog and walked on a leash with the dog, cat and the children. She became such a pet the local newspaper photographer came by for a photo shoot–made the front page! She never messed in the whole yard except for a tiny corner for her bidness; she would not leave the yard unless on a leash. She was an interesting and loveable pet and she surely kept the kids occupied for the six months we had her. She knew many words and was easy to train. We named her, Rosie La Porcina. She grew too big on dog food; we gave her to a lady who had the room to keep her. A special hog like that you don't get in a hurry to eat.

I've sutured up many, many hog dogs. They came into the clinic mostly late at night. The reason was simple: the dogs were cut up trying to catch an ear of a cornered hog somewhere around late afternoon or early evening. By the time the men caught up with the dogs and the hog, tied up the hog and loaded it in the truck, unloaded it in a trap, got all the dogs collected and checked and all the beer finished, it was midnight or later. Honestly, the damage could be done many miles back in the woods and there was no way to get to the vet hospital for at least an hour or two, especially if the dog was unable to travel well or got separated from the hunters. Many hog hunters slipped into ranches to chase hogs; the ranchers wanted them there as long as they respected the livestock and property; truth is hog hunters usually did less damage than a herd of hogs. It was a wild, death-defying tradition in Highlands County, if not in all of the cattle country of South Florida.

Hog hunters like to have lots of dogs. More than one has told me, "Doc, if it's gonna cost a lot, put 'im down, I got five more in the truck." Unbelievable lacerations were brought in; exhausted dogs with cuts and stabs anywhere on their bodies. As I inspected these dogs for wounds I always said something like, "Why I wish you'd look! This dog must be sorry; he's cut in the butt. Must ah been runnin' away." The boys would jerk their heads back to the dog's rump and lift the tail to look, saying, "Doc, he ain't never run from a hog..." Then we'd smile. He'd been had.

The wounds were usually nasty–both with contamination and in severity–because the simple ones had already been handled in the woods. It was not unusual to find sutures in them where they'd recently been sewn up. We used stainless steel suture material because it was non-reactive and easy to remove after the wounds healed. The hog dogs were not only tougher than most, they healed quickly. A common question after suturing a hog dog was, "Doc, whin can we use 'im agin?"

Years ago, I remember a hog hunter asking me at 1:30 in the morning what I thought the bill would be. I told him I thought it would be around $175 to $190, adding, "That's night call and all." He flinched. So while I continued suturing the sleeping dog, I asked, "What do you think would be fair?"

He replied, "Well, a good welder gits $25 an hour... we been here two hours..." (He left that suggestion hanging for consideration.)

In a few minutes, I said, "I tell you what; I'll do it for $50 if you'll pay the hospital expenses." (I left *that* hanging for consideration.)

Curiosity got the better of him and he asked, "Well, how much are the expenses?"

I swabbed some debris out of the contaminated wound and answered, "Right at 80% of every dollar I charge..."

Being a sharp lad, he asked how much that would come out to be. I said, "Divide $50 by 20% and it'll tell you what the bill should be for me to net $50."

He figured it out with a pencil on a piece of paper towel and said, "Why that comes out $250..."

"Yep", I said.

He said, "I'll take the first price you mentioned." Then as an afterthought, he added, "Doc, how'd you like some fresh pork?"(That was the end of the discussion. Yes, the pork roast was good.)

(One fella asked me, "What do I owe you?" I replied, "That'll be $10 for the surgery and $115 to clean the place up."

One experience will illustrate how a hog hunter thinks. On one foray into hog hunting, Johnny and I took my dogs out for a run on a cold winter night. The dogs jumped a medium-sized hog, which shot into a Cypress bayhead. I waded in while asthmatic Johnny hung back and smoked a cigarette. The dogs waded in chest-deep water as I hollered the customary, "Ketch 'im!" They kept circling a large clump of dense undergrowth. I couldn't see the beast, but shook the tree limbs, chunked in sticks, and hollered, all the while looking for a tree to climb, just in case... No hog. All wet and exhausted, I finally returned to the Jeep. Johnny only smiled as I walked up. I related as how I never found the hog and how he must have given the dogs and me the slip.

Johnny said, "Oh, the hog left about thirty minutes ago."

I said, "Why in the hamfat didden you holler at me?"

He replied, "Well, I hadn't finished my cigarette and I was enjoyin' the show."

Hog waller: usually refers to a spot where feral hogs have churned the soil, wallowed in it to get cool or to scratch their backs. Swine don't have sweat glands and over-heating is serious for them. In fact, if the hog has a choice in the matter they will not get dirty, but in confinement the options are limited. They do the best they can under those conditions. Hog waller can be interchanged with sow's nest when used of children's rooms "Y'all, this room looks like a hog waller–clean it up!" The proper reply is, "Yes, Ma'am."

Hold'er! Hold'im! or Holdup!: typically used when working cattle to tell the chute man not to release the cow or bull. While running cattle through a working chute at the rate of a hundred head an hour–or more, it gets pretty frantic. But if everyone does his job in a coordinated, rhythmic fashion, it can go like clockwork and, hopefully, without injury. In the old-style manually operated chute one man is on the head-catch, one on the tail gate (closing it to keep the animal from backing out or another from running in on top of the caught animal), and one on the squeeze of the side panels (to prevent jumping and hold them steady, etc.). On hydraulic chutes the man at the controls can open the front gate, squeeze the side panels as the animal comes in, simultaneously close the back gate and, lastly, pull a lever to lift the head to a working height–all done in a smooth and organized production line. But if something interrupts the rhythm of the operator or he loses his concentration, such as opening the head and/or back gate too soon or unsqueezing the animal at the wrong time, a wreck could ensue. The work has to be stopped, the pile-up unsorted, the bruised cowboys tended to and maybe catch the cow again before she gets lost in the already-worked herd. So, when a chute controller hears someone holler, "Hold'er!" or "Holdup!" it means to wait and not release the beast (i.e., turn 'im out) until the problem is corrected. Anything can cause a hold'er or holdup. Someone sees a bad eye, a growth, or the cow spits out the de-wormer (requiring the vaccination man to re-fill his syringes and repeat the action), or the cow is not pregnant; (i.e., open) and the palpator wants to be sure, or (and this it the worst distraction) a bunch of pretty girls comes to the pens to watch.

The ground vibrates, the steel panels clang at ear-piercing levels, cattle snort and blow, dust and dirt fill the air, and there are at least five ways a man can get bruised or maimed. It sure is a wonder that there aren't serious injuries every time the chute is operating. All kinds of injuries occur: teeth knocked out, arms and ribs mashed, broken and bruised, head and lips busted on any day that tough cattle are worked. Makes people wonder why these men do this work. It's hard to explain to the uninitiated. All I can say is that there is deep satisfaction in rollin' the cattle through the chute like well-oiled machinery.

It can be summarized by a statement I once told an audience: "Working commercial crossbred cattle efficiently is a coordinated, symphonic chaos, characterized by heat, humidity, flies, repetition, boredom, long hours, fatigue, and accompanied by moments of panic and utter terror–much like rearing children."

There has to be a vast amount of common sense in this work and an ability to alter a procedure if need be; i.e., to be quick on one's feet.

I recall a story told by my cousin who was staying in a fairly nice hotel. She called Room Service for a hamburger and it went something like this:

"Room Service."

"Yes, I'd like a hamburger sent up to room 903... I want just a burger on a bun–that's all. And a Coke."

"Ma'am, we don't have a plain burger on a bun... we have a burger basket. It includes lettuce, tomato, onion, fries, cheese, catsup and mayo..."

"All I want is a plain burger on a plain bun–that's all. Can you put one together on a little plate and send it up?"

"No, Ma'am, we don't have plain burgers; we have a burger basket with everything on the side."

"Can you hold something? Say, the fries?"

"Yes, Ma'am..."

Cracker Terms, Phrases And Definitions

"Okay, tell you what... I'd like a hamburger basket. Hold the lettuce, tomato, onion, fries, cheese, catsup and mayo."

"Yes, Ma'am; that's one burger basket, hold the lettuce, tomato, onion, fries, cheese, catsup and mayo and one Coke. It'll be up in twenty minutes."

Hold'ertail: a directive for a helper to grab the tail and force it up so the vet or someone can brand, apply insecticide, administer an injection, deliver a calf or palpate. When Brahma crossbred cows were restrained (hit the chute), their tail would "Ring and twist" (see term), to express their anxiety. Some more docile breeds were not as bad about switching their tails. Tails are rough, coarse and usually laden with dried manure. There's nothing like being hit in the face by a wet, filthy tail. The stiff hair could scratch or cut the cornea and that will ruin your day and several days thereafter. (You'd look like a pirate without the parrot the next day.)

How'er y'all doin? or the singular form, How ya doin'? Obviously, this is the usual greeting to a group in the pens or entering a Cracker's house. Upon walking in among a cow crew, it is a common greeting that is well understood. If someone is sick or has been hurt, "How ya doin?" is meant as a question in regard to the person's health. When someone is thrown from a horse or is cow-hooked, the common question of a friend leaning over the fallen man is, "You awrite?" If the man is out of danger, up and resting or getting his self back in order, one might hear, "How'er ya doin'?" The difference is degree; "You awrite?" is a little more immediate question after a wreck. "How'er ya doin?" after things have settled down (or the next morning when the fella can barely walk.)

A friend of mine was speaking of health concerns and made the following off-handed comment: "Ya know, it's ah little known health fact that stifled sneezes cause pot-belliedness." (This has nothing to do with the above–it's the only place I could work it in.)

How'dj'all do? How did it go? How did things turn out? Did you finish—and if not, why not? Did the cattle handle alright? What did the lawyer say about your case? I remember hearing this question at a fish camp frequented by Crackers in Everglades City, Florida, south of Naples. While resting before supper, sitting on a picnic table under a palm tree in the evening breeze, I noticed two fishermen on a fine flats boat trolling toward the dock. A sun-burned man came out of a nearby RV and, upon recognizing the boat driver he called out, "How'dj'all do?"

The answer rang back over soft breezes, "We dun reel good. We got two Snook an' ah $75 ticket frum the Park Ranger!"

How miny cows do ya reckon is in ther? a somewhat obvious question regarding the head count of cattle in a group. Reckon meant to estimate, guess, or consider. It was usually asked to estimate how long it would take to work the group. Answers ranged from Just ah' handful, Ah sackful, Ah few, Ah fistful, Ah little bunch or Over (*fill in the number*).

At an Alabama wedding reception, I met a man named Duge Cannon from Oklahoma. He was the kind of man that you would notice when he entered the room. He was naturally easy-going with a dry wit. He was asked by a less than sophisticated guest, "How many cattle do you own?" It's like asking how much money you've got. He deflected the impolite query with his usual humor and grace, "Well, there's a hundred or so on the north side of the house, several hundred on the west side of the ranch and a few more in the south pasture." Years later, I ran into Duge in Oklahoma. We caught up on visiting. He remembered the Alabama incident and confessed his deception. He said, "I got three steers named, A-hundred-or-so, Several-hundred and A-few-more. He rocked backwards as he laughed. (Oklahoma humor, no doubt.)

How miny people died in that wreck? a back-handed question asked about a less than cared-for vehicle. It was meant as a greeting, and was also a dig at his mode of transportation.

Cracker Terms, Phrases And Definitions

I heard tell of a young fella who told his dad that he just bought a truck for $200 dollars. His daddy replied, "That don't sound like much of a truck, son. Where do you intend to go in this vehicle?" The boy replied, "No wheres—it ain't got no motor." A variation of this type of humor was in reference to a man's horse. If a fella unloads a different horse than he ordinarily rides, one of the men might teasingly say, "How long has that horse bin sick?"

Humis: means high humidity. "Whou-ee, it sure is humis today," or "I'm hotter'n a toad under a cookin' skillet—it sure is humis."

Hut ch'all want? Sometimes simplified to "Ch'all want?" Sonny reminded me that this is what a Cracker waitress asks when summoned to the table in a small café. "Ch'all want sum-en'?" In north Alabama the phrase, Ch'all want sum-en, is spoken in a manner where the last word has an upward lilt–kinda like a pig's tail starting straight and ending in an upward curl.

Florida Cow Hunter's Handbook

Cracker Terms, Phrases And Definitions

I

I always take a bath whin I git a drink: As far as I can determine there is only one documented incidence where the phrase was used. It occurred in the fifties. Harris Sills, who we called Partner, and Sid Pearce, a descendent of a pioneer who settled in Basinger, Florida, were cow huntin' one time. They'd covered a lot of territory on their round-about when they came to an old railroad grade that had been converted to a road. Down the grade was an old railroad bridge that was still strong and useful. As they approached it, Partner allowed that he wanted a drink. The heavy rains had resulted in lots of water that was flowing through the creek, running swiftly under the bridge. On the banks of the grade, next to the bridge, tall grasses had grown up and Partner figured he'd get a drink there. He dismounted, hitched up his belt and jumped off the grade. Well, he went right through the grass mat and disappeared into the black water. The grass was actually a floating mass of vegetation that had been undercut by the strong current, leaving a deep hole next to the bridge.

Sid watched as his hat floated away and Partner's white head came up near the middle of the creek. Partner was spitting water as he surfaced.

Sid said, "Well, d*(expletive deleted)*, Partner, I didden know you wuz goin' tah take a bath."

That's when Partner replied, "I always take a bath whin I git a drink."

Speaking of hats floating off in the creek, I recall a late afternoon when we were going back to the horse barn after a full day of working cattle. As we approached a canal crossing, we could see that the water was high after the recent summer rains. Everyone pulled his boots back toward the back of their saddles, except me. I tried a new technique: I pulled my feet forward toward the saddle horn. The problems started at that point because the green horse I was riding thought I was about to bog my spurs in his shoulders. (See Bog.) He bolted forward, as he thought he was supposed to, leaving me tumbling off backwards into the canal. My hat floated off as the horse charged out of the water. There was a considerable amount of laughter as a result of this innovative procedure. Had I known about Partner and Sid at the time I would have taken a page out of Partner's book: "Y'all don't mind me–I always take a bath whin I git a drink."

I bin ta two county fairs an a goat ropin' an I ain't never seen nuthin' like that! Although this expression brings to mind a similar one from the movie, *Dr. Strangelove*, "Well, I've been to one World Fair, a picnic, and a rodeo, and that's the stupidest thing I ever heard come over a set of earphones." It found a place in Okeechobee and the surrounding counties. (I guess I used it too much.) I happened to Google it and found fifteen or twenty variations. I couldn't find where it originated.

It was often said in observance of some peculiar occurrence, such as the delivery of a two-headed calf or finding several dead cattle that had been lightning struck next to a fence. (If you want to get the full import of the statement, gather up a bunch of wild goats and just try roping them; they watch the loop as it comes toward them, duck their heads at the last instant, and dodge it with ease. It is really hard to rope a goat. I tried it some, finding a flimsy cotton clothesline rope worked best. I gave up after a while, since they acted like they were enjoying it a lot more than I was.)

Idee: Cracker pronunciation for idea; as in, "Y'all hav' any idee whin we'll finish up?" Two classic illustrations come to mind. A young man from Highlands County was courting a girl from a prominent Hardee County family. As I recall, he said he was getting friendly with the family by his frequent visits. Well, the time was right to ask the gal's father for his permission to marry his daughter.

Cracker Terms, Phrases And Definitions

The daddy asked the young man if he wanted to ride to town with him to pick up ranch supplies and the boy thought that would be a good opportunity to talk to Daddy about his daughter.

While they were riding in the Jeep Wagoneer at fifty miles per hour on a deep-gullied sand road, Boy asked Daddy, "I was wonderin' if you would mind if I asked your daughter for her hand in marriage."

The young man described the reaction this way: "Daddy slammed on the brakes, weaved around in the sand, 'bout turned over, and we ended up in a ditch alongside the road." He said, "I wuz sure I'd ripped my britches with him."

Daddy waved the dust cloud away as he faced Boy and said, "Boy, do you hav' any idee how much it costs to maintain that girl?"

(The names have been deleted to protect Highland County's Steve Hartt and Van Adams.)

The second story that is helpful in understanding the use of the word involves a traffic stop. A Cracker boy was driving a little too fast and the law caught him. The State Trooper asked, "Sir, do you have any I.D.?" The boy replied, "'Bout whut?"

I'd know'er anywher' or I'd know 'im anywher': a nonsense phrase often used as a humorous retort after some animal acted ugly or there was some sort of wreck. It seemed an appropriate understatement. For an illustration, when a seriously bad-to-kick cow at a dairy or an outlaw mare would catch someone unawares, kicking the taste out of their mouth, the fella might respond, "I'd know her anywher'." (Oh yeah? Why'd she nail you again?) I'd use the phrase in the pens when all the cattle were identified by an ear tag. Someone would call out the number: "She's number M 28." I'd respond, "Ol' number M 28; I'd know 'er anywhere..." (Habit, I guess.)

Another quote I use right often is similar to this one and used in the same situations: "Sort of reminds me of an old girl I usta know."

I don't care whut y'all say: a face-saving acknowledgement that someone else was correct in their assessment of a correction, situation or action. As an example, if a fella failed to tighten his cinch well and the saddle was slipping off kilter on his horses' back, one of the men might comment with an understatement, "Ah believe yer 'bout ta lose yer saddle." The rider could respond to the obvious statement, as he dismounted, "Well, I don't care whut y'all say, I'm gonna tighten my cinch."

I'd rather take a dose of mineral oil: an emphatic, though exaggerated way of responding to an unwelcome, but necessary, task that was unpleasant, tedious, dangerous, obnoxious or troublesome. For example, if a tractor broke down, the proper response was, "I'druther take a dose of mineral oil than to tear into that tractor engine." Ranchers often hate book work or income tax preparation, so it would be entirely appropriate to hear, "I'd rather take a dose of mineral oil than look for that missing 12 cents."

If I'da knowed (*fill in the blank*), I'da (*fill in the blank*): this has a wide use and appeal, similar to "If you'd ah asked me, I'da told you" or "I coudda told ya that won't work." (Below) The perfect example is the time I bought some new T-shirts. Several days later I found a little note that said, "Inspected by No. 19." I showed it to my wife and told her, "If I'da knowed they wuz gonna send sumbody to inspect my underwear drawer, I'da not bought those T-shirts."

If youda asked me, I coudda told you (*fill in the blank*) **or "I tried to tell ya:** phrases my mama used when something I'd already done didn't work out. Now what's funny to me is that Mama usually didn't have any idea I was about to try something. If it didn't work, she'd often say, "If youdah asked me I couda told you that wouldn't work." When she

Cracker Terms, Phrases And Definitions

said, "I tried to tell ya…" I'd reply, "But, naw, I wodden listen to you." Then, we'd laugh every time.

I hear ya cluckin' but ah cain't find yer nest: A phrase used when trying to find someone who is closeby. For instance, I would call Sonny to come select the correct equipment part for a repair or for his help in carrying it. He might not know exactly where I was in the maze of shelves and supplies, so he'd say, "Hey, I hear you cluckin' but I can't find yer nest." This phrase got a friend of mine in deep trouble with his mama one time. She was scolding him for some crack-pot stunt he had pulled and he tried her, "I hear ya cluckin', but ah cain't find yer nest." This was accompanied by a recently acquired sneer. That was the last time he sassed his mama and the longest his back-side ever stung.

I jus' luv dis kuntry: used to communicate how much you appreciate someone's courteousness or generosity. It can cause a double-take by the one hearing it. The last time I used it was when a cashier caught an over charge and corrected it. I spoke in my clearest East Pakistani accent, saying, "I jus' luv dis kuntry." She broke into laughing. As far as I know it has no Cracker connection, but I felt it might be a "good'un" to use. (See term)

I'm havin' a hard time gettin' gals to go out with me: a comment made by a Cracker cow hunter, named Jake, to his companions on one Friday afternoon. The story goes that lonesome Jake was speaking to his friends about how to get dates. One of them said, "I tell you whut, ol' Cooter is always goin' out with some fine women, maybe you oughta talk to him for some pointers or sumthin'." So Jake hunted down Cooter.

The next morning when the men arrived to saddle up for work, they heard some music coming out of the barn. They went in and found clean-shaven Jake in his Sunday hat, shined boots, new jeans and freshly ironed shirt. He had placed some aroma candles in various places around the barn, had a CD player with Kenny G playing romantic saxophone ballads and he was scattering rose petals all around the tractor.

Harvey asked, "Whut in the world are you doin'?" Jake replied, "Well, I talked to Cooter and he said tha first thing I had to do to get a woman wuz to do sumthin' sexy to a tractor."

Inerts: the proper name of substances that make or have no contribution to effectiveness or medicinal value, usually serving as a vehicle for the active ingredient; as in, "This product contains 3.0% active ingredients and 97.0% inerts." The reason I include the term will come clear in the following account. Years ago there was a flea product called ParaBomb – a carbamate or organophosphate. This type of chemical is an insecticide that is found today in powder forms such as Sevin Dust for Roses, etc. Those early years when flea control was very difficult, ParaBomb was a commonly used aerosol spray. Every veterinarian used it to eliminate fleas on pets coming into a veterinary hospital and, too, use of it increased over the counter sales since it was so dramatic in effect. We'd spray every flea infested dog. Hundreds of fleas would immediately die before the owner's eyes and fall *en masse* onto the table. It was dramatic and memorable. The truth be told, it probably was the 98% alcohol content which caused the rapid deaths. It acted as a carrier for the active portion, 2-3% carbamate. The carbamate was left as a residue for prolonged effectiveness.

One particular cowboy brought in a big brindle cur dog. The fleas covered every square inch of his body but were difficult to see because of his color pattern. I sprayed him down and went about making some notes on the medical record. The table was black from the hundreds and hundreds of fleas in the throes of death. It truly was a flea circus. The cowboy was impressed. He picked up the aerosol spray can and intently read the ingredients. He got a twinkle in his eyes as he said, "Them d*(expletive deleted)* inerts are rank, ain't they?"

Ironin' with a short board: a reference to fatigue from various causes like a restless night of sleep due to lower back pain. It was first heard when we had worked very late and had to go back before daylight. After sort of falling out of bed, one of the bleary-eyed men said, "I feel like I been ironin' all nite with a short board."

Ironing boards can be used for other activities. When my friend Berny Zellner, whom I mention in several places, obtained two female dogs and some cats over a period of time, it bothered me that he would have to take them to Auburn or somewhere to have them neutered. He really was not interested in raising pups and kittens. I also knew they could get killed in a heartbeat since they lived near a busy road. I hated the thought of his spending lots of money on the strays. He had given them a good home–the least I could do was neuter them for him. There were other un-neutered dogs and cats around so it was just a matter of time before a sack full of little ones would be joining the crowd.

I mentioned to Berny that I could spay them at his house. We put our scientific minds together and came up with a plan. I pilfered the Small Animal Clinic (one could do that as a Staff member) and located a half-bottle of liquid used in gas anesthesia machines. I met Berny at his house and arrayed a stunning assortment of surgical tools and supplies. Berny got out some string and the ironing board and we set up in the kitchen.

The first thing we did was eat lunch, which was common for us when beginning any project. With the smell of pimento cheese on our breaths and occasionally burping cookies and iced tea, we took two Dixie-cups and poked holes in the bottoms of them. In one we put surgical sponges and cotton balls. We then slipped the other inside, thus forming a chamber of absorbent material. We dripped the anesthesia liquid on the cotton balls and held it over the nose of the patient, just like chloroform in Jack-the-Ripper days. When the patient had progressed to the proper depth of anesthesia, we tied her on the ironing board and progressed with the surgery. The recovery room was the hall floor and the garage, mainly because one of the dogs had rolled in something.

Some got up quickly and walked around our feet; others slept peacefully. All surgeries that day were successful.

You may think that we were callous and unprofessional. But the anesthesia and technique were excellent, the patients were kept pain-free, didn't know what happened, the recoveries were uneventful, and we had plenty of iced tea and pimento cheese sandwiches. What else could you ask for?

One thing I've learned as a veterinarian, one can do amazing (or at least adequate) medical work in less than ideal conditions. (Ask missionary doctors!) The patients did well until Berny tried to remove the skin sutures. He chuckled, "They scratched me some. They didn't go for it."

I am reminded of the tale told to me by a Cracker while we were on a water break in the cow pens. He said, "Doc, you see them cow dogs over ther' by tha trailer?"

"Yeah, whut about them?"

He said, "They're not only good cow dogs, they're crackerjack coon dogs, too."

"Oh? I had no idea."

"Yeah," he explained, "All I hav ta do is show 'em tha board I use tah stretch an' cure tha coon hides an' they'll tree a coon that size. One will come git me while tha others keep the ole coon in tha tree." (By this time I knew I was in for a good leg pullin'.)

After a pregnant pause he continued, "Yeah. Last week I made ah mistake an' carried the wife's ironin' board out on the back porch and them dogs took off like all gitout. I didn't see 'um for three days. Then one come and got me. I follered 'er out and them dogs had treed ah 'gator."

Cracker Terms, Phrases And Definitions

It cain't be dirty 'cause it ain't touched tha ground: a reply to kids' reaction ("Uh-h-h-h-h-h, gross, yuck," etc.) when they first see cow manure on the veterinarian's glove during rectal palpation in cattle. Hunter (pronounced in Alabamian as Huntah), my wife, learned that manure stained coveralls was proof I had work and wasn't carousing around. She saw these stains as brown gold or the sweet smell of money.

It don't take much to make us happy: As far as I can determine this phrase was first used on the Kissimmee River near Lorida, Florida (pronounced *Low-reed'-ah*). It occurred when Robert and I were fishing out of a fine 22-foot Stratos bass boat. The fishing action was slow that afternoon as dusk began creeping toward the horizon. At times when the fish are slow to bite, men become reflective.

Robert said, "Ya know? It don't take much to make us happy."

I gave him a few seconds to expand on that statement, as he usually did and for me to try another cast, "Whutta you mean?"

Another long pause as he concentrated on reeling a zigzagging top-water plug toward the boat, "Well, it's this away; we're fishin' out of a $22,000 boat."

"And..." I injected.

"Well, we haul tha boat on a $1000 trailer, pulled by a $34,000 Suburban and we're fishing with $90 rods and reels."

I cast at the edge of the water near a little bush and took up the track, "Yeah, an' we got $500 worth of plugs, worms, line, spinner baits, hooks, tackle boxes, weights, extra rods and reels, an' a cooler full of sandwiches and drinks."

We fished for another few minutes before he added, "Yeah, and we got life jackets, flashlights, trolling motor, extra batteries, flares, and inspection stickers."

"An' fishin' licenses", I added. Another ten minutes went by without a word. I finally said, "Ya know, it only costs eighty-percent more to go first class."

After another ten to fifteen minutes, he said, "I figure it's cost us about $59 a fish over the last four years."

I think he's got C.O.D.: I thought the acronym referred to O.C.D. (Obsessive Compulsive Disorder). When asked about it the speaker said, Naw, he's got C.O.D... he owes me $10.

I tried ta tell ya: an often used expression following one's bad decision. In fact, the speaker may actually have tried to warn the fella. But my mother used it in the following manner: "Well, I tried to tell you that wouldn't work, but naw, you wooden listen to me." Most (if not all) of the time she had no idea of what I was going to do. *But she never said, "I told you so…"* She used, "If you'da asked me, I coudda told you," and I would mimic her, "But no… I wooden ask you." We'd both smile, she got the point and it became a family joke.

Itsah long ways frum his heart: describes an injury that is minor or insignificant. Say, a bull's horns have to be tipped to remove its sharp points so he won't damage another animal or man in the pens, occasionally the procedure cuts into the sensitive portion on the horn. This procedure is often complicated by the uncooperative attitude of the bull toward restraint. Just as the clippers are about to be closed, the animal jumps, throwing off the angle of the cut. When it is a little too deep, the consequent bleeding is minor, usually stopping in a few minutes. This area is called the quick — much like cutting one's fingernails too short. The cowboys would briefly evaluate it, and conclude, "Don't worry, itsah long ways frum his heart." They also used this in sarcastic understatement, as when a horse steps on an unguarded toe and elicits the feeble, quivering response, "Un-n-n-h-h-h-h-h… Good thing itsah long ways frum my heart."

Homicidally dangerous bulls (and cows) with a history of killing were usually completely de-horned. The surgical

Cracker Terms, Phrases And Definitions

procedure left only the base of the horns, about 2-5 inches. Yes, there was some bleeding. The stump sometimes spurted blood for a time since the blood pressure was elevated during the handling of the renegade. *It was a long ways from his heart* but looked much worse that it was. In reality, these bulls, many of the huge Brahman bulls in particular, were terrors and would in fact go for anyone or anything in their reach. This radical means of de-horning was the simplest way to prevent that threat, though a de-horned killer could still maul a man pretty badly. (If he didn't die, he'd sure wish he had...)

The Crackers didn't tolerate killers much. The problem with the de-horning method was too much bleeding at times. So at one ranch the cowboys came up with a solution. They tied a stretchy nylon cord around the base of the horn, near the head. They took a flat piece of wood and inserted it between the loop, twisting it so that a tourniquet was made, putting pressure on the supplying arteries and veins under the base of the horns. Though difficult to describe, the result was a piece of flat wood in the middle of the bull's forehead, with the cord twisted like a fence post wire used to pull tension on the end post. In effect, it was a figure-eight tourniquet-loop, between the horns. But how to remove the loop when the bleeding stopped? To run him back into the chute only raised the blood pressure. The solution: let the bull out to settle him down (i.e., cool his jets), get a .22 rifle and approach the bull outside the fence. The bull would whirl around, raising his head high ready to fight. Taking careful aim above the raised head of the killer, the shooter would skip the bullet off the wood, clip the cord and release the tourniquet. The tourniquet would fall off–problem solved! (I described this technique to some incredulous veterinary students. They thought I was making up a story. I tried to tell 'em... but, naw, they wooden listen to me.)

I wuz afraid he'd do that: an understatement, completely unnecessary as well as false, made after a wrecked plan. It sort of elicited smiles among by-standers.

One time I was de-worming a horse. Now, this involves restraining the horse and passing a stomach tube through the nasal cavity. If done correctly, the horse doesn't get upset, but it does take some practice. Green or untrained horses are easily frightened by it the first time or two. The reason tubes are passed nasally is that horses have an extremely complex oral and nasal anatomy. Oral passage of tubes is nearly impossible in the conscious horse. We had the nervous horse under an oak tree, with limbs not a foot above his head. He was restrained by what is known as a twitch, a device that applies pressure to the top lip of the horse, similar in theory to pain relief in acupuncture. (It is beyond the scope of this Handbook to completely describe the technique. Suffice it to say, a twitch gets the horse's attention so he isn't thinking about something going down his windpipe. The tube is passed to the stomach for introduction of the anthelminthic.)

The horse suddenly became alarmed and fractious. I looked up and saw (of all things) a monkey, positioned directly over the horse's head, staring from his crouched position in the fork of a branch. The horse had seen him and was about to become uncorked. The owner casually said, "I wuz afraid he wuz gonna do that," referring to either the monkey's propensity to get too close to the action, or the horse's being spooked by the unfamiliar sight.

If a bull tore down a whole fence, butted several cowboys, destroyed one side of a truck and escaped into the woods, there was usually the tongue-in-cheek, "I wuz afraid he would do that." Why no one ever warned us about the potential for any of these wrecks is beyond me. It did lighten the mood, I guess.

I wish you'd look at that: a phrase used in exclamation, astonishment, or humorous ridicule. If one of the men had to leave work that day for an appointment with a judge or a doctor, he'd come to work in nice jeans and dress shirt, with hair all slicked down. The men would immediately take notice of him, and one would say, "Well, I wish you'd look at that—ain't you a sight." The comment was usually followed by wide grins. No one would ever dare say, "You look very nice today." Sonny used the phrase when I came home from college during breaks. My skin would be an unblemished lily-white and my hands grown soft from easy living. It was his way of showing affection. (See Ain't you a site?)

In-KNEE-mah: a Cracker pronunciation of enema. Mrs. Dorothy Hicks was the housekeeper and part-time veterinary assistant at the first hospital where I worked. Miz Hicks was as faithful as the day is long to Dr. Frank Handley and the Handley family. In those early days, Dr. Handley would be on the road almost all day—six to seven days a week. His clients would bring in a sick or wounded dog, and leave it there until Doc had a chance to examine it when he returned. Miz Hicks would meet him at the door, with, "Docta Handley, somebody brought in a sick dog. I already gave him an inKNEEmah." She was very kindly taking the poor dog's mind off his problem.

That reminds me of the story told to me by my step-father about the veterinarian called to treat a bloated bull. Where he heard it I don't know.

Years ago there was a little community built on a river. Fertile farms dotted both sides of the river flood plain and there was a little draw bridge in the middle of the town. A bridge tender lived next to the bridge; his job was to raise the bridge when boatmen blew their whistles to signal their request to pass under the bridge. It happened that the bridge tender quit his job in order to run for county commissioner. He traveled to all the residences and farms to ask for the citizen's vote in the forthcoming election.

He approached one farmer, introduced himself and began a short talk about the election, his plans for the community and to ask for the man's vote.

The farmer cut the comments short asking, "You used to be the bridge tender, didn't you?"

"Yes, I just quit to run my campaign," was the reply.

The farmer said, "No! There ain't no way I'll vote for you."

Puzzled, the bridge-tender-turned-politician asked, "Why won't you consider voting for me?"

The farmer said, "Well, it wadn't too long ago that I had a prize purebred bull. He wuz really sumthin'—tha best one around here anyways. He got bloated on a bunch of horse feed and I called the vet out to treat him. The vet got here and looked him over. He said, 'I have to give this bull an enema—he's so bloated his gut is swollen. If I can relieve his gas obstruction, he'll be alright.' So he went to his truck and fumbled around several minutes. The bull wuz getting' worse by the minute. So I went over and askt him whut the delay wuz. He said, 'Wellsir, I left my funnel at the house. I don't have anything I can use to pour the soapy water into the tube.' My grandson wuz standin' there and he said, 'Grandaddy? We got that old World War I bugle in the attic. Cain't we use that for a funnel?' The vet said, 'Yeah, that'll work fine.' So my grandson goes in, gits the bugle and brings it out. We gathered up the buckets of warm water, the vet puts in the soap, puts a tube into the bulls rectum and we poured gallons of warm soapy water down the funnel attached to the tube. Everything wuz goin' fine til the bull got squirmy. He bucked and frammed around in the chute and finally broke the gate and run off down the highway at a full gallop. The soapy water and gas began to blow out the bugle makin' all kinds of noise."

The bridge tender asked, "What does that have to do with your not voting for me?"

Cracker Terms, Phrases And Definitions

The farmer said, "Well, he headed down the road toward town an' whin he got close to the bridge with all that gas comin' out the bugle, you raised the draw bridge! He run off the end of it and drowned in the river. So, I'm here to tell ya I ain't votin' for nobody that cain't tell the difference between ah boat whistle and ah bugle up a bull's butt."

I wish he'd try that with me…: an audacious hot-air response to someone's tale about some past or frustrating circumstances or misunderstandings. The classic example is the story about the Cracker Sheriff that stopped a couple of fellas for speeding. The driver began to give a little attitude and the Sheriff reached in, pulled him partially out of the window and slapped him a couple of times. That pretty much settled the issue. The Sheriff walked around to the passenger side of the truck and told the passenger to roll down his window. He reached in, grabbed a handful of the passenger's shirt and slapped him a few times.

The man replied, "Whut wuz that for?"

The old Sheriff said, "I wuz just grantin' you yer wish."

"What wish?"

The Sheriff answered, "Well, tha minute I'd got in my car, you'da said, 'I wish he'da tried that with me!'"

J

Jawl-P? short form of "Did all of you go to the bathroom?"

Jerk a knot in his tail: to sternly reprimand in order to stop dangerous, foolish or any ill-conceived activity. Whup is a synonym. For example, if a fella was rowdy and about to get into trouble, someone might predict, "Sumbody's gonna jerk a knot in his tail." It was also used to indicate that one of the cowboys had put a stop to the activity of a mean bull, cow, horse or dog before it hurt someone. Other synonyms are: clean his clock/plow, adjust his attitude, explain things to 'im, pull his barn down, stomp the wax out his ears, ice his cake, thump his head, slap up side tha head, jerk or pull his chain, smack his jaws/jowls or give him a fat lip. Regardless of the circumstances, you don't want sumbody to jerk a knot in yer tail.

Job or jobbed: Example: "Y'all watch that red bull. He'll job his horns in yer horse, if you ain't careful." Also, "They fought rite ther' in tha parkin' lot like two cur dogs til Billy Joe jobbed him in tha eye with his thumb."

For example, many years ago I asked my covenant-adopted son, David, what kind of summer job he'd gotten. He said, "Jobbin' sow gators."

Whut? I investigated further. "What were you doin'?"

He said, "I got a summer job feeding gators an' harvesting eggs."

"Whut did you do?"

David explained, "Well one of your neighbors has a commercial alligator farm. He's got a big bunch of gators penned in a swamp. I'm harvesting the eggs from the female's nests and movin' them to an incubator. He's got a controlled environment hatchery. He says the survival rates are greatly improved with management. I go to the Okeechobee catfish processing plant every week to pick up frozen blocks of fish heads for feeding them."

I asked, "How do you rob the nests?"

"Well, I take a row boat out to the island in the middle and get a pole from tha boat. I slip through the underbrush and find a nest. I dig out the eggs and put 'em in a bucket. The sow gators don't go for it, so, it's dig awhile, job the sow gator back, dig, job 'er back. I can usually get a bucket full in fifteen minutes. They don't ordinarily follow me out to tha boat."

I asked him later why he took that summer job.

Cracker Terms, Phrases And Definitions

He replied, "Desperation."

The rest of the story is interesting: When he graduated from the University of Florida, he applied for a position with Ford Motor Company. He had to write down all his extra-curricular activities and jobs he had for the preceding four years. He figured if he left that summer job out, the Ford interviewer would question his resume or figure he wasn't a serious candidate. When they got to the Alligator-egg-harvesting-and-feeding job on his resume, they must have concluded, "This kid will do anything–we need him at Ford!" He took their offer and has progressed up the corporate ladder over the last decade. He has figuratively jobbed sow gators for Ford in Michigan, Scotland, Sweden, England and China. (The newly designed Volvo models, starting in 2001, reflect his influence on the team that re-styled the old box-like Volvos. Who'da thought it?)

Juke, jukin' or juke joint: Juke, a word that designates a tavern, dive, dance hall, honky-tonk, café, some eating establishments or a place where serious parties are in progress, especially on Saturday nights. Some Crackers pronounce it to rhyme with rook. Jukein'refers to the act of going to a juke, bar-hopping (as used in Wisconsin) or dancing, in general. Juke joint is self-explanatory. Some people spell or call it "jook."

I think of the Green Lizard, where they had a pile of beer cans out back, higher than fifteen feet. Annie's Steak House and The Watering Hole in Highlands County, and The Speckled Perch Lounge and Restaurant and the old Twin Oaks Café in Okeechobee, where there were few windows. There was also a dive on Lake Okeechobee, which had an openly racist and politically incorrect sign out front that invited hostiles to enter. It was not unusual, at these places, for one of the men to slip out to his or another's trailer, return with a piglet or larger pig, and turn it loose into the crowd. Everyone laughs and hoots, as a part of the affair, spending a considerable amount of time trying to catch said pig. The Watering Hole was the source of a story I found interesting. At the time the Pella Brothers owned and ran the establishment. In the lounge there was a large display case containing a huge boa constrictor. One Sunday during clean-up, one of the boys went to feed the dang thing. He opened the case door, bent down to pick up a dead rabbit to feed the beast. Well, ol' Boa decided to catch the nearest thing to him. He bit the fella on the head and immediately wrapped tight coils around him. Fortunately, there was a man working in the kitchen. He came out with a butcher's knife and proceeded to extricate the caught man from the coils of the boa. (See "that jus' ended it up.")

The Twin Oaks was the first place I heard the word "head-skin;" the term applied to the damage done to heads of those diving out of the small windows during fights. One particular juke joint and café in Durant, Oklahoma, comes to mind. The café has been memorable since a couple of motorcycle gang members decided to make a lasting impression with the locals. During the preliminary preflight discussions, one man slipped out and unloaded his horse while another got a rope. They roped meanest one of the gang members, tossed the rope out the window to the saddled cowboy, and dragged the roped man through the tables, out the window and down the parking lot at a full gallop. The next sound heard was the firing up of the motorcycles. (Technically, I would refer to that as a road rash café). I do not know if the fellas in Durant were Crackers, but it sounds like they could be... if they wanted to...

It is in such a Florida juke as I have described where Dennis (Minnerhead) McClelland first performed and invented what he called the Gator Crawl–a dance where he laid down on the floor, amid the other dancers, and rhythmically imitated a crawling alligator. How he kept the rhythm with the music, I have not been able to determine. He warned, "Y'all better watch it–they'll keep steppin' on yer hands and legs."

Cracker Terms, Phrases And Definitions

The McClelland's are said to be the sons of a ruling clan many generations ago. Somehow this is hard to accept with the image of Minnerhead on the floor, doing the Gator Crawl. It never really took off in popularity for some reason. One cowboy came to the pens one day without Minnerhead and his brother. Someone asked where they were. He said, "Aww-w, they bin drinkin' again."

The foreman asked, "How do you know they wuz drinkin?"

The cowboy replied, "I set intha truck for thirty minutes an' watched 'um try to kill a garden hose."

Juicy: a generic name for any cow that is lactating. It was common to prod a cow into the working chute while saying, "Step up, Juicy." To my way of thinking, any dairy cow is called, Ol' Juicy.

Jug or jugs: slang for a milk bottle for an orphaned or newborn calves, pups, kittens or foals. Jugs usually refers to the udder of the cow. "Boy, go to tha house and git a jug for this calf," is an example when used for a milk feeding bottle. When a calf is aggressively nursing a bottle, one might hear, "He likes his jug, don't he?"

Jugue: to jab, poke, job in, stick, punch, veer off, push, prod, nudge, insert, force or dig in. The proper pronunciation rimes with fugue. (See Jugueass Pond, under Meat stick.) Hubert used it to refer to cattle that turned back or toward a protective hammock in attempts to escape round-up. He'd say, "We wuz doin' fine until that yeller cow jugued into the bay head." He sometimes substituted jugued for sucked back.

Jump ah deer: usually referred to riding horseback, driving a vehicle or walking through dense woods in hopes of startling a buck from a resting place. Sometimes you only got a glimpse of a jumped deer. There is also a ritual for those who shoot at a buck and miss; it's the old cuttin' off tha shirt-tail of the one who misses the shot. I've seen places where three or four shirt-tails needed to be cut but it was too much trouble. I've even had my shirt-tail cut off for <u>not</u> shooting at a buck. I can well remember drawing up a little as the one with the sharp ear-markin' knife took a swath of my shirt while two fellas held me down. (It was a sphincter-tightening experience. Maybe they didn't like the shirt...)

I recall a story told originally by Patrick F. McManus in his book entitled, *The Grasshopper Trap*. He said something about what to do if you jump a buck before you get a chance to shoot. If there is a nearby hunter, rather than admit you were caught flat-footed (see term), he recommended pulling your hunting knife and run after the deer at full speed. When you give out of wind, stop, replace your knife in the scabbard and bend over to get your breath. When the other curious hunters approach and ask, "Whut happened?" say, "I'm gettin' too old to run deer down with my knife. I'm gonna have tah start usin' my rifle and shoot at 'em." Saves a lotta face.

Speaking of jumpin' a deer, I remember my friend, Berny Zellner. I refer to him above and under "Ratkillin'," too. (See terms). We hunted together on occasion; Berny was a woodsman. We deer hunted near the Milstead Research Center in East Alabama. I sat on a little creek while he found him a spot. I hadn't been there forty-five minutes when a fine buck eased out on the edge of the woods. I had a clear shot and took advantage of it. Berny heard me shoot, showing up in a little while afterwards. Well, we must have been more than a mile from the truck in the woods. Now here we were: a Ph.D. candidate and a Master's Degree graduate in Animal Science in the unbelievably thick woods, trying to retain balance while carrying a buck deer. (Let's put it this way, we weren't Cherokee.)

We decided that we would make a pole, carrying the deer like the old cinemas that show people carrying trussed-up animals (or humans in cannibal country). I like to have died climbing the ten-foot high sand-bank. Every movement caused the big deer to sway. We found that we spent more time trying to stand up than in toting. I was stumbling in the brush, the deer flopping around, swaying violently on the pole. (From first-hand descriptions I considered this activity similar to childbirth in intensity.)

Being very practical, Berny quickly had enough of carrying his load and 3/4s of mine, while dragging us both in the woods–by this time, in total darkness. He finally said, "Give me the danged thing. I'll carry him and you just try to keep up. Better yet, knock the brush down for me." He carried the buck out of the woods in the dark while I stumbled and talked to myself. I didn't seem to do much better; not carrying the deer didn't make my trip any easier. We walked through the deep woods in the dark that night. I was hoping that my gray hair didn't look like a deer's butt to some overzealous deer hunter.

If we'd written about this incident in scientific jargon, it would have read like this:

Our preliminary data suggests that the Pole and Sling Method of carrying a deer carcass is best suited for camp presentation only and is not a good method for general transportation. Our findings confirm that there is a significant positive correlation between Age Differential (A.D, see Figure 2) and Swaying (See Figure 4). There is high statistical probability that the Pole and Sling Method will be abandoned within 11.37 minutes of initiation under average conditions (P < 0.05%; See Table 5). Our findings suggest that the following formula can be used to determine the minutes needed to change to other means of transportation:

$$T = (A.D. + P.L. + P.S.P + ((D.D.W \times S.F.) - H.A.F. + (C.F. + 1/B.C. / S.F.$$

(Where T = mean time to abandon the method, in minutes; A.D. = difference in age of carriers; P.L. = carry pole length, in centimeters; P.S.P. = pole spring potential, in springs/minute/step; D.D.W. = dead deer weight, in Kg; S.F. = sway factor, in average sways per step; H.A.F = height above carrier's footing, in meters; C.F. = conditioning factor of carriers, in hours/week spent in conditioning exercise; B.C. = bush concentration, in average number of bushes per square meter; and, S.F. = stupid factor, i.e., character, attitude and/or vocabulary)

(Note: our preliminary data do not include quantitative alcohol consumption, which greatly affects S.F.; See Tennessee Memoirs by J. Daniels; Bibliography, page 219.)

Berny was reliable, trustworthy, conscientious and funny. We enjoyed each other's company. (See ratkillin')

Jumpin'-off place: refers to the flat world concept. In context it could be heard as a tongue-in-cheek expression, as in, "Son, that man's ranch is west of Palmdale. It'sah regular jumpin' off place." This also brings to mind a concept about soil quality. "Tha land wuz so poor ther' all it did was hold the world together." And, "All his land is scrub and patches of sugar sand."

Sugar sand refers to the white granulated sand found in scrubs. It actually often looks like granulated cane sugar. Little grows on it but over the years some plants adapt to it and thrive. Florida Scrub is a type of land in Florida. The sandy soil is thin and contains little plant nutrients. The plants are specialized for that type soil and are not resilient when disturbed. The friendly Florida Jay lives in these barren-looking places. In reality this land type is a highly specialized ecosystem. Many areas are pure scrub. Silver Springs near Ocala is pure rough pine scrub. It is not unusual for some ranches to have all the land types of Florida.

Jus' like a duck... he wakes up ina new world ever' day: descriptive phrase of what happens when "First cousins

Cracker Terms, Phrases And Definitions

keep marrying" (See term). This was used to indicate that the individual was a little too laid back when it came to remembering schedules and being responsible. I use it in response to someone asking, "How are you doing?" I reply, "I'm just like a duck; I wake up in a new world every day." Sometimes I substitute, "I'm jus' skatin' away on the thin ice of life." (Yes, they smile when I say it.)

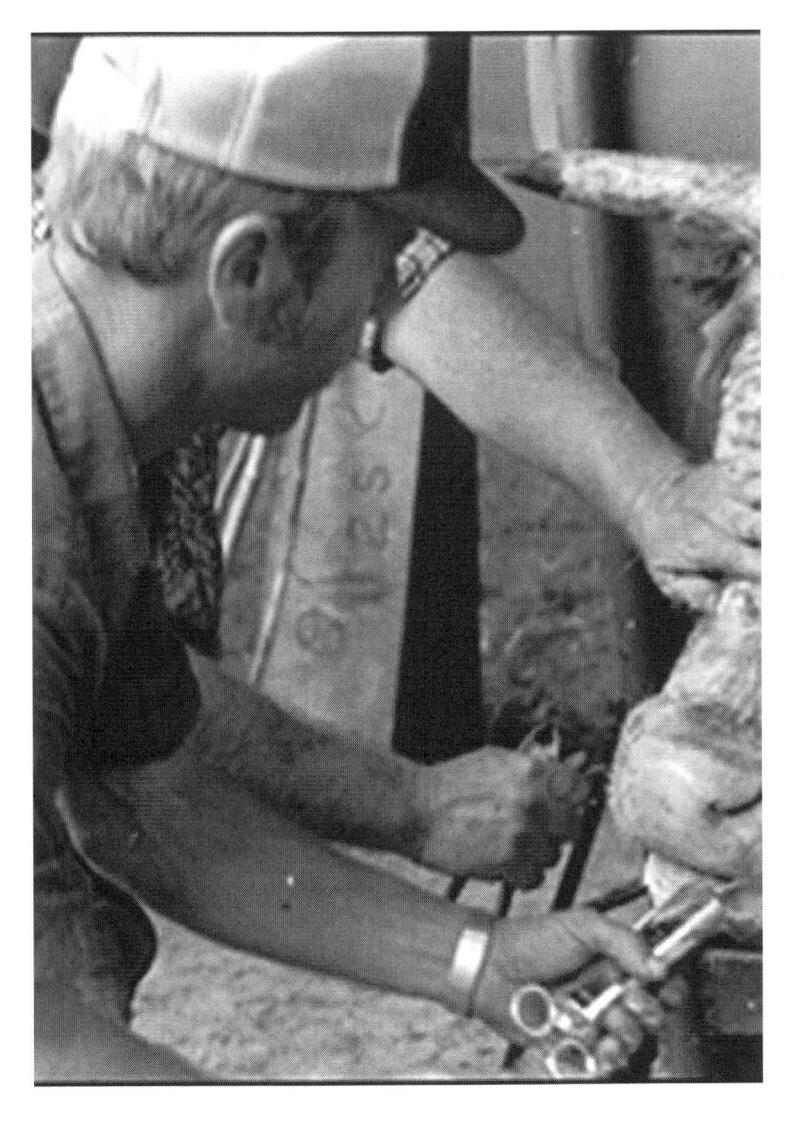

K

Katy barred tha door: an expression which probably originated in the forties. It first described taking precautions, but has come to mean an uncontrollable break-out. An example might be, "Whin tha bull broke tha fence, it wuz 'Katy bar tha door'." The meaning here relates to the fact that the herd escaped the pens after the bull broke out. (That ended it up is a synonym phrase. See the phrase for meaning.)

Ketch'im or ketch'er: a directive to a catch dog to actually grab or catch the nose or ear of a belligerent bull or cow in an effort to control or return the animal to the herd. It did not mean the dog would always catch the nose or ear, since it could mean a command for the dog just to harass an unruly individual. The term was also directed frequently to hog dogs when catching wild hogs. Some cow dogs and hog dogs are difficult to remove from a caught animal. In that case, one might hear, "Yeah, I had to pry his mouth open with a crowbar." Some hog hunters literally carried an oak hammer handle or similar device to pry dog's mouths open and release the caught hogs. Handling catch dogs is an art as well as a skill. Every cow dog is a little different in attitude, skill and determination. A pack can revert to a primeval killing mob. Frequently a man has to ride into the fray and crack his whip right next to the dogs to make them get back. If you ever have a whip crack right next to your ear, you'll quit what you're doing, too.

I am always amazed how tough these dogs are–especially hog dogs. Old heavy boars are an absolute terror when they come after you. A tough set of hog dogs is needed to off-set a boar flashing four-inch razor-sharp tusks. Hogs can kill dogs in short order under some conditions.

Stories circulate about dogs continuing to work in spite of broken or bruised bodies and legs or nasty cuts. Though that seems cruel and doesn't happen much, there are times when the dogs and the men are separated. The dogs just keep

Cracker Terms, Phrases And Definitions

going until help arrives. There is such a thing as blind loyalty, too. Some dogs will fight to the death for their masters. In some of these cattle and hog situations, I don't know which are the craziest–the dogs or the men. It also amazes me that cowboys and cur dogs have some of the same characteristics with both sharing attributes like tenacity, fearlessness, speed, perseverance, endurance and pure meanness when the need arises.

L

Laid up, lay-up or laid-out or laid back: Laid up usually means to be incapacitated or resting, as in: "Wher' you bin?" "Oh, I bin laid up with the colly wobbles." meaning he was sick with some obscure malady or laid-up as in taking a rest from the pain and fatigue of working cattle. Another context the cowboys rarely used with laid up referred to the honeymoon trip. The obvious use of laid out was when a fella was knocked silly in some sort of animal-related wreck. "I jus' happened to look out and see he was laid out rite ther' in the pens; calves walkin' all over him." It was also used to refer to carousing, rambling, jukein', revelry, riotous behavior, chasing girls, etc. It might be used in a question, "Whut y'all gonna do? Ya gonna lay out all night?" They sometimes used it in a tongue-in-cheek comment where some poor young fella was nearly worked to death after two weeks of 4:30 am to 9:00 pm days and showing signs of ragged exhaustion. Near the end of the day, the young man might be asked, "You gonna lay out all night, drinkin' and carousin' til daylight?" It was always said with a smirk, but not always appreciated.

(Laid back was easy going and taking life as it comes–the opposite of high strung or tightly wound.)

A story was told that a preacher was talking to a young fella about missing the Sunday service. Preacher said, "Well, I guess you laid-out all night an' that's why you missed church."

The fella replied, "Nosir. An' I got the fish to prove it."

Lasses: a contraction of molasses. It could be heard sometimes when a cowboy talked about some horse feed, "Yeah, he ain't been eatin' good, so I put some 'lasses on his feed this mornin'." It might be used to describe how slow someone was moving, especially on a cold morning, "Y'all are movin' as slow as lasses this mornin'."

Lauzie: a substitution for the word, Lordy and meaning the calling upon God in some context as in an oath or for emphasis. I first heard the expression in a Cracker situation in a story by a Cracker from Arcadia, Florida. It seems a family reunion was called and was well attended by most of the family members. The usual routine was the men sat outside talking while the women prepared the meal. The children did what children do at these affairs. When called, everyone came to the table, though sometimes meals were eaten on tables (or laps) outside under shade trees. After the meal, the men returned to the porch, yard or some gathering place, while the women did dishes and cleaned up the kitchen. In the story the women had finished the dishes and were sitting around a big table, talking and drinking sweet iced tea. All ages were gathered for the fellowship. One particular young woman had just recently married a local boy. She was seated beside her aunt who was in her eighties. Somehow the conversation got around to the relationships of and differences in men and women. Curiosity got the better of the young woman and she asked her aunt, "Aunt Bess, whin does a woman start losing her interest in sparkin' and kissin', you know, in neckin' and such?"

Eighty-year old Aunt Bess replied, "Lauzie, child; yer gonna hav' to ask sumbody older'n me."

The terms kissin', sparkin' and such remind me of what I overheard when a couple of cowboys were talking about one's daughter and her boyfriend. The conversation was something like: "Well, I wuz headed for tha barn. I wadn't payin' no mind and stepped out on the porch... ther' daughter wuz with that lo-rent boy kissin' on her right ther'... it sounded like a litter of coons suckin' on their mama." (Though I have never heard that sound the thought of it remains vivid in my mind. That must have been some serious kissin'.)

Leathers: Many cow hunters carry a ball of rawhide leather for making some minor repairs on their saddle, etc. The leather is most often coiled or folded strips of thick leather, long enough to make a rein that has broken or for making the cracker of a cow whip (if it can be trimmed narrow). The cracker section of a cow (or bull) whip is often made of a finely braided (or tapered) synthetic material like nylon or parachute cord attached to the thin leather tip. Interestingly, the crack heard when the whip completes its circuit is a supersonic breaking of the sound barrier. I have seen an old timer with a round piece of raw hide about one-foot in diameter use his pocket knife to trim a continuous narrow strip, round and round from the leather until he had enough for a leather rein or whatever he needed. The curled strips will straighten during use.

Cow whips are made this way as well. Long strips are cut, broader at the start of the trim and narrowing toward the end. Then, four (or more) of the ten- to twelve-foot long, tapered strips are braided into a long whip with a bigger diameter at the handle end and narrow at the tip with a cracker portion at the tip. Wooden handles are affixed to the big end, either by incorporating the handle in the braid or attached in some other fashion.

Leave me a shot: a common request from a cowboy when a veterinarian finishes treating a horse, bull, cow or other ranch animal and the vet leaves a shot to be administered by the owner the next day, or at the prescribed time.

R. B. Elder comes to mind when I think on it. Being fresh out of vet school I joined Frank Handley's clinic in Highlands County. Mr. Elder called one day, asking for one of us to come out to his ranch on Skipper Road. He said his Jersey cow was down again. I think Dr. Handley knew every animal in three counties; he told me, "Get you some calcium and go out an' pump her up. She lets every calf on the place nurse her to the point she gets low blood calcium. She gets down from it every year about this time." So I loaded up with all the necessary plunder to treat a milk fever cow and proceeded to the Elder Ranch. Sure enough when I arrived Ol' Juicy was broadside in the pasture. We drove up to her. Mrs. Elder followed in the truck and watched.

The cow had classic signs of low blood calcium: she was cold to the touch, her nose was dry, and she had no tears. She was lying on her side, weaker than a sick house cat and not responsive to any stimulation. She was nearly comatose and in need of immediate help. We hooked up a bottle of intravenous calcium, inserted a needle in the jugular vein and slowly dripped the life saving calcium solution in her. Giving I.V. calcium is not without risk since too rapid an infusion can kill a cow. Toward the end of the bottle, I returned to the vehicle and drew an injection of a potent antihistamine solution. The side effect from I.V. injection of the drug acted like adrenaline and often got the cow up rapidly. She was a little slow in her response to treatment so I figured it would help get re-booted, so to speak. (It was always better to leave them standing when you left the ranch; it left a better impression.)

As the last drops of the calcium solution dripped in, I told R. B., "Stand back, I'm gonna give her another shot to get her up."

He looked surprised, stating, "Doc, there's no way in (*expletive deleted*) she'll git up before dark. She always takes about an hour or two to get back on her feet."

I put the syringe on the inserted needle and injected the antihistamine. I backed off about ten feet next to R. B and we watched. Nothing happened—for about 30 seconds. She elevated herself from her side, started looking around, batted her eyes, and her nose suddenly started sweating. Tears started flowing from her eyes and she belched the trapped gas from her rumen. Her breathing became increasingly pronounced, sounding like a steam engine that had just been put in gear, as she became more and more animated. She struggled a bit getting to her feet, then bolted out into the pasture, bawling blindly and kicking at an imaginary pack of wolves.

R. B. said, "Whoa-a-a, Doc! You better leave me a shot of that for the ol' lady!"

Mrs. Elder leaned out of the truck, responding, "You better git one for yerself, R. B." She said it straight-faced.

From then on R. B. always reminded me, "Doc, bring one of those shots when you come."

Let me know: My vet partner taught me this phrase and I find I still use it today. His reasoning was based on the fact that treated animals may or may not respond to whatever he'd done for them. In effect, he was shifting responsibility for the health monitoring, care and future treatment of the animal to the owner or manager. He developed this because of the culture. There seemed a tendency for some people to assume that once the vet had left the premises there would be no complication and it was all settled after that one visit. Some of the owners stopped paying attention at the end of the treatment.

The significance of the phrase dawned on me when I overheard what he said to an owner that called the clinic several says after a surgery. The man said, "Doc, he ain't been eatin'."

Dr. Handley quizzed him, "How long?"

"For five days, since you left."

"Why didn't you let me know? The last thing I said to you wuz, 'Let me know how he's doin'. Why did you drag around for five days?"

Of course, the fella admitted his negligence, "Well, I got busy."

But Handley didn't let him off the hook, repeating, "Why didn't you let me know?" He proceeded to fuss a little more, but then immediately loaded up the vehicle and went to see the horse. He was in an unconscious habit of saying, "Let us know" or "Let us know how he's doin'." He even said it to owners when they took their animals from the hospital after the simplest of procedures, such as rabies vaccinations. It meant, "The ball is in your court" or "I am turning the responsibility for supervision over to you." (Y'all *let me know* if you don't understand this definition.)

Lemme ask ya this: a preparatory phrase appearing just before a question, which is usually in a humorous context. A perfect example occurred when a Cracker was driving through a little town with a visitor that wadn't from around there. The passenger was curious about the area since he was from Oregon. Well, the Cracker started bragging about the little town. He said, "Well, I'll tell ya… this is one fine town. We got a café up the road a piece where you can go git a hamburger, then walk down stairs, shoot pool, git a tattoo, while yer gal friend gits a tan and her nails done." The visitor looked sort of fishy-eyed. The Cracker continued, "You know, whut I like about this town is you can go anywheres in the world frum here." By this time the visitor began to get the wafts of dry humor. They stopped at the second of the town's two stop lights and both men happened to notice two handmade signs saying, WEDDING RECEPTION and below that: YARD SALE. Both signs had an arrow pointing to the right. The Cracker never missed a beat saying, "Lemme ask ya this: wher' else could a fella go an' attend a weddin' party and buy tha gift at the same time?"

Let tha hide go with tha hair: a slang phrase meaning one should not worry about the small details. It was usually used to indicate that there was a downside or side-effect to whatever was being planned. If a few calves were accidentally mixed in with the cows and there was some reason that we

Cracker Terms, Phrases And Definitions

couldn't sort them out, such as an impending thunderstorm, someone might use it to indicate we wouldn't worry about it right then. It is close in meaning to the phrase, "Don't worry 'bout the mule, jes' load tha wagon."

Let tha air out his tires: used to indicate that someone has been beaten up, has had his ego deflated, or lost face because of an accident or a prank played on him. It was also used to indicate that someone was about to get his bell rung, a knot jerked in his tail, cross into Fist City, get a fat lip, or a "knot on his head," etc. (See terms) A prime example was when a fella was asking for trouble and someone was commenting on it, as in, "I guarantee sumbody's goin' to let tha air out his tires."

Like a country boy on his honeymoon: a phrase that was heard describing a particularly pleasurable experience. For example, if a fella was enthusiastic about a big fish he'd recently caught, he might say, "Boy! I wuz like a country boy on his honeymoon. I wanna try that again!"

Speaking of honeymoons, the reason I know that there is a similarity between Kentuckians and Florida Crackers is from what my Kentucky cousin told me once. She happened to be working on the staff for a Kentucky educational program one summer. It was a remedial schooling effort to bring some slow children up to their grade level. Parents could enroll their child in the program by filling out an application. Pam's job was to supervise and help applicants. She told the family that one lady filled out the questionnaire and handed it to her. Pam scanned it to be sure all the pertinent questions were answered. When she came to the question of gender, she got hysterical. Under Sex, the woman had written in tiny letters extending out into the margins, "Yes. Once in Calhoun, Kentucky." (Cracker people just think differently.)

Limb-hit: used to describe mental dullness, as in "That ol' boy acts limb-hit." The term brings to mind getting smacked in the head by a limb pulled and released under tension for passage by the front horseman or by one going up a steep path in the mountains. Acutely limb-hit persons can show pain and disorientation. Synonym phrases would be, "He's three puppies short of a pet shop." Or, "His butter dun slipped off his biscuit." "Shur nuf limb-hit" is generally reserved for the slow learner or the uneducated, although the highly educated can be limb-hit. I wonder about some members of Congress.

Literd, lightered, litern, fatwood, heartwood, heart pine or starter wood: All Cracker and Southern names for the heart of pine where the resin concentrates in dead pine tree, whether standing or lying on the earth. Literd can still be found throughout Florida. It will light even if wet, provided one gets it hot enough. The wood can be found throughout various regions of America. Some of the early homes in this country were constructed by heart pine board 20-24 inches wide. The wood is particularly resistant to termite, moisture and wood rot. When most of the wood is gone and the resins have collected in limb junctures the piece is called a 'literd knot'. Literd knots are frequently used to describe other things: "He needs a literd knot upside his head." "Tha danged rattler crawled rite up to my bedroll. I laid 'im out with a literd knot." It can be used in exaggeration: "I wish you'd look! That baby ain't bigger'n a literd knot."

I got a funny looks from time to time when I carried literd knots in my suitcase on flights to New Orleans. I really was taking it to start romantic fireplace fires. I told the baggage checkers it was for my sick and ailing grandmother who couldn't afford kindling, but wanted to smell a literd fire just one more time before she passed. It worked except for one trip. I got the same baggage checker on another trip. "I see your grandmother is 7 still ailing," he said. I quickly said, "Naw, man, I'm courtin' a gal." He let me go.

Load up! or loaded up: the common phrase to direct cow dogs to get in the vehicle. It could be used to tell a man or a crew to get organized and go to a work site. ("Y'all load up and meet us at tha back pens by 9:00.") Loaded up often meant one was ready to go. "Y'all ready?" could be followed by a variety of answers, such as, "Shoot! We wuz loaded up ah hour ago." Sometimes it was used in humorous fashions: "That danged ol' muddy dog loaded up in the front seat of Mama's new car; she like to have killed him." Or,"We went to Granny's house an loaded up on apple pie and coffee. I'm gonna need a fence stretcher to git my belt loose."

I recall a real character named O.B. Cantrell. O.B. was about 6'6" and thin as a rail. He spoke in a slow, deep and deliberate voice. By the time I knew him, he'd been retired from the Fire Department at the Sebring Airport for many years. O.B. had a nice little ranch on a shallow lake and spent considerable time training colts, cow, bulls and his dogs, too. He had a Cracker horse named Mickey. Mickey was black and gangling. Mickey got the colic regularly about three times a year and O.B. would ask me to come by his place and de-worm Mickey. O.B. also brought the horse to the vet hospital when it was really busy. The first time, Mickey was saddled and standing in the back of a flat-bed truck. The bed must have been four-feet off the pavement. I couldn't figure how we'd get him off the truck. I asked O.B. if we ought to get up in the truck, and commented, "There ain't much room."

"Doc, I don't expect you to do that. Mickey can git out by hisself." He proceeded to open the back gate and bellowed, "Mickey! Come on!"

The old horse jumped out of the truck like a dog. We took care of him and when finished, O.B. walked him to the back of the truck holding only the mane and said, "Mickey! Load up!"

The old horse straightened his body square with the back of the truck, stuck his nose close to the bed, hunkered down on his back legs and jumped up into the truck bed with no obvious effort. The stirrups slapped his sides as he landed. He made a tight turn around and looked at O.B. as if to say, "Okay. Now whut?" O.B. grinned like a dad whose son had just won a gold medal.

On one trip to his house, he presented a green-broke yearling that needed treatment for intestinal parasites. This colt was really skittish, too. I reached for his nose and he went into orbit. O.B. said, "Just hold on, Doc." He walked the colt to a tree that had a fork in it about head high on the colt. He stuck the colt's head in the fork and said, "Now, Doc; do whut you want to with 'im." The colt was a perfect gentleman from that point. Upon looking more closely at the fork in the trees I saw the bark was worn thin where he'd tied and trained more than one animal. O.B. had the time, patience and talent to train his animals. It was a pleasure to work for him even though he had a bad habit of wanting to set under a shade tree and visit for an hour or two. I always had to tell him I had more calls to make and couldn't stay. (He offered to sell me a choice acre on the lake beside his house. As far as I know he never offered land to anyone else. I was honored... and I turned it down. I knew we'd be visitin' every time he saw me come home and he wouldn't understand I wanted to rest when I got there. He was a fine old man, but I had figured him out: O.B. was lonesome.)

Loan applicashun: a phrase overheard while standing in line at the snacks counter at a Highlands County cinema. A young, sun-burned Cracker man came up to the counter beside me while I waited for my order. He looked very serious as he said, "I'd like a loan applicashun for a great big popcorn and coke." The girl just grinned at him as he reached for his wallet.

Lob shot: a tale was told on Hubert Waldron's brother Curtis. Several men were on a hunting expedition in Montana. Curtis made a spectacularly long shot at an elk with his high-powered rifle, which by the way he enjoyed shooting near people who were sighting up a shot. (Sonny said, "It'd make yer britches legs twitch whin he did it.") Well, as with all hunters, there was considerable discussion after the shot. Sonny allowed it was pure luck, while Curtis declared it was pure skill. In mock frustration, Sonny said, "Curtis, ther ain't no way you can hit anuther elk that far away again." Curtis replied, "It don't matter how far they are, I jus lob the bullets in." Sonny couldn't stand that so he said, "If you can make a shot like that agin, I'll kiss yer butt in downtown Okeechobee and giv ya an hour to raise a crowd!" (This long distance shooting became known among the crew as a Lob shot.)

Long in tha' tooth: referring to the age of an old horse. As horses age their teeth wear off and, in order to have effective teeth, the teeth grow longer to replace the portions that are worn off by eating grasses. The expression is used to indicate a subject is "long in tha' tooth" meaning the horse, dog, or man is old. For example, Harrison Ford, the actor, is long in the tooth. The age of horses (and cattle) can be fairly accurately estimated by the time of eruption of the incisors. Why should we never look a gift horse in the mouth? Because he might be a little long in tha' tooth.

Looked like a buzzard roost: a teasing, descriptive phrase used by a person to describe something that is overly done. I first heard it when two men were talking about the up-coming holiday. One was a little irritated at the insistence of his wife for his purchasing a Christmas tree and setting it in a base so she could decorate it for the children. He casually said, "Whin she got done with it, it looked like a buzzard roost," referring to the homemade artificial snow. Gull roost and pelican roost are synonymous.

Looked like both knees were shoved up the front of 'er dress: as far as I know this was a one-time expression used by my daughter in regard to a well-endowed young woman wearing a low-cut formal dress. I've thought about it some and consider it a typical Cracker phrase, though it is rarely used. (Yes, I have used it on occasion.)

Looked lik' two monkeys sewin' up a football: the phrase has a history. I've heard it only one time from a Cracker. It was about midnight on a Saturday when I was called to Basinger, between the Kissimmee River Bridge and Panther

Ford in Okeechobee. There was a night light showing in front of the old dilapidated closed grocery and gas station. Four rough-looking men were standing out front; one was trying to keep the filly under control while the others were drinking some adult beverages from brown paper sacks. "Here we go." I thought. (You never know how things will go in such a situation. Sometimes Crackers and brown bags don't mix well.)

A green filly had stuck her foot through the grill work on a truck. (Why they decided to halter break a filly in the dark I'll never know, though the brown paper sacks might have had something to do with it.) She had a nasty laceration on the inside lower left hind leg. She was flighty and easily spooked. I gave her a tranquilizer to "cool her jets" (See term) and carefully eased in under her from the right side so I could get access to the cut. I was able to block the pain with a local anesthetic with about three or six tries. The slightly "gassed" fella (See term) who was holding the filly was a little unfamiliar with green horses and I spent more time dodging his feet than the filly's. One of the other men stood back about five feet and held a sorry dim flash light so I could see–some of the time it was even close to the area I was trying to suture.

I was able to cautiously start the suturing. On the third stitch, one of the men said, "Y'all look like two monkeys sewing' up a football." I laughed but didn't take my eyes off the filly which could come "uncorked" (See term) at any moment. Then as I started to tie the next suture, I felt a warm alcoholic-tainted breath on my neck. The fella holding the flash light had slipped in close behind me as I squatted under the filly. He said, "Approximate–don't strangulate."

That's a surgery truism. I said, "Where in the world did you hear that?"

He said, "Doc, I wuz ah Navy Corpsman for eighteen years. I sewed up more sailors than I could count and most of 'um

Cracker Terms, Phrases And Definitions

were drunk." We finished, they paid me and returned to the brown bags.

Looks like he sleeps onnah barrel: a description of a bow-legged man, as in, "He's so bow-legged he looks lik' he sleeps onnah barrel."

Looks like ah three-chicken job: an obscure phrase related to chimneys in Cracker houses. It is seldom used now but referred to the cleaning of the soot from the inside of the chimney. The soot and residues from burning wood often coated the chimney and would under some circumstances catch fire. Cleaning out the soot could be done by dropping a chicken down the chimney. The flapping wings would knock excess soot off the inner lining. Obviously, there shouldn't be a fire in the fireplace, the chimney should be big enough for the chicken to attempt flying down, and some preparation for a sooty, half-crazed chicken running in the house should be anticipated. A three-chicken job indicated a big chimney.

Lo-rent: it generally means a person, place or thing is cheap, useless, run down, dilapidated, or worthless. It can be used in reference to an individual with poor character or an outlaw. The words are spoken as one, as in, "Her' he come on his ol' lo-rent horse." or "I swear, whut such a purty gal sees in such a lo-rent fella like that makes no sense to me." Repairs to equipment, trucks, saddles and pens can be less than ideal—even when good supplies are available. A lo-rent set of cow pens will have sheets of roofing tin, barbed or hog wire, cabbage fans or old shirts in the fence holes to keep the cattle from escaping. (In all fairness however, sometimes there is no reason to shut down the whole operation to re-build minor damage. We simply fixed a temporary blind by plugging the hole with any available materials, including our bodies and faces, so the crew could keep working. (Some faces were better than others in spooking cattle away from fence holes.) The blind served to cover or plug the opening so the cattle wouldn't see it as a place for escape. The real permanent repairs would occur after working was finished.)

In addition to lo-rent pens, one could have (or see) lo-rent ranches, cattle, cattle or horse trailers, day workers, cow crews, saddles and horse rigging and have lo-rent lawyers, bankers, vets and even preachers. I remember hearing a Cracker lady idly comment, "If all these little girls jus' knew whut they wuz in for whin they get married to one-ah them lo-rent boys, they'd not be in such a hurry." Out West, a rawhide outfit is a synonym for lo-rent outfit.

M

Makin' off or makin' out like: to slip off, avoid, hide from, leave, ease off, sneak away or mislead. A good example is, "He eased off to his truck like he wuz makin' off with the church supper." Also, "All the time he wuz makin' out like he didden know ah thing about horses."

Mash: a synonym for push, injure, twist, turn on or press, as in, "Hey! Mash tha starter an let's see if she'll fire up." Mashed was also used for stomped, hit, smashed, rolled, tumbled, crushed or injured in any number of contexts. "How'd ya mash yer thumb?" "Aw, ah ol' hog bit me."

Do not confuse the word mash with corn mash used in the making of whiskey. Some Crackers refer to whiskey as mash. One story told to me used mash for corn liquor. As the story goes, a preacher was walking to church when a rough looking man stepped out of the bushes carrying a sawed-off shotgun and a jug of mash whiskey. The man held the jug toward the preacher, saying, "Hey, man! Hav a drink." The preacher said, "Oh, no sir, I don't drink." The man spoke more firmly, "I said hava drink!" and shoved the barrel of the shotgun into the preacher's stomach. The preacher was understandably upset. He said, "Okay, Mister. I'll have a drink. Just relax." He proceeded to pull the corn cob out of the jug and swallow a big gulp of the clear liquid. He immediately started coughing, got acute indigestion, retched and bent over in severe pain. After he recovered, he said, "Mister, I don't know how in tha

Cracker Terms, Phrases And Definitions

world you drink that stuff!" The man retorted, "Here, hold the shotgun on me an' I'll hav a drink."

Maypops: a worn or slick treaded tire. "Whut kind of tires you got mounted on yer truck?" "Them's Maypops." The term was used when kidding a man about his nearly bald and worn tires: "Son, them maypops ain't gonna last too much longer." It was very common to reuse bald tires during and after the war. People called them may pop tires. They could pop anytime from excessive wear. When the treads began showing, they simply recapped. This was practiced well into the mid-1950's. If the tires are exceptionally thin, they may be referred to as, WillPops. Maypop may also refer to the old engines used in tractors or boats. The engines were single stroke types and often back-fired due to accumulated, unspent fuel. The old time fishermen often heard these maypop boat motors. In the Ten Thousand Islands there was a boat named, *The Maypop*. It was said everyone knew its coming even before it appeared from the mangroves.

Meaner'n ah snake: a warning to denote vicious temperament, disposition or character and as a term for describing the potential for personal injury; as in, "Son! That bull is meaner'n ah snake." A variation was, "He's meaner'n a wampus cat." (I don't know what that is, but it sounds mean.) Recently I heard a variation, "He's meaner than a welfare recipient on a soda cracker diet."

I call to mind an incident when a Cracker helped me move my furniture to Florida many years ago. He was a trucker and had just returned from long distance driving. I happened to mention that we were moving. He said he'd move us in his semi-trailer if we'd pay the gas to Florida. His reason for the offer was so he could take his family to Disney World. Since this was considerably cheaper than a professional mover, I took the offer. I followed him in a little Chevrolet truck, carrying yard tools and an assortment of odds and ends. The only incident on the trip was when we crossed the Florida State line and he had to go into the inspection and weigh station for semis. On the radio, he told me to follow him. I did. He talked with the officer. I noticed they looked back at me but it didn't mean anything at the time. Roger pulled out and I stopped at the scales when the officer flagged me down. I was thinking Roger had told him I was following. No. The man asked me if I was carrying any agricultural products or contraband.

"Whut?" I said.

He then directed, "Sir, please step out of the truck and remove the tarpaulin." He inspected everything and I loosened my belt, figuring I was in for a cavity search. After the officer determined I was not a smuggler, he released me. (Roger had told the man, "Naw, I'm not loaded. I'm just carrying some furniture for a fella. But I think that man back ther' in tha white truck is carryin' some fruit from California.")

A Cracker told me what happened to him when he and a friend were stopped for driving over the speed limit. The trooper said he clocked the boy at ten miles an hour over the speed limit. The boy politely questioned the ruling by the trooper. His passenger buddy interrupted, saying, "Officer, I learned a long time ago not to argue with him whin he's been drinkin'." The trooper invited the driver out of the truck for a little balance demonstration, but he soon realized the joke.

These two incidents perfectly illustrate friends that are meaner than snakes.

Meat stick: a stick, often a trimmed cabbage palm limb, trimmed and sharpened at both ends for cooking meat. The steak, ribs or other meat was stabbed with one sharp end and the other end was imbedded in the earth near the cooking fire. When a cabbage palm was used, the frond portion was saved to serve as a surface where the meat could be laid so that it could be turned or rotated for placing the uncooked side next to the fire. Meat sticks were commonly used among Crackers in the woods. The drippings would fall to the edge of the cooking fire, causing little sizzling flare-up fires that

Cracker Terms, Phrases And Definitions

soon were self-extinguished. Crackers would take wild sour oranges or grapefruits for marinating or flavoring the meats. Many carried a little salt for the purpose of cooking meat in the woods. The meat stick made from a cabbage stalk or limb was similar to one used to poke cattle down the chutes in the cow pens, as in, "Boy, go cut a cabbage stalk and poke them cattle along." In both uses, the palm fan was cut off. The difference was that the stick used to poke cattle along was rounded on both ends. The sharp edges along the stalk were removed.

One meat stick story of notoriety was the particular one that is responsible for the naming of a favorite nooning place, i.e., a place where noon meals were eaten by cowboys. Some of the favorite places to rest and eat were called dinner hammocks and were well known by that name. As the story goes a cow crew had nooned at a little place on the banks of a shallow natural pond. A fire was built, coffee started, meat sticks were prepared and each man cooked a piece of meat. One particular man was tending his meat stick, trying to place it just right for best cooking temperature, when he inadvertently backed into an empty meat stick that was stuck in the earth near the fire. Hoots and laughs spread throughout the crew. Finally, one thoughtful man decided to name the place, Jugueass Pond. It stuck, though it is sometimes called, Jugueass Slough. (See jugue) The place is still called that by the old timers. It is a little northeast of the Williamson Ranch, about eight miles north of Lake Okeechobee.

Partner Sills told of a time when the cowboys camped out in the woods while cow huntin'. He said it was really hot that year. The men would leave before daylight or at first light, come back to camp about noon, eat a dinner, sleep a couple of hours and head out to work until dark or sometimes after dark. He recalled one story: at the noon meal of fried meat, rice and gravy, swamp cabbage stew, lima beans, biscuits and coffee, all the men found shade for long naps during the most intense heat of the day. After a bit, one man awoke a little earlier than the rest. He eased over to cut a cabbage fan from a cabbage palm some eight feet tall. He cut off one of the stalks, trimmed the broad fan-portion off, cut off the sharp edges on the stalk and rounded the ends. It made one fine stick, about four-feet long. Partner said that a few more men were waking up. This is a critical time for a Cracker cowboy; all kind of tricks and pranks are played at this somewhat vulnerable time after a deep nap, when one is not fully awake. The culprit went over to one of his buddies who slept in deep sleep, hat over his eyes and face, hands folded over his stomach. He took the palmetto stick and whipped the sleeper several times, awakening him so confused and disoriented that he crawled out into the brush. All the time he was being whipped the poor fella heard, "By hob, I'll teach you to run rabbits." The cowboys hooted at the novelty of the remark usually reserved for a bird dog that switched from bird hunting to rabbit running.

Milk foam on his chin: While dressing out a buck I had brought home for the freezer my stepfather came to watch the activity. He rolled his cigar, watching me all serious-like. Finally, he said with a straight face, "Well, I wish you'd look at that."

"Whut?" I said.

"Why, that buck was nursing his mama when you shot him. The milk foam is still on his chin."

Yes, before I could think, I looked to see if the milk was indeed on his chin. No milk, of course. He chuckled as he walked off, and I felt had.

Mineral box: a small shed-like structure built to house mineral supplements for cattle. These look like small trough-boxes (about 4' X 2' boxes and about 5" to 6" deep), covered by a tin roof to keep rains off the loose mineral mixes. The trough is mounted on posts about the height of a cow's natural head position. In this way, cattle could stick their heads in under the roof and lick the mineral mix. The mineral included salt, phosphorus and trace minerals, various vitamins and, sometimes contained a protein supplement to promote growth and meet mineral and vitamin needs of pastured cattle.

An interesting story goes with mineral boxes. During the days of World War II, my step-father bought lumber and made several mineral boxes to place in pastures on the ranch. At the time combat pilots flew training missions from Homestead or other air force training bases to the Avon Park Bombing Range located about fifty miles from the ranch. On the return trips to Homestead, many still had live and unused ammunition. The new mineral boxes with bright tin roofs shone enticing like sparkling diamonds on the green background of the pastures. In order to return with the whole nine yards of ammo used, some got the bright idea to strafe the boxes with .50 caliber bullets. (The term, "whole nine yards" refers to the length of the ammunition belts in the planes and has nothing to do with football.) The selected target boxes were ripped to splinters and kindling. My step-daddy kept replacing these shot-up boxes but it became a pure nuisance. Rather than raise a ruckus about it, he wrote the commander of the base a nice letter stating something like,

"Dear Sir: I have noticed that the boys are shooting up my mineral boxes. In support of the war effort, and as long as I can buy more lumber, tell them to have at it. Sincerely, Frank Williamson, Okeechobee, Florida." (See That jus' ended it up.)

Mineral sup: slang for mineral supplement. The old time cattle on undeveloped and unfertilized pastures often suffered from mineral deficiencies, such as cobalt, copper, iron and phosphorus. Between these deficiencies and ticks, mosquitoes and internal parasites they could decline to a poor body condition and would look terrible. Instead of normal brown or dark hair many would be thin and have a reddish tinge to the hair. Some were so gaunt that one or two men could catch and hold the skinny cow while one gave a concoction of supplements in liquid form, along with a de-wormer. It would be common to hear something like, "Y'all catch that yeller cow an' give 'er ah dose of mineral sup."

Mite near: to be approximately, opposed to, near, almost, close in proximity, close to or nearly, as in, "That cow mite near killed me." Or "You mite near messed up." and, "It's mite near four miles to the barn." A synonym is purt near.

Move ta Hardee County: Hardee County, Florida is a great place to live, though in typical Cracker fashion, surrounding counties sometimes kid about it and others as well. A story circulated about Hardee that I thought hilarious. It seems that a local Cracker man went to the doctor. He was told that according to the findings and laboratory results, he was affected by a terminal disease. He asked, "How long do I have, Doc?"

The doctor replied, "Well, you have ten to twelve months—probably a year."

The fella was concerned, asking, "Ain't ther' anythin' you can do fer me? Ain't ther' some new treatment or somethin'?"

"Naw," was the reply.

He pressed the doctor, "Ther's got to be somethin' I could do."

The doctor pondered a bit before answering. "Well there is no treatment but there is something you can do."

"Whut, Doc?"

The doctor continued, "I'd recommend you get married to a chain-smoking, red-headed divorcee who has two teenage boys and move to Hardee County."

The sick man said, "Is that gonna help me?"

The doctor replied, "Naw, but it'll seem a lot longer than a year."

Mother's Friend: a reference to a product used by expectant and new mothers for the abdominal stretch marks caused

Cracker Terms, Phrases And Definitions

by pregnancy. It was misused by the cowboys and some southerners in general, after a big meal which has distended their abdomen. In context: "Man! We best break out tha mother's friend. My belly's tighter'n a tick." Somehow the visual of a bunch of bloated men rubbing a greasy salve on their distended abdomens struck me as funny. What can I say?

Motherlode: the biggest concentration, the source, or an unexpectedly high amount or number of something. It was especially helpful in communicating to another that you have found more than what you needed or what you were looking for, as in, "Lookie he-ah, Hub! I found the motherlode of saddles in tha back of tha store." Or, "I'll be John Brown! I believe we hit the motherlode of wasps whin I jerked the tin outta tha trash pile." Or, if one goes to a bar-b-que and finds a feast, one could complement the cooks by saying, "Boys, y'all hav' gathered the motherlode here, ain't ya?"

Mulletwrapper: a synonym for a local newspaper, as in, "Y'all seen tha last issue of the mulletwrapper?" Synonyms referring to newspapers include "The Pretender," "Gossip Sheet," etc.

Another variation of the term includes bird cage liner. A Cracker professor at a southern veterinary school (Yes, there are some...) was once asked to review a colleague's technical paper.

He read it diligently and commented, "Too slick."

The preparer said "What do you mean, 'Too slick?'"

He said, "Tha paper is too slick for my parrot cage."

(This is the same Cracker professor who examined a goat that was suffering the effects of eating the marijuana stash of some rural hippies. His recommendation was, "Put on some Grateful Dead music and check it in the mornin'. It'll be fine." It was.)

Murgatroyd: an old name from the 40's made popular by Bert Lahr in an early movie. We used on the ranch to indicate that we couldn't remember someone's name or as a greeting. When Sonny, my stepbrother, would say, "Zat you, Murgatroyd?" he knew perfectly well it was me but he said it as a joke of sorts. We also used it for people who made a mistake in judgment: "Whut you reckon ol' Murgatroyd wuz thnkin' whin he drove off into tha bayhead? Didden he remember the last time he tried it?"

My dog wooden eat that: usually spoken with a sneer, it's a rejection of some meal or prepared dish. I first heard it in Sabinal, Texas, when Hubert Waldron decided to try Mexican food. He'd eaten pork, chicken or beef for a week because in his mind that was the only things on the menus that looked like real food. I had ordered a plate of enchiladas, a tortilla with fried beans and rice. He decided to step out and try it, too. When the girl brought the meal, she was wearing an oven mitt as she sat the plate before us. He immediately reached to adjust the plate and burned his fingers, since the plate was straight from the oven. He took one bite, pushed the plate away with his fork and said with the proper disdain, "My dog wooden eat that."

N

Narrah-eyed: slang for narrow-eyed, "pig-eyed" or "possum-eyed." (See terms) It was occasionally used to indicate a man who was sneaky or underhanded. It could refer to a cross-eyed individual, as one cowboy commented, "That fella is so narrah-eyed he could poke both eyes out with a pencil up his nose."

Needed killin' or needs killin': a phrase usually reserved for some kind of outlaw, whether man or beast. For example, if a crazy wild boar cut up one or three of the catch dogs and the hog hunters finally had to kill it because it was so mean, one might say, "That sum(*expletive for female canine* *deleted*) needed killin'." I have been told that this phrase is considered a legal defense in Texas. "Now, Sir, would you please tell the court what you were thinking when you shot the victim?" "Well, I'll tell ya exactly whut I wuz thinkin': He needed killin'. He wuz sorry." (Case dismissed.)

Speaking of needed killin', I used to tell a Carl Hurley joke about his little hometown. He said that the Post Office had a Man Wanted for Murder sign posted. He said four men came in to apply for the job. One said, "Yeah, I'll kill 'im."

Needs lead: I have only heard this phrase one time in all my years of cow-working. It was said by one typical Cracker cowboy. The context was in reference to a poor sick cow. She was nearly dead–she just hadn't quit breathing. She staggered into the chute and stood there weakly. She had no teeth, her gums were white from severe anemia and she had a large growth under her neck. I was pondering the best way to tell the men she was beyond hope when one of the raw-boned cowboys said, "Doc, she needs lead." Knowing that lead is toxic to most creatures, I must have had an odd look on my face. He smiled and said, "Right between the eyes. A .22 would do it." In other words, she needed to be put out of her misery. The only synonym was, "She needs iron," which meant to strike a killing blow with an iron pipe or other similar object to put the poor thing out of its suffering.

Neetsfoot oil: Neatsfoot oil is yellow oil rendered and purified from the shin bones and feet (but not the hooves) of cattle. Neat in the oil's name comes from an old name for cattle. Neatsfoot oil is used as a conditioning, softening and preservative agent for leather. In the 18th century, it was also used medicinally as a topical application for dry scaly skin conditions. It does make chapped hands softer and helps for preparations for a trip to town on Saturday nights. (I never tried it or axle grease for hair-dressing… though I think it'd work and certainly would have a unique smell. Perhaps its best use in this category is for comb-overs.) Prime neatsfoot oil or neatsfoot oil compound are names for a blend of pure neatsfoot oil and non-animal oils, generally mineral or other petroleum-based oils.

Neatsfoot oil is used on a number of leather products, although it has been replaced by synthetic silicon-based products for certain applications. Items such as dry boots, baseball gloves, saddles, horse harnesses and other horse tack can be softened and conditioned with neatsfoot oil.

If used on important historical objects, neatsfoot oil (like other leather dressings) can oxidize over time and actually may contribute to making the leather brittle, whereas the newer silicon-based products don't. It also may leave an oily residue that can attract dust. (I'd rather have dusty boots than water-soaked feet from standing or working in mud and water.) On new leather, it may cause darkening (even after a single application) and doesn't look good on suede leather, and thus may not be a desirable product to use when the maintenance of a lighter shade is desired. Neatsfoot oil is more beneficial for routine use on working equipment and is often used to oil sign-writers' brushes (pencils) that have been used in oil based paint as this oil is non-drying and can be easily washed out with solvent at any time. By oiling the brushes it reduces the build up of pigment on the metal part of the brushes holding the bristles. (Another fine example from my extensive storehouse of barely essential information.)

Next thing ya know (*fill in the blank*): a phrase used when one is trying to express a warning. An example could be, "I told y'all if he got hooked up with them boys tha next thing ya know he'll be in trouble."

While I was at Auburn I met a man with a pure Cracker mentality named Dr. Tom Powe. Tom heard the students talking about a bull from the Enterprise and Monroeville, Alabama, area. He asked who the owner was. The students told him it was a man named Wilson. Being familiar with the area and the family, Tom went out to the Beef Barn to look at the bull. He returned, gathered the students together and said, "Y'all should spare no expense on that bull. Do a complete laboratory blood profile, a full examination with radiographs and do several biopsies of the lymph nodes."

This was contrary to his ordinarily conservative nature. The bull was dying from lymphoma. The students looked puzzled. Why would he recommend a full medical and laboratory work-up with biopsies on a bull that was obviously dying?

One of the students asked, "Dr. Powe what is your reasoning for spending the money for these tests?"

Tom explained. "I know Bud Wilson and his wife Paula. Bud is bad to fool around. If we spend his discretionary income on this bull, he won't go out an' buy a Corvette or some such toy. If he did that *tha next thing ya know* he'd be runnin' aroun' the road houses and the joints... He'd get hooked up with ah sweet young thing and Paula would find out... I know Paula. She'd kill him where he sits. She'd only stop shootin' when she was re-loadin' tha shot gun. So, by spending his discretionary funds, he can't get involved in this behavior an' Paula won't kill him. Gentlemen, by doing these expensive tests we will be savin' Bud's life." (Made sense to me.)

Nigh or nir: slang for near or close to; as in, It's nigh on to dinner time or Tha bulls mite nir tore down the pens."

Noonin' hammock or dinner hammock: a place where the men stop for lunch when working cattle. Some places have a permanent name of Dinner Hammock. The location was usually a central place, easy to spot, had lots of shade, firewood and water nearby. A long dinner was a good-news-an'-bad-news deal: The good news was a comfortable respite (and a nap) from hard work in the heat and humidity. The bad news was we'd work 'til "dark-thirty" to make up for the rest. (See term)

Not nirsomuch or not nirasmuch: not nearly as much or "the person in reference to the phrase doesn't have any idea yet what he got into." The expression is often used when trying to communicate that more of something will be needed since we ran short or "Just wait until he/she has the whole story." The best example happened when a man came to visit us at our home. He was an executive for Connecticut Mutual out of Hartford. He was discussing appraisals and loans for ranches in South Florida, which was his business. The conversation lulled a bit.

My stepfather said, "By the way, you ought to see the plaque that the boy gave me." I had just graduated from college. I was so thankful for the support and encouragement my stepfather had shown over the six-year education. In honor of him, I had a brass plaque made for him, telling him how much I appreciated his guidance and encouragement during the long years of schooling. I was surprised that he was so pleased with it and that he wanted to show it to the executive. I went to the wall in the office, removed the plaque and presented it for the executive's inspection.

He read it twice, looked at us both and said to my stepfather, "Well, Mr. Frank, I expect you're really impressed with this."

I couldn't stand it, saying, "Not nirasmuch as he <u>will</u> be whin he gits the bill for it."

There were hoots of laughter—my stepfather laughing the most.

Not now: although this is a common response to some questions, one instance of its use was classic. Austin (Austie) Heacock was a former assistant in my veterinary hospital, but after graduation from high school, he joined his family's insurance business. Sonny gave me an old boat for use on the lake behind my house. From the first day I had trouble with it. The motor was inoperable and there were some weak spots in the fiber-glass. After spending money for a motor and repairs, it still gave me trouble. I happened to ask Austie, who was the insurance carrier for everything, "Austie, if I was to drive down the highway at sixty miles an hour, an'

Cracker Terms, Phrases And Definitions

tha boat jus' happened tah come off the hitch, is it covered (*for damage and loss*)?" He never missed a beat in his reply, "Not now...."

Not worth ah rat's _(highly offensive word for posterior)_: something that is considered worthless. An example could be, "I pulled it outta the box an' it wuz broke. it wadden worth ah rat's (highly offensive word for posterior). Or, "Whut's the prize for winnin' the calf ropin'?" "Oh, I think it'll be thirty rat's (posterior) an' a jar of guava jelly."

Now, howcumiszat: Now, why is that? Now, can you explain this to me? or How did we get in this situation? We didn't use the phrase much but when we did it was questioning a repair or why the adjustment we made didn't work. "I put the part in just like we took it out, but the danged ol' tractor won't turn over (i.e., start), now, howcumiszat?" The phrase could be used is jest. If a cinch was loose and a saddle rolled over to the point a rider fell off, someone might comment, "We wuz in a tight whin Ol' Clarence decided to fall off his horse. Clarence, howcumiszat?"

A modern example of the phrase is found in the following:

One Cracker noticed that another had a small lap-top computer on his kitchen table. He asked, "Whut in the world are you doin' with a thing lik' that?"

The man replied, "Oh, it's ma girl's outfit; she's tryin' to teach me how to git caught up in the world. She sez I can git cattle prices an' tha weather forecasts."

"Wellsir, show me how it's dun," said the visitor.

"You can do it! It ain't any harder than tying a calf down," came the answer.

Visitor said, "Naw, you show me."

So the man pressed the power button and the thing came to life. The request for Password came on screen. He typed in "JuniorBubbaCharlieFredClaudeGatorTallahassee."

Visitor was astounded as the screen changed to the desk top. He said, "Whut kinda password is that? You typed in all our cow crew? Howcumiszat?"

The Cracker said, "Well, whin we wuz settin' it up it said, tha password had to be six characters an' one capital."

Now, this is tha way I remember it, That's the way I remember it, or, I remember it this way: an interesting phrase indicating that a story teller was absolved from any responsibility for truth. I was recently reminded of this phrase by Wes, my nephew in telling tales about hunting or working. A fella could go through a whole story and have a listener in the group say something like the phrase or even correct the teller by saying, "That ain't tha way I remember it." Now the interesting thing to me is that this common Cracker phrase is used in a highly perfected art form by politicians in Washington, D.C. It really didn't matter what the variation was or if the facts were exactly correct, it was the way he remembered it. How can you question that since that might be the way he remembers it? Usually, everyone would grin or laugh with the one who said the phrase because he embellished it without restraint.

It is similar to the old story about the car wreck at a four-way stop. According to Carl Hurley, deputies were trying to sort out who was at fault. One noticed an old man sitting on his front porch near the intersection of the country roads. They decided to ask him for an eyewitness account of the accident. One asked him, "Sir, did you see tha wreck?" The old man replied, "Yep." "Could you tell us what happened?" "Yessir. Well, it seemed to me that they both got there at the same time." (How are you going to question his analysis since that's the way he remembered it?)

Now... you gotta say sumthin' nice: a response to a negative comment. In the south in general you can say anything about a person if you follow it with, "Bless their heart." I recollect an example that happened when I criticized a young

Cracker Terms, Phrases And Definitions

woman in the presence of my wife in our small church. Before the worship service a large group of young people came in and sat in every available seat. The front row had several of these college-age youths. One particular young woman sat on the end seat toward us. She was wearing sandals and a fashionable short skirt. After the hymn she removed her sandals, crossed her legs and rocked her foot up and down while unconsciously flashing a very attractive foot and leg as it rocked. I happened to be seated at such an angle that her leg and foot were all I could notice as I attentively tried to watch the pastor delivering a stirring sermon. After the service I mentioned to my wife, "I've never seen such. That child had her shoes off in church!" All we could see was her ol' foot flipping up an' down.

My wife said, "Now. You've got to say three nice things about her."

I studied on it a moment and responded, "Well, she did have her Bible with her. That's a positive sign." I continued the thought, saying, "… and she really was enjoyin' the hymns and listened to the sermon…"

"And…" said my wife.

"She closed her eyes durin' the prayers. So I guess she had some faith."

My wife responded, "Now that wasn't so bad, was it?"

I said, "Yeah. Well that means to me she is open to the Lord; maybe he can work with'er (long pause) an' she'll learn to keep her shoes on in church and not rock 'er bare foot an' leg on the front row."

Then, I had to say three more nice things about her. As my Grandmother once said, "It jus' takes sum people longer than others."

"But that's jus' me," is a synonym phrase of "bless his heart."

I am reminded of the story where a new preacher took over the reins of a little country church. He hadn't been there very long when a man named Bubba, a scoundrel, died in the little community. The deceased man's brother, Rollie, came to the Pastor and said, "Now, I know you all have big plans for building a new church. I know my brother Bubba wasn't well thought of, him bein' in the liquor business and all… But if you'll preach his funeral and say something really nice about him, I'll donate $100,000 to the church building fund. The Pastor said he wanted to think about it because he had heard the deceased was real rogue. The dilemma was whether to go against his training and principles or to do the funeral and accept the offer of a sizeable donation toward the new church. He finally agreed to do the funeral.

The extravagant funeral day came, the preliminaries went well and it was time for the Pastor to say the words over Bubba. He began by saying, "Bubba was a lying, cheatin', theivin', conivin', no-account, outlaw of a man." The congregation gasped as he paused. He continued, "But next to his brother, Rollie, he was a livin' saint. Amen."

(Sorry about this, but the above prompts my recollection of the pastor when, in the middle of his sermon, a woman in the front row shouted, "Glory to God!" This shook the pastor and the whole congregation as they hadn't been accustomed to such outbursts. He collected himself, found his place in the sermon and continued. Upon reaching a particularly important point the woman again shouted, "Hallelujah! Bless God!" The pastor was so flustered at the outbursts he looked down at the woman and said, "Sister, what seems to be your problem?" She answered, "Preacher, I got religion!" The pastor replied, "Well, you didn't get it here, so cut it out!")

A modified version of this phrase is, "If you cain't say sumthin' nice about someone, say-it-reel-fast."

Nursin' a hoe: used to describe the posture of grass hoers. In the grove, years ago at least, hand-hoeing of the weeds around the citrus trees took a crew of men to stay ahead of the grass growth. Day in and day out, it was tedious and repetitious work. When taking a break, it was common to see men leaning on their hoe handles. The end of the handle was under their arm pit, the opposite hand holding the end of the handle near the arm and chest. This allowed one to rest while leaning on the hoe. The men called it nursin' tha hoe. "Boys, y'all better quite nursin' tha hoe. I see tha boss man comin' in tha gate."

O

Okempucky: a brand name for a fastener lubricant. I first heard okempucky in Oklahoma at the brood mare stables. It was used as a lubricant in the rectal palpation of mares for pregnancy. This word may have originated in Nebraska or the mid-west where the word okeypuckie is used with an entirely different meaning. As I understand it, it was used there to designate a sickness, as in, "Man, I feel bad; I guess I got a case of okeypuckie." I am not sure if that is the only use.

I introduced okempucky to Okeechobee and Highlands Counties in 1970. It became so common among the ranches and the veterinary hospitals that everyone knew what it meant. Since chapped hands were so common due to the type of work we did we used skin cream and called it okempucky.

Odes: oh'-dis, it is a local pronunciation of oldest, usually meaning the oldest son. When you approached a group of Crackers working cattle, and wanted to know who was in charge, you'd ask, "Who's Cap?" meaning, "Who is the leader of this outfit." If the father or manager was present, someone would point to him; if not, they might say, "Well, Finis is odes." (I once had a bulldog I named Odes. He wuz crazier than ah outhouse rat.)

Odiferus: a slang word for odiferous, smelly, rotten-smelling, stinking, or foul smelling. Usually the word is used in understatement, as in, "I wanna tell ya–that dead calf wuz plum odiferus." This means the smell was over-powering. When a cowboy came to a gathering, such as a party or dance, and having been to the barber who put copious amounts of hair tonic on the individual, one might say, "Boys, I wish y'all'd come her', he smells plum odiferus."

Older'n dirt: extreme age; a contraction of 'older than dirt', as in, "That bull's older'n dirt; we ought to sell 'im."

Ol' man (*fill in the last name*)'s boy: a response to the question from one asking a person's name. I use this comment often and most of the time it gets a hesitation and a laugh. For example, when the one asked doesn't know the name he will resort to this deflection. "Yeah, we went to Billy Johnson's house to look at his horse for sale." The question might pop-up, "Who's Billy Johnson?" My answer, usually without thinking, is "Ol' man Johnson's boy." It didn't help identify the fella but it surely caused some smiles. Of course, if one knew the game, he'd say, "Which ol' man Johnson; the preacher or the one in prison?"

Oh lordy: an expression rarely used in the context I first heard. It was a Cracker boy who'd just graduated from the University of Florida, School of Agriculture. He said, "Y'all hav' heard of graduatin' *Cum Laude*? Well, I graduated *Oh Lordy!*" I knew exactly what he meant: he, like me, was surely glad to get out of college with a degree.

The University of Florida had some intelligent engineering students, too. On occasion I would study in the room where all the reference materials for the School of Engineering were kept. It was quiet, lightly peopled and a great place to study. One night I had need of the restroom facilities. After selecting a suitable stall and situating myself, I noticed a message neatly printed on the back of the stall door.

In the middle of the door, eye-level, were big 3-inch letters that read: "READ BELOW."

Cracker Terms, Phrases And Definitions

Under it was an arrow pointing downward to another, but smaller, "READ BELOW."

Another arrow pointed toward a much smaller, "READ BELOW."

Downward another smaller arrow pointed to a small box containing very small letters with a neatly printed message. It was difficult to see; one had to bend closer to read the words, "You are now using the restroom at a forty-five degree angle."

(I was unable to verify if the writer was of Cracker origin. What did men think when they entered the restroom with a fella on his back under a stall door carefully writing this message?)

Onest: vernacular for once, as in, "Onest upon a time, I remember we had a speckled bull that wuz meaner'n ah snake."

Ordah: a contraction of ought to, as in, "We ordah tie our horses outside the pens. These bulls are a little rank." One Cracker once tied a plastic gallon milk-jug to a dairy cow's tail for fun. The cow would have none of it and pulled out, running through fences for the woods. The Cracker casually observed this unanticipated phenomenon, commenting, "I ordin-na done that."

There's a tale about a Cracker boy who was asked by his teacher to give a sentence using auditorium. He studied and came up with, "I had to go to the outhouse, my zipper hung up an' I coudden get my britches up an' I coudden git 'um down–I ordahtore 'um."

Other'n that, he's doin' good: The phrase was generally used as a summary of a situation or condition. "Yeah, after he got out of the hospital, he's mighty sore, but other'n that, he's doin good." The best example of a contorted usage occurred when a man brought in a seventeen-year old dog. The poor thing was brought in on a folded and soiled blanket. The dog had severe cataracts, terribly infected teeth and gums, had bed sores and was unable to control his bladder and bowels. I commented, "That poor ol' fella sure is in bad shape."

The man replied in absolute seriousness, "Yeah, Doc, he cain't see, cain't git up an' walk. I think he's totally deaf an' he cain't control his functions; but other'n that, he's doin' good."

Outtened his lights or outten yer lights: a phrase meaning "to knock unconscious or render semi-conscious", as in, "Whin tha head catch came loose it thumped him under the jaw; boys, it sure did outten his lights." Another example is, "Stay clear of that bull, he'll outten yer lights."

Outside!: a loud call to the man in control of the catch chute when working cattle. It simply meant, "We're done with her, turn her out *of the chute*." Real sporty fellas might holler, "Release the hairy beast!" (Same idea.)

P

Paintin': contraction for painting, as in painting a house, barn or some other thing. Painting isn't a favorite activity of the cowboys. They'd do it but it wasn't something they enjoyed. I am reminded of the story I was told about a local Cracker artist that had developed quite a reputation for his natural painting talent. A local wealthy woman came to his house one day. She asked him if he would paint her portrait. "The only thing is I want you to paint it in the nude."

He said, "I don't think ma wife would go for it."

She replied, "I'll pay you $500."

He looked at her beady-eyed and said, "Well, I hav' to ask my wife."

He went into the house and returned in about fifteen minutes. He said, "She says it'd be alrite with her but you'll have to let me wear my socks so's I'll hav' a place to wipe my brushes."

Cracker Terms, Phrases And Definitions

Part tha cattle, partin' cattle or partin' gate: to sort cattle into pens for working and treatments. A partin' gate is a gate in the cow pens that can be opened or closed to move cattle in the desired direction. A four-way part means the cattle are sorted into four pens; for example: cows, calves, bulls, and steers to sell. A partin' circle is a circle in the corner of four adjacent (or more) pens where cattle can be parted into any one of the four pens. This allows one or two men to open and close gates to sort a continuous stream of cattle coming down the chute or alley way. One can part out cattle from a herd or part into a particular pen.

One of the tougher jobs in this occupation is parting wild cattle in open pasture or a fence corner. It requires a crew with some cow sense, disciplined cow dogs and horse riding skill. I learned this at an early time (and received a dog cussin' which I've never forgotten) for getting in the way of selected cows that needed separating from the herd. One man rides in amongst 'um, selects the cow (or bull), and eases her toward the edge of the herd. Cattle run around her and the rider as the crew makes an opening for her to go. As she passes, they fill in the area with riders so the whole herd won't try an escape or take after her, as the Crackers would say it. The problem is many parted cattle will try to re-enter the herd, so a fella has to watch the herd and behind him as well. This is a place where good dogs can be helpful. This ballet is similar to "pilin' ants" (see term).

Patootie: a humorous word for the afterbirth of the cow. While working with a veterinarian in the Gainesville area, we worked cattle, horses, mules, hogs, dogs and cats. Crackers inhabit the area. (Yes, just outside of the Gainesville city limits.) One Friday night, a Cracker named McKinney borrowed his neighbor's telephone and called for help. His little farm was deep in the rough woods near Alachua, just north of Gainesville. His cow was having calving difficulty. Arriving after sunset, we spent a considerable amount of time trying to rope the solid black running crossbred Angus cow–with a weak flashlight, in the pitch black darkness, in underbrush, amid sink holes. (Try that sometime.) We finally caught her in a corner. It was the old little-cow-big-calf problem. After an examination we knew she would have to have a Cesarean.

The C-section done under flashlight went amazingly well. She was up and out of the area very rapidly. We said our goodbye and "Let us know how she's doin'," loaded our gear and drove to the nearest café for pie and coffee. I felt sure she would be fine.

Mr. McKinney called early the next day and started the conversation by saying, "Doc, her patootie is hanging out! It's atouchin' the ground and she's steppin' on it!" Dr. Dudley slammed down the phone, shook his head in self-disgust and said, "Mr. McKinney just called; tha cow we did the C-section on has her omentum out–her incision is dehisced." (The omentum is the free-floating portion of the abdominal lining. It serves as a pouch for the small intestine and acts as a device that protectively wraps around the intestine during inflammation or puncture wounds.) It surely sounded serious. We raced up there, breaking all speed limit laws.

The cow was in a pen when we arrived, standing there calmly chewing her cud and obviously contented. As she turned away, we saw the afterbirth hanging out of the birth canal. The normal placenta was being expelled. Mr. McKinney called the afterbirth tha Patootie. Showing relief in our faces, we laughed out loud. I have used the term for many years; sometimes for anything I can't remember the name of. (I'm not making this up either.)

Pawed up: to be torn, disturbed, stomped, upset or trampled. It was used to signify the ground had been trampled by running cattle or horses. A piece of paper can be pawed up if trampled. A cowboy might say, "I kin tell tha ol' horse is sick 'cause tha ground wher' I tied him is all pawed up." Pawin' the ground generally referred to a tied horse that was in pain

Cracker Terms, Phrases And Definitions

or discomfort. Bulls will paw tha dirt when mad, ready to fight or trying to impress the ladies.

Peel tha hide: injure the skin in some way or a description of the effect of a very strong substance. The term could have two meanings. Firstly, in branding, a firebrand would work if the hide was precisely seared but not heat damaged. In other words, the red-hot iron could be firmly applied to the hide and quickly removed before damage was too deep to the layers of the skin. The brander often tested his branding by scraping a fingernail over the branded area—if it peeled away precisely in the touched area the brand would be a good one. If it did not, the brand was too light and would require a touch up.

The worst thing one could do was to over-heat the skin or scald the hide if it was wet. We generally never branded wet cattle because there was a tendency to scald the brand site. The steam would blister the area around the brand, resulting in a disfigured brand. It was an art form sometimes developed by trial and error; but one who was new to the procedure wouldn't know for a time whether his branding technique was good until he saw the healed hide or had some coaching by an experienced brander. Well-done fire branding was done quickly and efficiently, with a minimum of trauma and discomfort to the animal or the human. It is one of the oldest surgical procedures done by man, along with castration and circumcision. So in this context, peelin' tha hide was a good thing.

I know there will be some who think this is a horrible procedure. Howls may go up from segments of unschooled society. And, yes, things have changed. Modern animal science has adapted other technology to permanent identification. In my mind, the ultimate irony is an image of a longhaired, dirty, liberal college student, in sandals, having various painfully applied tattoos and festering tongue, navel and nose rings, drinking Starbucks coffee, and carrying a banner against branding cattle. Go figure.

Secondly, in the other more common context it referred to the literal laceration and denuding of a portion of one's skin—especially on the knuckles, hands, shins, knees, face or arms. It was used as slang for a traumatic event. "Son! Them briars will peel tha hide if you ride through 'em!" Also, this phrase was often used to describe a martial difficulty: "They commenced to fight there in the parkin' lot and she jus peeled the hide offen his nose." or "Boy, her lawyer jus peeled his hide in court." This was not a good thing in general. A synonym, "barked the hide", referred to a milder damage done to knuckles while accomplishing some mechanical task, as in, "Did you have trouble takin' the pig out tha trailer?" "Yeah, he barked my knuckles a bit," A horse could run under a low tin roof at a barn and cause severe head or face laceration, as described by, "He peeled the hide back between his eyes."

Pea raid: Cracker and mountain language for parade, a procession or formal presentation.

Peein' ah drop at ah time: a phrase indicating being excited, cornered, under stress or fearful. The phrase came from observing cattle that were extremely upset in the cow pens. Some would become aggressive and defensive at being separated from other cattle. Taking a defensive stance, they'd charge the first things that moved in their immediate proximity—dogs, men, horses, or anything. When the particular bull or cow had run whatever it was out of the area, they'd turn around looking for another target while urinating very small amounts. The cause was due to an adrenaline surge in a fight or flight reaction. The cowboys misused the phrase, applying to any potentially exciting event like a party, "You goin' to the buckout?" "Yeah, I'm peein' a drop at tha time."

Will Rogers referred to this word when he wrote: "There are three kinds of men: The ones that learn by reading; the few who learn by observation; the rest of them have to pee on the electric fence and find out for themselves."

Cracker Terms, Phrases And Definitions

Peein' on mah leg: slang for, "Yer, kiddin' me, right?" This has been used on numerous occasions to express suspicion that one is being lied to, deceived, or set up for a joke. When a cowboy embellished a story about some recent happening, Frank Handley responded, "Boys, I think he's peein' on our leg" thereby indicating skepticism about the tale.

Many years ago, Dr. Henry Jones, a Mississippi veterinarian, remarked to our classmates, "The ol' timers in my country say the way to tame a mule istah pee on his legs." Dr. Ben LaRavia from near the same part of the country said, "Henry, if you can git that close to a mule, he ain't wild."

Peein' red and blinkin' at tha sun: a phrase used to describe the reaction to an old de-wormer called, phenothiazine. Phenothiazine was less than ideal as a de-wormer for cattle and horses with only a parasitic kill rate of about 45%; however, it was the only available drug in its time. With a good diet it would keep intestinal parasites at bay, but must be re-administered frequently to be effective.

There were some reactions to the drug. Firstly, those administering the drug had to take care to not get it in their eyes or on the skin of the face. It would cause an intense and painful dermatitis. It didn't last long but you'd look like a Yankee tourist who'd fallen asleep at the beach. The skin reaction was similar to that caused by creosote from fence posts. That would burn, too. The phrase, peein' red and blinkin' at tha sun comes from the reaction of cattle which had been given phenothiazine. It caused what is known as photo-sensitization." (Yeah, I know it's a big word… but hang on.) This is a liver reaction where the metabolism of the liver is affected and the breakdown of chlorophyll from plant ingestion is hampered and it causes an over-production of compounds called "porphyries" which are light sensitive. Sunlight contacts white coats or skin and causes necrosis (dead skin). Black or dark skin doesn't absorb the light and is unaffected. Photosensitization is the worst form of reaction from phenothiazine and can occur in other conditions.

The mild form, as the phrase denotes, is a light sensitivity, expressed as a discomfort of the eyes to sunlight and some discolored urine from the breakdown products of the insulted liver. So, occasionally, a phenothiazine-treated cow would go to the shade, pee red and blink at the sun. The Crackers were familiar with the problem though it wasn't common. They'd use the phrase to kid a fella that was not feeling well, as in, "Boy? You sure look bad... you peein' red and blinkin' at tha sun?" I heard the phrase used in the pens when a sick fella returned to work. He was asked, "How ya doin', Bill?" He replied, "Oh, I'm still peein' red and blinkin' at tha sun..."

Peein' up ah rope: a slang phrase for a futile effort. Dr. Handley used to find the "weak men" in a crew when working cattle. He was noted for going back in the pens and talking with young men new to the cow crew. He'd point out the weakness and time-wasting actions of the man, indicating it by, "We need to titen-up. I ain't got all day here... you need ta git over near tha partin' pen an' job tha cows as they come in (i.e., into tha alleyway toward the catch chute). Standin' wher you are is like peein' up a rope... Let's go!" (For another reference to "pee," see "Whutta you think?")

(Please excuse this foray into the "peein'" definitions. And, yes, I am aware there is another German slang word often used for "peein'," but we didn't use the German very much and, besides, "peein'" gets the point across....)

Pencil-nosed (*fill in the blank*): a description of a dog such as a dachshund or inbred dog or a general derogatory term for anything that wasn't particularly desirable or pretty. "Y'all go git that pencil-nosed horse and let's worm 'im" is an example. (Rare and locally used) I knew a man who called his dog, "Pencil." (I never knew why.) A "sharp-headed dog" usually was one that had a narrow head that came to a point.

People do strange things for money: I have said this same phrase to working people all over the southern U.S. and it rarely fails to elicit a smile. It originally came from a cowboy in Oklahoma who brought a young crossbred heifer to a veterinary clinic from a ranch about 35 miles away–at 3:30 a.m. She was having a difficult birthing and needed a cesarean-section. The bleary-eyed veterinarian asked the haggard, sunken-eyed cowboy, "How in the world did you find this heifer at 2:00 am?" The exhausted cowboy replied to the doctor, "Doc…, people do strange things for money…"

Perlue: the Cracker version of "pilau" an Oriental dish of rice boiled with fish, meat or chicken. Crackers make the dish with chicken, squirrel, rabbit, quail, fish, "scrub chicken" (see below), pork and beef or just about any meat. Often a Dutch oven was used--especially one that had a rim on the lid so that hot coals could be put there to heat from above. They would set up the ingredients and leave it unattended for an hour or two while hunting or working cattle and later return to a hot meal. Some of the camp cooks were able to bake good biscuits in the Dutch oven.

Pick tha scab: opening a particularly sensitive subject or persisting in holding on to a grudge, to re-visit an especially bad memory or is reminded of it by someone else. In this case, "Boy, let it go. Ther' ain't no need to pick tha scab over that gal. Move on!"

Piddling: the seemingly unorganized, but methodical and relaxed approach to a project or activity; not to be confused with the events occurring with the arrival of a new puppy. "Piddling" should not be confused with diddling or dawddling, since most piddling is done by people who actually are not wasting time (See the definition of "time" below); generally, piddling involves an activity that can be stopped at any time, is not absolutely essential that it be done by a specific time and no one is waiting on the piddler.

Mature, active individuals of all cultural origins and dialects can practice piddling. They generally accomplish much work but on a relaxed level. It is possible that a piddler can dawddle or diddle but generally a piddler doesn't – they are just trying to get some little projects done before something really important happens. Piddling is characterized by an enhanced sense of well-being and confident self image, whereas, when caught in the act diddlers and dawddlers know they are doing wrong, even though they won't admit it. Generally, most Yankees are piddlers, while Southerners are dawddlers and diddlers. However, very old Yankees can dawddle.

Pig-eyed: describes the small or under-pigmented eye of horses or other animals. It usually is associated with small or undersized round eyes of horses, but could be used to describe many other individuals, as in: "Bring that pig-eyed puppy along—maybe he'll learn somethin'." "Yeah she usta go with that pig-eyed fella from Hardee County." To a puppy, it could be regarded as an expression of affection, "Come her', Buck—you pig-eyed whelp..." It could be used as a preparatory adjective in cursing. I have heard it interchanged with "possum-eyed." (See "Cussinum")

Pile of guts: Totch Brown (See "Shakin' lik' a dog passin' a peach seed.") used the term referring to two men who wanted to run his crew out of an area of Key Largo. K. Irvin and Old Man Henry, in Totch's words, "pulled right up to our landing like it belonged to them. K. had his .30-.30 laying across his knees in plain sight and Henry had a double-barrel shotgun across his..." He continued, "What a load of nerve those two men had, and what a pile of guts to go along with it–sailing up to our camp in an open boat, guns across their knees...." (Enough said.)

Piney-woods rooter: a wild hog.

Pipe it in: a phrase used in context with isolation or distance. An example is, "They live so far back in tha wood, they hav' tah pipe in sunshine." It is closely akin to the phrase, "They lived so far back in the woods, even the Presbyterians handled snakes...."

Pizzle-sprung: to indicate a bull has damage to his reproductive organ, such as breakage, deviation, nerve damage,

Cracker Terms, Phrases And Definitions

hematoma (blood clot), scar tissue or some other condition that prevents the individual from breeding. The term is common in England, Australia and New Zealand in regard to rams and bulls. It can be used in a tongue-in-cheek fashion when not feeling well. For example, "Man, this flu has got me pizzle-sprung."

Plantin' periwinkles: while attending a social affair at a lake house at Crooked Lake, near Frostproof, Florida, I noticed a thick patch of scrawny periwinkles next to the house. I asked the host if they could be transplanted, as I had a bare patch of sand that needed some cover. He told me how to transplant them: "First you need to park your car in the sun an' let it heat up a bit. Then run through the patch and jerk up handfuls of them—roots and all. Throw them in the trunk and slam the door. Leave them in the trunk for three days. Take 'em out, throw them where you want to plant and let 'um alone for a few days. Then when yer ready to set 'um, run the lawn mower over the pile. Ever' few days or so, run through an' kick sand on 'um… they'll do jus' fine…" (I knew he knew what he was talking about since he is a respected attorney. It worked, too.)

One of his fishing buddies told me how to cook "skip-jacks", a boney trash fish not worth keeping for food. He indicated, "Tha best way to cook skip-jack was to nail the fish to a one-inch Cedar board that has been cut to fit a big roast pan. Put the mounted fish in the pan, cover with a gallon of white wine, place a cover on the pan and bake at medium heat for the time it takes to drink three or four beers. When ready, remove lid, remove nail and fish; eat the Cedar board and drink the wine.

Plunder: a word used for "gear, equipment, supplies or tools", etc. "Gather yer plunder and meet me at the pens. We got to rebuild a gate." It sounded like you were among Viking raiders, but it meant one was to bring what ever was needed to do the job at hand.

Pole barn: a barn structure made with poles (I threw in that obvious definition as some don't make the connection). Old style Cracker barns, stalls, pens and cribs were made with split rails which could also be used to make fences. These buildings often had shingles for the roof, but galvanized tin roofing was quickly adopted when it became available. These barns and out-buildings had big support poles of litered pine and the split rails were stacked in an alternating fashion, like split-rail fences, to make pens, stalls or storage rooms. The newer pole barns were based on big poles put in at the corners with careful plumbing and leveling. Then, headers were attached to the poles, rafters attached to them and tin applied for roofing. They were simple to construct and sturdy and served as dry quarters to store feeds, fertilizer vehicles or other equipment. Many use the same construction for horse barns. Tin on the out sides defined rooms.

Polin' hogs or polin' calves: to insert a pole into the rectum of a thin or poor pig or calf and subsequently elevate it to the level of ripened cabbage palm berries, allowing it to eat the berries. I first heard this in the cow pens where two Crackers were talking. One asked his friend what he had been up to. The reply was, "Oh, jus polin' some yearlings at my house..." Of course, I had to know what that meant, so I asked what was polin' yearlings. He described it in detail and they laughed that I didn't know it was a joke.

It did figuratively describe how thin the particular animals were since the image that came to mind was the actual physical effort it would take to lift a pig up on a pole to the berries of the cabbage palm; it could only be done with the littlest and skinniest of animals. This phrase was also used with puzzle-gutted, possum-gutted, puny and whelp, as in, "I expect we'll have to pole them puzzle-gutted yearlin's." etc. (See "puzzle-gutted")

If a daddy told his son to go get a post and "pole up the cattle in the chute", he meant for him to shove a pole behind the cow or bull, between two fence boards and in front of two strong fence posts, to prevent the individuals from backing up or turning around. Which side of the post you stood on was important—standing behind the post as you inserted it into the chute left you protected. However, if you stood in front of the post or pole and missed shoving the far end in front of the post on the other side, when the animal backed up, the post would send you forward like a catapult. It only took one experience to figure it out… if you survived.

Ponder or ponderin': to mull over, think about, consider, study or analyze. "Whut'er you doin'?" "Oh, just ponderin' whut we ought to do with the yearlin's." My wife is a ponderer. She thinks about things like what to do about self-serving politicians, world peace, or the meaning of life, etc. I ponder, too… things like, "How do they get tha fillin' in Twinkies?" and "Whut happens if a fella is scared half to death… twice? Is he dead?" The synonym for ponderin' is studyin', as in, "You studied any more 'bout how many cows to put in the marsh pasture?"

Popped lik'ah can of biscits: used to describe any "pop" noise from gunshots to broken brogan laces. I heard an old Cracker tell about living in town. He said, "You can tell whin daylite is comin' 'cause you can hear canned biscuits poppin' all up an' down tha street."

Poor doer: an unthrifty or under-weight animal of any age. (See "puzzle gutted" and "skinnier nah ah earth worm with his guts slung out.")

Possum-belly or Possum-bellied: having a rounded stomach or abdomen; though rarely used it was most often in a description of a pot bellied individual cow, horse, catch dog or man. Sometimes affectionately, as in, "Y'all tell ol' possum belly to come to tha pens whin he's finished eatin'." "Possum-gutted" and "gut-sprung" are synonyms.

Prime his (or her) pump: the phrase is based on the old method of getting the old-style hand-cranked pumps started. The sucker leathers found within the pump dry out from disuse. In order to get suction, wetting the barrel and piston by pouring water into the outlet of the pump will cause the leather washers to swell and seal. The phrase became common when referring to starting anything. "Doc, give 'er sumthin' to prime 'er pump..." meant to treat or medicate a cow, for example. Another, "Boy, you look like you need yer pump primed this mornin'." After de-worming an anemic calf, the parting comment might be something like, "That ort to prime his pump." The phrase was common.

Prop it up: Only one documented instance using the term in Cracker context occurred after WW II. In a little town—so little that sunshine had to be trucked in–a GI returned from the war in the Pacific. He'd received all his back pay at discharge since he'd been in action in remote regions. Upon arriving in the states, he purchased a big green Indian Motorcycle. It was a huge thing with lots of chrome and shiny things attached. He rode it home. When he arrived, he made several runs up and down the main road. Dust hung in the air. Sand was flung hither and yon as he rode back and forth in front of the assembling children and on-lookers. One old man, Mr. Ledbetter, was watching from the porch of a little grocery. He rarely said much but when he did talk it was pretty dry. Up and down the road the proud GI went, dust flying, sand scattering onto the sidewalk. He finished his display with a dramatic figure-eight in the middle of the road. Riding over to the little crowd in front of the grocery, he stopped, pulled a piece of a board out of the saddle bags and put the kick-stand down, propping the machine on the wood so it would stay upright. Waving at the dust, one of the red-faced kids turned to Mr. Ledbetter and asked, "Mr. Ledbetter, whut do you think 'bout all this?" Mr. Ledbetter spit in the sand and replied, "Well, I don't want nuthin' that'll take ya to hell on ah teaspoon of gas and whin ya git ther' you'd hav to prop it up...."

Pulled ah (*fill in the blank*): a term that only has significance when one knows the characteristics of or the story behind the

Cracker Terms, Phrases And Definitions

person, place or thing referred to in the phrase, as in, "Yeah... whin he got mad he pulled a Clint Eastwood on him..." For example, when I first started running heavy equipment I didn't appreciate the Florida soil types and the massive weight of the machines I drove. More than once I bogged a dozer or sprayer tank down in mud and/or muck. It got so, for a time anyway, when someone went to the barn to get a tractor to pull something he was driving out of a bog, you'd hear them say, "Well, I pulled ah Howard." (Only they sometimes pronounced it "Hiard") To "pull a Jake" was referring to one of Hubert's cow dogs that could come "uncorked" on a rank cow or bull. (See term) I suppose you could say that "tried", "acted like", "imitated" or "copied" are synonyms for "pulled."

Pulled ah Zorro: a rarely used phrase indicating a job was done much faster than expected or that someone came earlier, did some job or service and quickly departed the premises. In context, cow crews often worked a group of fat cattle early, while it was cooler. The smaller and tougher calves were worked later in the morning. The "odes" will tell someone to meet them at the pens at 9:00 am adding, "We ought to be ready to work calves after we finish tha mama cows." If a veterinarian showed up on time and the crew was sitting in the pens, obviously finishing much earlier than expected, the vet might ask, "Y'all break down?" "Naw, we pulled ah Zorro" meaning, "We got in, made our 'Z' an' got out." (Remember how Zorro the masked swordsman would make his "Z" mark and jump out a window? He got in, made his mark and got out... Same idea.)

Pullout or pulled out: a directive or description of an action, respectively. "Whin y'all see tha cows come out the swamp, pullout for tha gap between tha hammocks—they'll head for the marsh. Turn'um back toward the fence..." or "Y'all pullout at daylight, we'll meet ya ther'." The meaning here is "leave, go, go ahead, head for, run or drive toward or gather up your plunder and meet us at some location." It could be used as a disgusted warning of sorts, as in: "I'll tell ya—that gal is plum crazy... if you jus' got ta marry her, pullout..." "Pulled out" is past tense, as in "He pulled out about thirty minutes ago."

My grandson was bored one day but reluctant to go outside by himself since he was from the big city. I knew he would be totally safe in our neighborhood—we don't have to lock our doors; so I said, "Pullout, boy." Every one listening laughed at the use of the unfamiliar term, which I thought expressed precisely what he should do.

Pump 'im up or pump it up: to restore health, deworm, resuscitate, bring back to life, revive or get someone up-and-going. It was slang for getting something back to normal. The common use was something like, "Boys, let's give that cow some fluke medicine... maybe that'll pump 'er up." Also, "Sumbody'll hav' to go by an' pump up Jack. If we don't, he'll sleep 'til noon." "Prime 'er pump" has the same connotation.

Puny: to be born late or immature, as in "runt of the litter"; to be underweight, inferior, slight, unsightly, unpleasant or weak. In the South the word is used to describe boys or young men, as in "That boy sure is puny." or, "Son! He's puny." It can be used more objectively, as in, "Boy, your trailer payment this month is purty puny."

Pure-dee: a variation of the word "pure", meaning unadulterated, totally, complete or completely, and "to be full of" or "filled with." Uses varied but always indicated a large amount of something, as in, "That woman is pure-dee mean whin you git her riled." One variation would be, "I wuz pure-dee scared whin the lightnin' popped ah pine rite next to us..."

Purty'n ah speckled birddog puppy: This phrase has special meaning to me as I used it when describing Hunter, my wife, when we courted. I'm not sure that they used that description where she comes from, but I think she appreciated it. Come to think of it, she's still that way.

Cracker Terms, Phrases And Definitions

Purt'nir: a contraction for "pretty near," meaning "approximately" or "close to," or "almost" as in, "That calf purt'nir broke my leg whin he kicked me." Or, "It wuz purt'nir daylite whin we found 'em." (I can see their faces if I had translated that sentence as, "Well, it was very near nautical first light whin we first observed the cattle.")

Put yer dog on a string: a directive to tie up a dog on a strong leash. Loose dogs in the pens can cause considerable disruption. Cattle and dogs aren't always friendly to each other, especially if a cow has a calf by her side. Most mature cow dogs, except pups on "OJT" (i.e., "on-the-job-training" programs) will find a place out of the way, such as under a catwalk or outside the pens in a shady spot. Loose dogs can put the men in danger when a cow or bulls selects a man as a secondary target after running the dog away. Those that disrupt the working activities are tied, put in a horse or cow trailer or introduced to a loud whip crack near their butts. (This encourages them to "gitout tha way.") Stubborn (or extremely stupid) dogs have been known to have cattle prod touched to their hind ends to "get their attention."

Synonym phrases are; "Put them dogs on the scales", "Stick 'em in the trailer", "Shut up yer dogs", or "Git them dogs outta here." Smart working dogs stay out of the way until an outlaw bull or cow becomes a threat to the men. They live for those moments when they'll hear, "Heah, ketch 'er, Bubba!" and be called into service. After the belligerent cow or bull relents in their attacks on the men, the dogs go back to "stand-by status." Funny how some mature dogs will fall sound asleep in the turmoil. They'll lie broadside, occasionally rising up to look around. One might get up, shake off the dust and dirt and find a new spot. But the minute someone goes to a horse to put cattle out, they're up and with wagging tails trot up to the riders, ready for action.

One of the best dogs I ever worked with was "Boss", a Blue Heeler. When palpating on the Triple G Ranch outside of Sebring, Boss would sit quietly by my side. If a cow stalled at the chute, he'd run up, turn his head sideways and nip her in the flank between the boards. This encouraged her to step into the chute. If a cow stalled in leaving the restraint chute, he'd reach up between the bars of the chute and pinch her flanks again. It got to be routine, I'd point to a cow and he'd run up and "encourage her" to step up. I thought I'd demonstrate this to his owner, Russell Lowe. I said, "Hey, Russell, watch this." I pointed to a stalled cow. Boss did the trick again, right on cue, and the cow stepped up into the chute. This went on for another hour or so and Russell finally said, "Hey, Doc. I spoke with Boss and he said he wanted to know where tah send his bill for his services."

Puzzle-gutted whelp: a term applied by Crackers to unattractive animals, especially pot-bellied children, dogs, pigs, calves and colts, as in, "Look at that puzzle-gutted whelp; ain't he sorry?" Its origin has been lost in history. Some have suggested that it came from Medieval England where sorcerers used sacrificial animal intestines to divine the future. In that context, a "puzzled gut" was the term used when the gut reader was stalling for time, turning to the king, saying, "Without doubt, 'tiz a puzzled gut I see. What wilt happen, I know not. I canst tell Thee naught, O Your Fullness."

"Whelp" always referred to a small creature. The probable meaning is that the puzzle-gutted puppy, for example, was pot-bellied from malnutrition due to intestinal parasites. That was how we always used it, so I suppose you could assume it to be synonymous with pot-bellied. (If you have read this far, you know by now I don't have any idea what it really means.)

Puzzlin': describes a situation not easily solved or remedied; to give thought to. The best example I could think of was the tale told about three Crackers trying to get the length of a literd post. They had one man trying to stand on the post while two others tried to hold it upright. The fella on top was precariously balanced and holding a tape measure down beside the post, trying to get a measurement while the two below were struggling to keep the post still. A man rode up, got off his horse and asked, "Hey! Whut are y'all puzzlin' about." One responded, "We're tryin' to get the length of this literd post." The onlooker suggested, "Why don't y'all lay it down and measure it on the ground?" One said, "We ain't tryin' to get how wide it is… we want ta know how long it is."

Q

Quick on tha trigger: to be ready, to not hesitate, to not be caught "flat-footed" (See term). The phrase was often used as a description of a man who responds hastily to a sudden or unexpected action. "Y'all be ready 'cause whin them cows see you, they'll pull out for tha hammocks; we'll never get them all if they git scattered. Whin you hear us comin' be quick on tha trigger or they'll take it away frum ya."

This phrase makes me think of Duge Cannon (mentioned under "How many cows do you own?"). He told me a story I thought hilarious. He said he and a friend were quail hunting one time. He indicated they were hunting Mexican Quail. They are very fast runners, according to him, and a fella had to be quick on the trigger to get a shot at one. He said, "The last time we went huntin' we had a rough day. We hadn't seen birds all day. On the way home late that afternoon we rode up on a huge covey of birds crossing tha road–there mustah been thirty birds in the covey. Well, we stopped the truck, got out an' took a couple of quick shots; by the time we got the cork back in the jug, all tha birds were gone."

Quilled 'er: "Has you quilled 'er yet?" The origin of this obscure, rarely-heard phrase was in Clearwater, Florida, described by an old country practitioner of the medical arts in the forties. As told to me by my stepfather the story goes like this: A young physician fresh from medical school moved to Clearwater to start his practice. During his early tenure, a black lady came to the office one morning, requesting that the doctor hurry to her house, as her youngest daughter was having a difficult time delivering her baby. She had been in labor since early morning. The lady added, "Well, the midwife is gone somewher's an' we cain't git her… so we come to you."

The lady situated herself in the front seat of his auto and patiently waited for him to get his medical bag together. She pointed out the turns while heading to the "quarters", an old term in Florida meaning the black section of town. Upon arrival he was escorted to a back bedroom with a young, healthy looking girl on the bed, groaning in acute discomfort. He examined her. She was a little on the skinny side and her abdomen was large with what appeared to be a fine baby. He tried several obstetrical approaches but at last, after a considerable amount of time, he was getting desperate. In the stress of the moment, in the darkened bedroom, with a squalling girl every time a contraction hit her, he was sweating profusely. Things were getting serious.

He noticed that another woman came into the bedroom. She whispered something to the Mama. Well, Mama having seen all the fruitless activities of the young doctor quietly approached his side.

She said, "Docter, does ya want me to go git Hattie?"

"Hattie? Who's Hattie?" the exasperated doctor asked.

"She bees tha midwife for the quarters. We use her most all the time. She ought to be back tah home by now."

In an irritated tone, shaking his head in frustration, the doctor said, "Yeah; go git Hattie." He needed a break.

In about 20 minutes a petite black woman came into the bedroom. She was dressed in a freshly starched white uniform, her short sleeves standing out like unfurled sails, and her immaculate nurse's hat pinned primly in place. He later admitted she did look professional.

Not saying a word to the doctor, or even looking his way, she walked to the bed, poked the girl in the belly in two or three places and asked the doctor, "Has you quilled 'er yet?" "Quilled her?" responded the confused doctor. Upon hearing his query, the skinny little midwife gave him a glance of undisguised contempt and huffed out of the house. In a few minutes, he heard all kinds of clamor from the chicken house. One poor hen squalled especially loudly. He peeked out the little window in time to see the efficient Hattie stand up satisfactorily holding a few tail feathers. She expertly selected a suitable one, produced a pair of scissors and neatly trimmed the feather, making a tube like a soda straw. She came in, pulled a tin of snuff out of her pocket, jabbed the straw down in it, collecting some in the end of the quill. She then went to the head of the bed to the squalling girl, bent over and blew the snuff into her nose. Well, the girl began a fit of rapid sneezes–back-to-back hard sneezes! To his amazement, the baby began to exit the birth canal. He assisted Hattie in the delivery of a healthy baby boy.

He mentioned the technique of "quillin'" to his colleagues but they weren't willing to adopt it. (I am not making this up... either.)

Florida Cow Hunter's Handbook

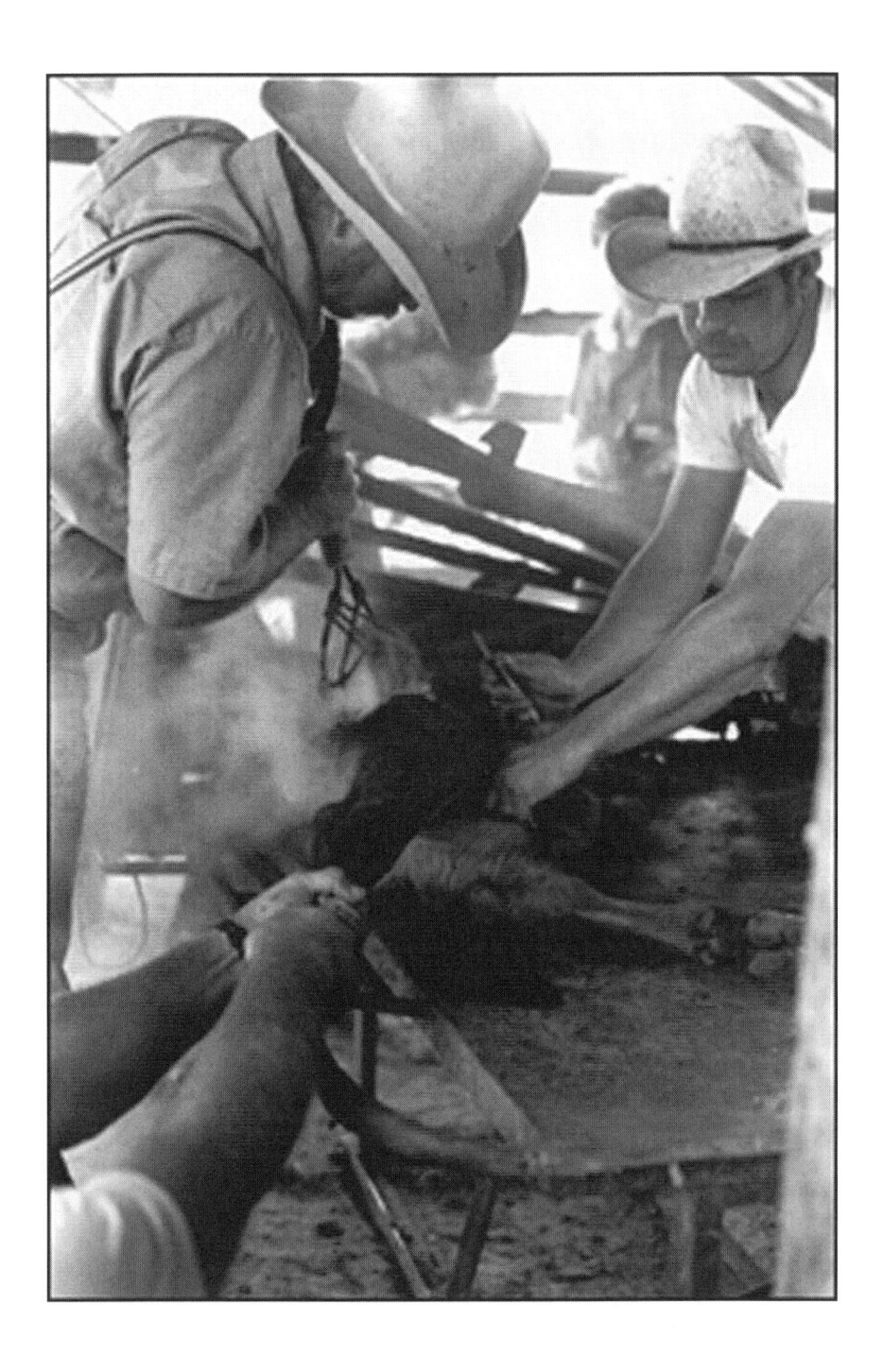

R

Rank: a slang word for tough, mean, out of control, dangerous, aggressive, thick, unmanageable, wild or having a bad odor. Examples: "These cattle are rank, ain't they?" "I stepped in a fire-ant bed; they're rank, I wanna tell ya!" "I don't think he knew how rank that boy can git whin he gits riled up." "The briars wer so rank we come out of there." And, of course, "Boy the taxes on cows are sure rank, ain't they?" The typical use might be, "That boy wuz so rank whin he wuz growin' up, they had to potty train him at gun point! He's tha only kid I know that flunked out of home school."

Rat cheer: this phrase has nothing to do with cheerleaders or rodent racing. It means "right here", as in, "Wher' y'all gonna eat dinner?" "Ratcheer." It could be modified somewhat if the responder is pointing, as in, "Wher you want us to put this?" "Rat ther."

Ratkillin': can be used literally or figuratively. In literal "ratkillin'" a man is planning to kill rats that infest his feed barn or feed storage area. When they have an ample food supply rats will have a population explosion and take over very quickly; extermination is in order. This is accomplished by poison baits or by use of firearms. Crackers often let the children learn to shoot during this activity. It trains the child; under supervision, is a whole lot of fun and accomplishes a needed service (well, depending on the level of expertise of the kids). The easy way of rat extermination is to "hire" wizened barn cats, most of which are "wilder than nose hairs." I have known men who buy cases of .22 "rat shot" for pest control. Rat shot is miniature shot gun shells that work in a .22 caliber pistol. It's fun and keeps one's eye sharp in practicing shooting. The hardware store bills it out as "rodent control materials."

Let me digress a bit. In my technical research, I had the greatest helper a man could ever want. Berny Zellner was an Animal Science graduate and took the job of Manager at the old Ruminant Nutrition Unit just about two miles from my office. It was an old dilapidated facility but it worked well for my purposes. We were able to house four pens of about twenty-five steers each for testing various by-product diets. It had equipment, silo rooms, manure handlers, plenty of room and pastures where a small herd could be kept. Auburn's Milstead Research Facility was being finished at this time, but I could do my projects at the nearby old facility and Milstead was about twenty-five miles away from the campus.

Berny was a real Cracker, a highly intelligent one, and very enjoyable to be around. He always wore a baseball cap, jeans and boots. Hunter said he was really handsome; I never noticed. We hit it off immediately and quickly moved into a mutual trusting of each other. He was a little stand-off-ish at first, but we became close friends. He had cow sense and the common sense that I needed during the technical organization. He had the knack of making things work while maintaining tight research methods.

But there was a huge problem with the old facility–rats! The varmints had moved in over the years, taking advantage of the abundant stores of steer feed. Berny was the first man I ever knew that when I asked what he was going to do that day, he off-handedly said, "Oh, I thought I'd have a ratkillin' this evenin'."

I was intrigued by this, so I met him one night to see what went on during a "ratkillin'." We drove to the barn and pulled up to the feed room, headlight's glaring into the barn. I lost count of rats at around eighty-four; rats piled out of the room like a Hindu Temple at feeding time. I think they killed many of themselves during the mad scramble for dark holes. It was a sight to behold. I understood what he meant then. Funny how a good ratkillin' can make close friends.

The figurative use of "ratkillin'" refers to wasting time, being idle, having nothing to do or hoping there might be an option in an otherwise boring day.

Example: "Whut you up to today?"

Cracker Terms, Phrases And Definitions

"Aw, nuthin'. We're fixin'tah hav' a ratkillin'."

"How 'bout goin' with me to tha market? I'm gonna sell some calves."

"Yeah. I'm ready."

Ratshot: a type of ammunition for small pistols like a .22 caliber. In effect it is a "tiny shotgun." Years ago, Crackers used ratshot in pistols for "changing the attitude" of aggressive and belligerent bulls. This was a time when Brahman bulls were more commonly used as herd sires. Some of these bulls were notorious about becoming defensive and aggressive. More than a few horses were gored in the hind quarters or abdomen by these outlaw bulls. Some were even killed by them. The burnt-face and speckled Rio Negro line of Brahman bulls was especially mean, but any individual could come "uncorked." These bulls would often head for the thickest brush or palmetto patches to hide or escape. Trying to move these animals out and back to the herds was a challenge. Here again, good cow dogs were an advantage. They'd "werkon 'um" until the bull *wanted* to return to the herd.

One time we had a bull that was especially difficult to move with the herd. The foreman brought a .22 pistol with ratshot. When the bull backed into the palmettos, tossed his head in warning and then charged out after the horses, hooking up high in the air with lethal horns, Sonny shot the bull in the brisket. It didn't take many of these lessons to educate the bull. The ratshot didn't hurt him much, but it surely did communicate that it would be to his advantage to return to the herd and not show his "country behind." (You'll have to look up all the terms you don't recognize.)

Registered: ordinarily used in reference to the cataloging of purebred animals in breed associations, I recall another use of the word during an introduction at a meeting where I was to speak. The university had sent speaker information before all the speakers arrived. The master of ceremonies got to my introduction. He began by reading my credentials,

Florida Cow Hunter's Handbook

paused and said, "Folks, let me put it this way: if he was a bull, I'd jus say 'He's registered....'"

Releef: The best illustration occurred during an exchange between a woman and a Ph.D. Poultry Specialist for the Extension Service, who just happened to be Cracker. (As I said, there are some Crackers scattered throughout academia.) The woman called the office, asking the secretary, "I need to talk with somebody that knows sumthin' about chickens." The call was routed to the Ph.D. He answered and she began, "Well, ma hens ain't layin'. They look all scrawny and frazzled. I uped their feed but it don't seem to help. I wonder if you could tell me whut's wrong with'um." The specialist asked a few questions. After a brief conversation, he said he would come by her house the next morning.

The next morning, The Ph.D. came to work about fifteen minutes later than usual. His office colleague saw that he was smiling. Interested he asked, "Well, what did you find out about the lady's chicken problem?"

The poultry specialist laughed out loud; then told what he'd seen at the "poultry operation."

"I went out back of her house to a little coop with a ten-by-ten pen attached. The hens looked bad, all ratty-looking and poor. There were four hens and eight or nine roosters. Every time a hen tried to walk a rooster would jump her and try to mate. As soon as he quit, another would jump her. The poor hens couldn't eat or walk or nuthin'"

"What were your recommendations?" asked the office mate.

He laughed again and said, "I talked to her so she'd understand; I told her, 'Git riddah all tha roosters but one–these hens gotta hav' sum releef!'"

Reminds me of an ol' gal I usta to know: a response phrase used in any number of contexts, usually with something unexpected, outlandish, vicious or ridiculous. A cow could jump right in the middle of a bunch of men, hook one or two

Cracker Terms, Phrases And Definitions

of them, chasing the rest to the fences, and someone would say, "She reminds me of an ol' gal I usta know." For example, a fat barren cow could walk by, where men rested under shade in the cow pens. In an off-handed comment, someone would say, "She reminds me of an ol' gal I used know."

It was used in any number of contexts, but most always seemed to fit the situation. It usually started conversations about some 'ol' gal' that everyone knew. In modified form a woman might use it as, "That bull reminds me of ma ex-husband." (Usually she wouldn't explain the significance. It was left to the imagination. Was it his muscled shoulders or neck, his color, attitude, stupidity, or some other anatomical part?)

Restmacase: colloquial "rest my case." Though rarely used, it is an excellent means of communicating that one has made his point without further explanation.

My introduction to the phrase was unique. To my knowledge, Carlos Falla ("Fah-yah") is the first Cuban attorney that has been severely impacted by the Cracker culture. Leaving Cuba with his family, just before Castro started killing all political enemies, including attorneys, the family made it to Miami. They eventually went to Highlands County, and established the Yucatan Ranch. The Falla family had to start from scratch in the cattle business since Carlos was schooled under the Napoleonic system of law. Carlos had two big-footed boys named Carlos (who I called Little Carlos or Carlosito) and Eddie. I knew they had been indoctrinated into the Cracker mind-set the first time I saw Big Carlos sic them on a running cow. (She was having a difficult time delivering her calf. In the middle of a 200 acre pasture, Carlos raced the pickup beside her as she tried to escape capture. He then yelled, "Whup! Ketch 'er, boys!" Off the truck sailed the two boys—one on the head, the other on her neck and shoulders. With dogged determination, they pulled her head around, tripping her, and brought her to the ground. We delivered the calf in the middle of the pasture—no ropes, no nothing.)

Little Carlos and Eddie were entirely different temperaments, though both had a short-fused Latin temper. Both were handsome, but Little Carlos was taller and tended to stay out of trouble. Eddie on the other hand seemed to always be where trouble brewed. For example, one night in Avon Park, Florida, someone threatened Eddie with bodily harm and questioned his parentage. Being eighteen at the time, Eddie had enjoyed an adult beverage or three and was slightly "gassed." (See term) He took charge of the altercation, and pulled a shot gun on the aggressive young man. Well, in Highlands County that particular reaction is not on the approved list of ways to settle disagreements—even if one "needs killin'." (See term.)

This story was related to me by Big Carlos. The details may be a little fuzzy in my memory but I remember the important parts.

Eddie came home one night to meet his daddy at the front door. Carlos said, "Ther he wuz, drunker than a skunk. I was so mad I could hav' keeled him. I took him in, threw him in a cold shower, clothes and all, and put on a pot of strong black coffee." After his shower, Carlos sat Eddie at the kitchen table and made him drink a pot of the rank brew, thinking it would sober him up some. He then put Eddie to bed, saying ominously, "Eddie, we'll settle this in the morning!"

As Carlos reached for the light switch Eddie asked quietly, "Daddy?"

"Yes, son?"

"Did you ever do something stupid when you were eighteen?"

(Carlos sheepishly grinned as he told me, "Well, I wuz not going to lie to the boy.") Turning, he replied, "Well..., yes, Eduardo, I have..."

Eddie buried his head in the pillow as he said, "I restmacase."

Riled up: to be fuming mad, livid, upset, "bent outta shape." "Don't mess with 'im, he's all riled up," is typical. "Burr under his saddle" is a synonym phrase.

Ring: was often used by the old time Crackers for head man, foreman, or leader. (See "Odes.")

Ride that horse as long as you can: meaning "Take advantage of that situation as long as possible." Sometimes it had to do with fortunate events. Or it could be used in humor. The most recent personal use of this diverse phrase was when an older man told a woman she looked like she was in her thirties when in fact she was forty-five years old. She just beamed at his comment. I spoke up, telling her, "Darlin', ride that horse as long as you can."

Ringing his tail: signifies agitation, such as a horse or cow rapidly whipping, flicking or swishing its tail. "He cum in the pens jus' ringing his tail!" It could be used to express anticipation or excitement: "Boy, I cain't wait til tha buckout (party)–I bet yer ringing yer tail, too, huh?"

Ring-neck or ring-necked cur: a particular color pattern on cow dogs. These big-chested animals were often red to tan and had a splash on their necks or an encircling of bright white hair around the neck. My only experience with these dogs up-close-and-personal-like was in Hardee County where for some reason I got too far away from the safety of my truck. Wayne Collier's four ring-necked cur dogs decided to bay me up like wolves on a bear. I could feel them grab my britches legs and the slight brush of their noses (and teeth) on my calves. Knowing that showing fear and running would seal my fate, I sucked up my courage and called them by a variety of phrases questioning their lineages. No effect — they smelled blood in the water. Wayne finally came to the fence and hollered, "He-ah! Let 'im alone!" The dogs quit their fun and went back to work. Still sweating a bit, I asked Wayne, "Whut you reckon got into them?" He calmly replied, "I guess something boogered 'em."

When I went to his mother's house, I'd blow my horn before I got out of the car for Miz Collier to come clear the way. She would to come to the door and holler, "Let 'im alone, boys… go lay down." I learned quickly.

(Inbred? Ah thank… That's the sort of thing that happens when first cousins keep marryin'.)

Ripped his britches: a misjudgment or stupid mistake. In context it was used to indicate a very bad situation.. "I wanna tell ya… tha second l got in tha saddle I knew I'd ripped my britches. That horse went cold jawed and lik to hav bucked my kidneys out." A man can rip his britches with his wife or girlfriend when he is thoughtless, stupid, inconsiderate or acting like a man who hasn't a clue — he only knows he's ripped his britches. (Many Washington politicians rip their britches with the people when they get into powerful positions. I am reminded of what Mark Twain once said regarding politicians: "There're lies, damned lies and statistics." Speaking of statistics, did you know that 49.632% of statistics are made up on the spot?)

Rippin' an' tearin': rapid action or re-action, angry outburst, or destruction of equipment or facilities, kind of like a fit or a huge hissy; probably comes from the activities in cow pens when cattle become belligerent or hostile, as in, "That ol' black bull come through here rippin' and tearin'." Another example could be, "We had things under control 'til he come rippin' an' tearin' up in that ol' truck."

Runnindown: attempt to catch something or someone or to complete a task; as in, "I didn't feel like runnindown the chicken that got my finger whin I cut it off with the saw." Or, "If he'd quit runnindown all them ol' gals, he'd be to work on time."

Roachkilt: indicating that a cow had run over an individual who was now wallowing on the ground in pain, looking much like a roach on his back in the throes of death. I heard that this term is used in professional football, where a lineman has applied a particularly effective block on a player. It is called, "a roach-kill block." This is not to be confused with the myth that the pointed toed boots of cowboys are designed for killing roaches in corners–though this does occur, it is an entirely secondary use of them. Saturday night activities such as this, as well as seeing who can swallow little green tree frogs, signify boredom or inebriation. I had a cowboy tell me one time the reason he wore sneakers instead of cowboy boots with his western shirt, hat and jeans was so people could tell the difference between him and a truck driver.

Rocky Mountain oysters, mountain oysters or fries, prairie oysters, calf fries, "Montana tendergroins" or bull fries: calf or bull testicles used as food. "Lamb fries" are lamb testicles prepared in the same way. They are often deep-fried after being peeled, coated in flour or crumbled soda crackers, pepper and salt, and sometimes pounded flat. This delicacy is most often served as an appetizer with or without a cocktail or hot sauce but Crackers prefer them crispy fried. Historically, the practice of frying processed bull or calf testicles may have originated in Spain, Mexico, Central and South America or even in Italy. They are common to Canada, Oklahoma, Texas, Idaho, Colorado, Arizona, Florida and any ranching area in this country. In Spain and Mexico they are called "criadillas" or "huevos de toro" (literally "bull eggs") in Central and South America. In fact there are some Western commercial eating establishments that provide the delicacy. The way we collected them was during the castration of bull calves in the pens. The castrator pitched them into a clean bucket and at the end of the day the testicles were put into plastic bags and frozen. On occasion, a cowboy would drop a sack full by the hospital for the Handley Clan. It wasn't unusual for Handley to say, "We're havin' bull fries tomorrow afternoon, y'all come by." His trick was to remove the covering before the meat had fully thawed. The covering would peel off easily while the tissue was still semi-solid. He'd then cut the meat into finger-sized strips. Then he'd crush soda crackers, coat the strips of meat, and sprinkle with salt and pepper and deep fry in hot oil. We'd eat them hot and crisp. Not bad at all.... In my mind this food is much better than pickled "tripe" (rumen), "sweetbread" (pancreas), "lights" (lung tissue), fried brains and eggs and hoof- or horn-gelatin desserts. When I was in Bolivia one time, the natives prepared a "bar-be-que" for me, which included everything but the bellow of the bull.

S

Sackfull: a large amount, or a bunch. "They come by here with a whole sackfull of yearlin's." Also, "We gathered up a sackfull of plunder and headed for camp." A sackfull of dogs or big-footed boys means a large number. (See "plunder" and "big-footed.")

Saddle soap: a compound containing mild soap and softening ingredients such as neatsfoot oil, glycerin, or lanolin. It also contains bee's wax to protect leather. It is used for cleaning, conditioning and softening leather, particularly saddles and other horse tack and for boots. (See "neetsfoot oil") Of course, it didn't work well on water-soaked boots. We had to let them dry each weekend and apply water-proofing of some kind before Monday morning. It wasn't unusual to see boots lying in the sun on a Cracker's porch. Saddle soap surely smells good.

Sand road sport: a reference to someone over-dressed in fancy or odd clothes. It wasn't frequently used but was understood by all by observing the person.

Saucered an' blowed: an old reference to coffee ready to drink. Saucers used to be more like a bowl and one let the coffee flow into the saucer and blow on it to cool it. Though I am unsure where it started, I have heard it used in Florida, Kentucky, Tennessee and Texas. In my family the descriptive phrase was also used figuratively to state any particular beverage was ready to consume.

Cracker Terms, Phrases And Definitions

Say... buddy: a phrase synonymous with "Howsit goin?" The following story illustrates its use. A friend and I were sent by the Animal Science Department of a prominent southern university to Columbus, Mississippi, to a meat packing plant to collect liver samples from slaughtered research cattle. The purpose was to show the benefits of a particular diet the cattle had been fed. When stopped at the intersection just outside of town, a truck pulled up on the passenger's side of the university vehicle. I was driving and Berny was the passenger. Berny casually looked over into the grizzled, scarred, hairy, harsh face of one of the meanest looking men you could imagine. His eyes were steel blue and looked right through you. The home-made prison tattoos on his bare arm shone brightly in the sun. A shotgun was situated in the gun rack of the truck.

Berny swallowed hard and said, "Say? Buddy. You wooden happen to hav' an extra spit cup, would jah?"

The fella never took his eyes off Berny as he reached under his seat. After fumbling a bit, he came up with an old McDonalds coke cup. (We thought he might be feeling for a pistol.) He reached out the window, handed the cup over and nodded.

Berny took it with a nod and in a hoarse broken voice he said, "Thanks."

As we drove off Berny said, "Son, I had tah think fast. That man was mean-lookin'. I saw he had a pack of Red Man Chewing Tobacco on the dash of his truck and figured I better make friends quick." I guess Berny figured if the man thought we chewed tobacco, we must be alright.

The only other example I can remember is the time that a friend of mine was sitting in his car waiting for a buddy to come out of the dorm at a southern university. Bill noticed a young man's head bob out of the downstairs window and look all around. The fella closed the window and shortly therafter the front doors opened and out walked a nearly nude college boy; all he was wearing was an athletic supporter which only covered the front vitals. He casually walked up next to Bill's car, opened the trunk of his car and pulled out a pair of shorts. As he pulled them on he looked at Bill and said, "Say? Buddy...."

Scared mah mule: a phrase that indicated a situation where danger or injury was probable, imminent, unexpected and/or barely avoided. For example, if one were to walk into a set of cow pens, heading for the chute area, and unknowingly pass by an enclosure containing a mean bull, there would be a high probability that that would scare your mule. That is to say, the bull would come after you, creating at the least a high level of adrenal gland activity. One might dress up the phrase: "I experienced the reflexive physiological phenomenon called 'the fight or flight reaction.'" One's mule can be scared by bad bulls, cows, steers, boar hogs, dogs, cats, wasps, hornets, snakes, men and women, thunder and lightning, near falls or wrecks, or a Sheriff's Deputy (or lawyer) having a blue colored warrant in his pocket. Standing before a judge in court will also scare your mule. (Trust me on that one.) I don't know how old the phrase is nor where it originated. A synonym phrase is, "boogered my mule." (See term.)

I remember a time when a man named Robert was working on our house. He was a sheet metal specialist and made all kinds of custom-made copper rain gutters for houses and tubs and drain pans for the air conditioning companies. While he was working one day he started reminiscing about the time after he first bought into his sheet metal business. He said, "I hadn't been in business for two weeks when the Sheriff came by and had a little talk with me. He punched his finger on ma chest and said, 'I'm watchin' you, Robert. If you start makin' whiskey stills, I'm comin' here and takin' you to jail.' It scared me so bad it was six weeks before I made my first still." I ain't makin' this one up either. It proves the adage: the best way to make people fish is to put up a "NO FISHING" sign. I'm not sure Robert even thought about it until then. He further related that the way he did it was make a copper funnel, wait a month and get that sold; then make the bottom or copper cooling coil and sell it, etc. Apparently he was never caught with a complete still.)

Saucy: to be colorful, opinionated or outspoken, as in, "She's a purty gal, but Saucy! I wanna tell ya!" Another meaning is to be full of meanness, vindictiveness, venom, irritation, aggression or anger. "Just 'cause I borried yer saddle, don't mean you need to git all saucy about it." (See "venomous.")

Scrub chicken: a term referring to fried or cooked Gopher tortoise, now considered an endangered species.

Scrub cattle: descendants of the old wild Spanish cattle, also called *Criollo* (pronounced, *cree-yoyo*) or *Andalusian* cattle and refers to a type of cattle with characteristics similar to the original wild cattle in Florida. These cattle were smaller than modern breeds. Some herds still have a trace of these bloodlines, but most of the characteristics and color patterns have disappeared. The Florida Seminoles, and probably other native Florida tribes, herded the scrub cattle left or lost by the Spaniards, starting 300-500 years ago. Synonyms include "woods cattle," native" or "Cracker cattle."

Settin' on my assets: a term made locally famous by Finis Harne of Wauchula, Florida. Finis (We pronounced it as "*Fine'-us*.") was a true Cracker cowboy, bowlegged and rough around the edges, but a finer man cannot be easily found. He was the kind of man that would stop in the middle of the road to talk with you. He was a horseman as well and reared some fine working colts. When Finis retired many years ago, we happened to cross paths. He was wearing a new off-white Stetson and smoking a long cigar. I greeted him, "Hey, Finis, how'er you doin'?" He grinned, puffed and rolled his cigar, then said, "Oh, Doc, I'm justa settin' on mah assets." Boy, I miss Finis. He was a good man. There was none better at keeping bad bulls or cows off your back in the pens.

Speaking of assets, I heard a Cracker cattlemen say, "We don't make any money in tha cattle bidness but we make it up on volume." (Think about it.)

Set in tha gates: an expression I've heard only a few times. The context was my step-father bragging on my mother. She'd done something that was thoughtful and helpful for us and he commented, "I think I'll go set in tha gates an' brag on you to tha elders." We laughed when we realized he was using an Old Testament reference to the elders of Israel who would sit in the gates of the city and judge issues. I use it but have never heard anyone else say this expression. (By the way, my wife likes it when I say it—it's right up there with "I wooden take a million dollars for that woman." See term)

Shakin' (tremblin' or quiverin') lik' ah dog passin' ah peach seed: a descriptive phrase connoting nervousness or anxiety, and which originates from the observation of a dog vigorously and continuously straining to pass some obstructing foreign object from the colon.

In a book entitled, *Totch–A Life in the Everglades*, Totch Brown, a true Cracker, tells of life in the Ten Thousand Islands of lower west coast Florida. In one tale he relates how an odd-behaving panther followed him and three other terrified fishermen. He wrote, "The panther let out a bloodcurdling squall." As they knew this tenacious and constantly growling cat was trailing them, they rowed away from their net with Totch holding a window-weight that was used for an anchor. He wrote, "While Bert paddled from the bow, I had the window weight in my hand ready for action, but the action probably wouldn't have amounted to much because the cat had me shaking like a dog passing a peach seed."

Yes, in fact dogs do eat peaches. One of my neighbors moved to Highlands County from Atlanta. Six weeks after the relocation she asked me to look at her Boston Bull Dog. Her complaint was her dog wasn't able to eat without vomiting. We recovered six charcoal-black peach seeds. We know the dog had them lodged in the stomach for six weeks (or more), 'cause there weren't any peach trees in Highlands County.

Sharp-shooters: a Cracker reference to biting horse flies. The vicious little things can fog out of the grass in certain places and worry a horse and rider to death. Sharp-shooters and mosquitoes can drive cattle out of an area. Cattle will sometimes move into or under brush, myrtles, Cabbage Palms, etc. to scratch these tenacious biters off their bodies. I am not sure but it could also be synonymous with "deer flies." All I know is the dang things hurt when they bite.

She's down, Doc… she ain't goin' nowher': this phrase comes under "Famous last words." Many, many times Cracker ranchers and small farmers would find a cow down in a pasture trying to have a calf; sometimes it was sick, but for whatever reason she was reluctant to get up and run away. I'd get calls to come "look at 'er 'cause she needs help" and I would automatically say, "Get her in the trap or caught and I'll be there in thirty- to forty-five minutes." I'd hear the famous last words, "She's down, Doc; she ain't goin' nowher'." For some reason, upon my arrival–whether it was just me, the car, the commotion, astrology or the crowd that gathered to watch or for other unknown reasons–a good many of these downer cows would find a miraculous burst of strength and pull out for the woods. I finally got wise to the behavior and I'd say, "Y'all get a rope on 'er an' tie her down so she can't pull out. Whin you get 'er caught or in tha trap, call me back an' I'll come on." (See "trap")

Cows aren't dumb; like horses, they think differently and act instinctively. When I was on the staff at Auburn we had to care for paralyzed dairy and beef cows. It was a chore at times because they often didn't respond to lifting and care. We had a device that could be attached to the wings of the pelvis, clamped on and fastened to a hoist. In this way we could lift a 1500-pound cow to relieve the pressure on massive muscles. Like elephants, large animals don't tolerate being down because of muscle damage.

This was done two to three times a day when we'd take them fresh feed and water. We had a particular dairy cow that just didn't seem to respond. After ten days in this condition it was usually a hopeless effort.

The students made regular "barn checks" at 9:00 pm, midnight, 3:00am and 6:00am. Critical cases were given constant monitoring–all others were checked for anything out of the ordinary. One of the students came into my office at 8:00 am and said, "You know that old downer cow we have been lifting for the last week?"

"Yes, what about her," I said.

He said, "Well, I happened to peek at her on the 3:00 barn-check; she was up and eating hay–but the second she saw me she laid down."

She was fine. We figured the old gal thought when she laid down someone would bring her fresh feed and water. (I knew a fella who said his grandmother was like that. He expressed it as, "She kinda enjoys poor health.")

Shire-down: a slang word for "shower-down," meaning to speed up or push harder. For example, when pulling a heavy load, one might be instructed, "Whin you hit that soft place in tha pasture, you better shire-down on it or you'll never make it through." This meant you should mash the accelerator to gain speed before hitting the slick area to keep the momentum of the equipment and not get stuck. "Pour tha coal toit" is a synonym. (See "bog")

Show 'er tha gate: a directive to someone controlling a parting gate to open it and get a cow's attention to an escape route. She would head for the opening to move into the selected pen.

Shuck, shuck off or shucked out of: to remove an outer layer of garments. "We shucked off our clothes an' hit the water," is an example. On hunting trips lasting several days Crackers would sometimes take a bath or go swimming on or near the last days. One might say, "I need to take a bath or go to town an' git a wildlife permit to keep ah Buffalo."

One of the meanest things I remember about this was a story told by Hubert Waldron. He said all the boys shucked off their clothes and went swimming. It was uneventful until it came time to dress. One of the men bent over to pull his britches up as someone behind him threw a handful of muddy sand and muck on his behind. After colorful remarks and laughs, the fella, shucked his clothes again and returned to the water.

"To git pulled out tha shuck" refers to an old expression related to de-husking corn on the cob. It figuratively meant to be taken advantage of, pulled down a notch, dressed down, beat up or corrected by a superior.

Shaugh, you ain't nuthin: a fondly teasing phrase that contradicts what is evident. I first heard it used by my Irish grandmother in Kentucky, when I appeared with my hair combed and slicked down, in a white starched shirt, with sleeves sticking out like little sails over my skinny arms. She'd say, "Shaugh, you ain't nuthin'." She knew I knew I looked nice; this was her way of telling me so. I used it a lot, especially when someone had put forth a great effort.

SHOE-ou-OU-U-tee: though somewhat difficult to explain, pronunciation and inflection are critical to the proper use of "shoot-tee." Using larger letter to indicate higher inflection, proper usage should be something like: "Well, SHOE-ou-OU-U-tee! I wish y'all'd look at that." It was an emphatic drawn out variation of the exclamation, "Shoot!"

Side tha cattle or side'um: a slang term directing a rider to place his horse beside a herd to keep them moving in a desired direction. Cows react predictably to a horse and rider. If a rider puts his horse directly behind a cow, she'll veer off to one side or the other to keep the rider in view because she can't see directly behind her. A running horse, for the same reason, will hold his head high and turn it slightly to watch something behind him.

Sidled: the term used to describe the oblique approach of one individual to another, as in, "Yeah, he sidled up next to me, said he wanted to take the day off and could he borrow $10 for gas money." Often this word indicated guile or shame.

Sillykick or silly kicked: to be kicked by a cow, horse or man and be rendered semi-conscious. (See "roachkilt") The best example I've ever heard of is a true story about a local dairyman, named Nick Bishop. There was notorious, Ol' Number 1098 that was meaner than a snake. She was a big cow and seemed to relish intimidating people. The cows were milked and then turned out into the feed barn for grain feed before being let out to pasture. They stuck their heads into stanchions or holding devices which served to keep them immobile. Treatments and vaccinations were done while the cows ate. In order to get to the feed the cows put their head into open head catches, which locked as they lowered their heads to eat.

Ol', Number 1098 was a killer cow. She could rearrange various body parts on unsuspecting souls with cobra-swift kicks. She'd ease her head up, get the windage and range to target, make adjustments for trajectory and earth rotation and, especially if you were not paying attention, deliver a kick that would "knock the taste outta your mouth."

On the day in question the manager, Nick Bishop, wasn't paying attention as he came down the line of cows. She knew it and nailed him right on the knee cap with a sillykick. "WHAP!" It sounded like a baseball bat hitting a country ham. Nick was flung back to the fence behind the cows. He bent over in severe pain, holding his knee and grimacing. After a bit, when he had caught his breath, he awkwardly straightened his body, hobbled up behind 1098 (out of range, of course) and, with a weak little-old-lady-on-her-death-bed soft-broken voice he wheezed, "Heh... heh... is that the best you can do?"

Cracker Terms, Phrases And Definitions

Sired: soured, spoiled, rotten or deteriorated. This slang has nothing to do with the breeding of animals; the word was frequently used as a synonym for spoilage, etc. One of the best examples occurred near Lake Placid, Florida, when my partner was called to do an autopsy at the Westby Ranch just west of town. Leonard Godwin had found a dead cow in the pasture and was concerned about the cause of death and whether it was a contagious herd issue. He called Handley to do the necropsy. They drove up, Frank got out his gear: rib cutters, autopsy knife and sample bottles with formalin for tissue specimens. He said he suspected the cow had been dead too long. As they walked up beside the carcass, he thumped the rib cage with the rib cutters. Out ran two fat possums from a hole in the abdomen. Frank grinned and said, "Leonard, I believe she's sired... we're wastin' our time here." So they went to the house and drank coffee.

Sitin' in: vernacular of "sighting in" as in sighting in one's rifle. There are various ways to accomplish this. Most of the time, the shooter will rest the barrel of his rifle on a solid object, a truck hood, a table or tree.

You'll hear phrases like, "How much you reckon tha bullet will drop in 400 yards?" or "Should we salt the bullet so the meat won't spoil by tha time we git to 'im?" The phrase can be used in a modified form in a figurative manner, "Son, whin he met her, he set his sites on her right then and ther'." Obviously, this does not refer to shooting at the woman; it means he was interested in pursuing a relationship.

A similar term "in the crosshairs" is an expression of literal sighting-in on an animal, "I had 'im right in my crosshairs and missed; I reckon my sites are off," (See "lob shot") or as a figure of speech, "I musta knocked my sites off" is an acceptable excuse for missing a shot by reason of the disturbed seating of his rifle scope. It is therefore, is a logical justification for the missed shot.

Skinnier'ern ah earthworm with his guts slung out: this phrase is used only to indicate thinness, debilitation, gauntness, puniness, emaciated body condition or the conclusion of inspection of a creature, usually bovine. "That calf is skinnier than a earthworm with his guts slung out." "Earthworm" and "night-crawler" are often used interchangeably.

Smartest dog: for example: A Florida man drove his fine truck to the local 7-11 Mini-Mart. He parked in front of the doors and got out, leaving his dog in the front seat. The dog was alert and interested in what his master was doing (after all, there might be a rat killin' fixin'ta break loose). It put its front feet on the dash and perked its ears in rapt attention. The truck model, a Ford 150, had an automatic light turn-off feature where the lights would turn off after a few minutes. As the man passed the counter the clerk said, "Sir, Sir, you leff your lights on!" (All he could see was the dog looking intently his way.)

The driver didn't pause, or even look his way, "Aw, tha dog'll turn 'um off."

The confused clerk glanced at the truck from time to time, and, sure enough, after several seconds the truck lights went out.

The man was approaching the counter just then when the amazed clerk pointed toward the truck, "Sir, that's the smartest dog I ever saw!"

Smellin' like a barbershop: a phrase describing a man who had recently attended the aforementioned establishment. The barbers used to apply Tiger Lily, Vitalis or some other odiferous hair tonic to the freshly cut hair and comb it down "tighter than a duck's wing." "Smellin' like a lily" means almost the same thing. Many of the old time barbers had a mantra of sorts when they finished the haircut and removed the apron from the customer, "Tell'um wher' you got it, boy." (I guess they wanted a little free advertising.)

Cracker Terms, Phrases And Definitions

I am reminded of the Cracker boy that enlisted in the Air Force. He had no particular skills so he was made a barber (After all, what kind of skill does it take to skin all the heads of the new recruits?) Pretty soon he was promoted to Airman 2nd and moved to another base. By this time he had become somewhat skilled at his job.

One day the Base Commander came in, settled in the chair and dosed off as the anxious Airman gave him the weekly regulation officer's trim. Airman noticed there was a prolific amount of nose hairs showing from the Colonel's nose. So, wanting to be helpful, he took the electric clippers and buzzed into the hairs thicker'n the weeds in a June garden. It must have felt like a bumblebee going up his nose because the Colonel jumped straight up and in no uncertain terms voiced his opinion of the Airman, his clippers, his future and even his mother. (That was the last time the Airman tried to go above and beyond the call of duty.)

Snub: to pull close to or near, to make something snug, to restrain, to tie up, etc. When a horse was "actin' ugly" it was often offered, "Why don't we snub 'im to a post?"

Snuff money: a small amount of money set aside for minor purchases or weekly needs. Susie Glass (mentioned under "Cans ya see my finances?") introduced it to us. Suzie rarely needed her full pay check since her position included room and board, so she asked my step-father to keep her money until she needed it. For a few weeks after Susie started work at the ranch, she didn't draw any money, but one Friday, after pay checks were distributed to all employees, Susie came to my step-father and announced, "Mr. Williams, I needs sum snuff money; let me hav' $30." It was often heard on Fridays, "Suzie, you gonna need some snuff money this week?" Sometimes she'd respond, "Naw, Mr. Williams, I gots plenty of snuff this week." The term caught on and became part of our family's vocabulary.

So, if I have it right, the royalty checks I receive from sales of this and my other books, I can correctly say, "They keeps me in snuff money..." (I didn't realize the influence Susie still had on my vocabulary from fifty years back. Incidentally, Susie never got it right the whole time she worked at the ranch. She always said "Williams" for "Williamson.")

So sore ya cain't touch it with a powder puff: an obvious reference to the tenderness of an injured part of the anatomy. For example, one of the crew happened to be run over by a bull in the pens and the next day showed up limping badly. A buddy asked how his leg was feeling. He replied, "Man... it's so sore you cain't touch it with a powder puff."

Soak ma feet in cold water: refers to the old treatment for an acute foot problem in horses. The inner sensitive layers of the horse's hoof, where the horny hoof is attached, become inflamed due to toxic compounds produced from over-eating grain, lush grasses or other problems. Severe founder could actually cause the loss of the horse's hoof. It is generally related to some imbalanced body chemistry, injury, infection or absorbed toxins. The old Crackers would take a sore-footed horse and stand him in a creek or simply spray the front feet with cold tap water at the first sign of lameness—especially if it had over-eaten grain, worked extremely hard or for any reason where the horse got rapidly sore in both front feet. So, in order to make light of being full or to complement a cook, one might say, "Boys, we'll hav to stand in cold water befor' we slough our toenails."

Sold! An exclamation at an auction indicating buyer will accept the offered price or trade. It comes from the livestock market auctioneers as they call bidding to a halt, indicating the last bidder won the bid. I heard a tale about two Crackers that worked a particularly successful sales plan. One of them had an old fashioned hearing aid. It was the kind that had a battery about the size of pack of cigarettes and was carried in the front shirt pocket. It had an ugly wire running up to the inserted earplug. You couldn't miss seeing it. Well, it seems

Cracker Terms, Phrases And Definitions

the one wearing the hearing aid always worked the main floor while the other would work up in a balcony showroom. They had couches, soft easy chairs and other nice stuff–both up- and downstairs. The man with the hearing aid would go over to help the customers. The price tags were purposely left off so he would have to ask his "boss" upstairs. When someone was interested in a couch, for example, he would diligently look all over it for the price tag. Not finding one, he'd holler up stairs, "Hey, Roy! How much is this couch?" His cohort would holler back, "$950." The hearing aid "artist" would tap his battery, adjust it a little and say, "The boss said, '$550'." This was followed many times with an eager customer saying, "Sold!"

SON! Son! or son: often used as an exclamation, before a comment, as in: "SON! That's the biggest gator I ever saw!" or, as in one word of amazement, 'SON!" It could be used in a question, "Son? What in the ham fat are you doin'?" Also, "son" could be used when there was puzzlement, "Look how tha rope is all knotted, son," or simply, "son…" when observing a curiosity in disgust or awestruck amazement. Inflection had everything to do with its intended use. In California, especially among the surfer society, the word "Dude" or "dude…" is interchangeable with "Son" and "son." Using the above examples it would be "Hey Dude! Where did you get the rad surf board?" Or as, "DUDE! Put some clothes on…", "Dude… that's gnarley…", "Dude?", meaning "What are you doing?" or simply, "Dude…" meaning don't do that, stop, or "Dude." meaning "Hey, howzitgoin'?."

A perfect example of the use of "Son!" occurred with David Schock, my "UAS" (my Unofficially Adopted Son). In his early days at a summer job, as already referenced under "Desperation," David frequently traveled in a raggedy Datsun-like pickup truck from Avon Park to Okeechobee. There was a fish processing operation where he'd pick up frozen fish parts left over, transport them to Avon Park and transfer these fifty-pound blocks to a freezer on an alligator farm. As needed, he'd thaw some of the blocks, grind them to smaller parts and feed the alligators. The use of the term occurred when he was returning from Okeechobee and was stopped by a Florida State Trooper for a non-functioning tail light. The trooper approached the vehicle, swatted in front of his face and said, "Sir, I stopped you for having only one tail light." He paused, looked back at the tarpaulin over the blocks of fish, tried to worry the smell away and asked, "What are you carrying?" David replied, "Fish guts...." The trooper said, "Son! I wus gonna give you a ticket but I can't stand tha smell! Get out of here and get your tail light fixed!"

There was a man that smarted off to a trooper one occasion when he was stopped. As the trooper approached the window, he rolled it down and said, "Whut'd you stop me for, I ain't got no donuts?" (With that amusing phrase, he won a night in the local jail.)

Sounds like ah warble fly: a phrase from the book *All Creatures Great and Small.* In it James Herriot told of an experience when a farmer was trying to get young wild heifers into a pen for vaccinations. Dr. Herriot said all the neighbors came to help. The heifers weren't cooperating. One neighbor suggested that he could get the services of a young man living near the farm. "He can make a sound like a warble fly—that might get the heifers to move into the pens." (Warble flies pierce the skin on the back of cattle and deposit eggs which develop into larvae. The hide is damaged by the larvae when the larvae hatch and leave a hole. Apparently the adult warble fly of the English variety makes a unique sound.) The group secured the services of the lad and sure enough the heifers ran from the sounds emanating from his mouth. Dr. Herriot commented, "He seems like a handy fellow to have around." "Yes", replied one of the men, "but that's about all he can do." (I know this has nothing to do with the theme of the book but I am sure I have met some of that young man's kinfolk in South Florida. If you hear the phrase, "Yeah, but that's about all he can do," I was probably the one that started it there.)

Sounded lik' a cork comin' out a jug: a "pop" or "fum-m." I had an emergency call years ago that was memorable. We had an aggressive young veterinarian on what is called "preceptorship." He was really excited about his first delivery. I went along to guide and keep the owner happy. (They didn't particularly like new-comers.) We arrived at the little ranch which had a shallow lake with a pine thicket around it. The Angus cow was running loose, which is always a thrill. She was obviously in labor, stopping to strain the baby out. We got lucky on that one and caught her on a rope in the pines. Many cows amazed me because they were docile at the moment of delivery. However, after delivery–they'll catch anyone standing around the calf.

We had her tied to a fence post and the young doctor was trying to put obstetrical chains on the calf's leg so we could apply traction. I felt the calf's head–he was coming fast. We'd made the trip and I knew we'd not get paid if we didn't produce some expert care. I told young doctor, "Hurry up... she's about to calve." He fumbled around a little longer and I was having a devil of a time holding the calf inside the cow. Finally, he had the O.B. (obstetrical) chains in place and the calf fell out with just a little light tug. Everything was fine. We went back to the hospital. Dr. Handley asked how it went. I said, "I held it back as long as I could and when Gregg pulled on the chains it sounded like a cork comin' out of a jug..." (We used the phrase to describe delivering puppies or kittens as well. It always made someone smile.)

Sounds lik' ah dirt dauber in ah beer can: a high-pitched, whining sound made by dirt daubers in a..., well, a tin can. It was very descriptive and evoked smiles when properly said.

For example, a small motorcycle makes that high-pitched buzz at high rpms, and as it goes by, you might hear, "He com' by here, soundin' lik' ah dirt dauber in a beer can."

Our son, David, worked in London, England, a couple of years. He once used the phrase among a covey of Brits. He said they were totally lost in its meaning, being stunned into fishy-eyed silence. Maybe it would have been more appropriate to use "warble fly." (One can substitute "fruit jar," "tin can" or "mail box" for "beer can.")

Sow Coon: I remember a true story about an Okeechobee Cracker listening to the radio. There was a vivid description of the damage done by a cyclone, which in those days was often interchanged with words like typhoon, hurricane, tornado or twister. After listening to the graphic description and turning off the radio, he commented, "Them damn sow coons are rank, ain't they?"

Split tha blanket: to separate, divorce or part company, as in: "Yeah, they split tha blanket 'bout three months ago."

Squashed and squished: We had a considerable discussion about the use of this word. Someone had squashed a bug on his arm. Another corrected him and said, "You should have used 'squished.'" To settle the argument, one of our cow crew, Partner, was elected as arbitrator of this serious application. He allowed, after deliberation, "Well, you ate 'squash', so 'squished' is the best word for what you do to a bug." That seemed to meet with everyone's approval and resolved the dispute.

Squawl: to yell, holler or call out. Panthers, Bob Cats, dying rabbits, tom cats, and such can squall. My mama could squawl when it was time to eat dinner.

Stall sour: "cabin fever", as in, "Girl, yer mama is plum stall sour. I got to take her to town." "Stall sour" comes from observations of horses kept in close confinement for too long. They get saucy from inactivity. It's similar to the conditions of college students after studying three solid days for final examinations or when someone is in the hospital for a protracted period of time. In that instance, I include here a comment I heard from a Cracker. "If my wife is ever in intensive care on her death-bed, I'm gonna go in, pat her on

Cracker Terms, Phrases And Definitions

the wrist and say, 'Honey... how about going out for dinner?' That'd get her up for sure!"

From this, I am reminded of the tale told many years ago about a minister under an oxygen tent. Tubes ran here and there into his body and a soft beep of an ECG could be heard in the background. The head Deacon approached his bed quietly, slipped his hand under the tent and patted the old minister on the hand, waking him. He then said, "Brother, you'll be delighted to hear that tha Deacons voted six to four in favor of prayin' for yer recovery."

Standin' around: a phrase usually coupled with a qualifier, indicating wasting time. "Whut 'er y'all standin' around for; we got cattle to work." Or, "No need for all of us standin' around; some of you go get more cows." Other variations indicate that one was inactive, as in, "Well, ther' I wuz, jus' standin' around, mindin' my own business whin she came by an' hollered at me."

A perfect example occurred when a bunch of us green vet students went on our first farm call. The clinician was a mean character; he didn't like people anyway and was noted for his ill temper. He shouted at us, "Whut'er you standin' around for? Do sumthin'—even if it's wrong!" (We did and it was.)

Statue, Myrtle: a quirky contraction of, "Is that you, Myrtle?" Sonny often said that to me or someone who came in the shop before he could identify them. I'd walk in and hear from the back office, "Statue, Myrtle?" I think he got it from a Cary Grant movie from the forties–why he used it, I don't know. It did work well, however. I was so impressed with the name I used it for a dog once.

I heard that there is another phrase, "Halo statue?" which is used when answering the phone near New Orleans, meaning, "Hello, is that you?" (The same people holler out the windows there, "Lou-EE, wher' yat?" meaning, "Louis, where are you?")

Stepped init: to make a bad decision or a colossal mistake and have an unexpected and unwanted result. It came from the cow pens in Florida and farms everywhere else. It refers to the soiling of one's boots (or any footwear) by stepping in manure. When used figuratively, it is used as kidding. "Boy, whin you bought that gal a ring, you reely stepped init," could mean that the fella had no idea the repercussions of his action. Synonym phrases are, "fouled yer nest," "got a bull by tha tail," "it was Katy barred tha door," "that ended 'er up" or "it wuz all over but tha shoutin,'" etc. (See the terms)

I am reminded of a Harvard graduate who was running for high office against an uneducated and rather "rough around the edges" opponent in a mid-western state. The Harvard man hired a video company to make a television promotion showing him walking among cattle in a farm lot while having that far-away look at the horizons. The idea was to give the impression that a Harvard man was a truly exceptional man of vision. The opponent responded by questioning the Harvard man's qualifications, "since anybody ought to know a fella ought to look down at the ground when he's walkin' in the cow pens." Because of the rebuttal, the Harvard man lost the election. In a way, "he stepped init, didden he?"

Stirup, stirout or stirrum: "Get up out of bed and get to work!" as in, "What time y'all gonna stirrup?" "Oh, 'bout daylite." A variation of this term is "stirout"; to "stir out." "Y'all go by the bunk house and stirout the crew." "Ther's so miny dogs here, you cain't stirum withah stick." When referring to cattle it would be used as in, "Alrite, I want y'all to stirum out tha hammocks and take em to tha marsh."

An item or event can "stirup" memories. For example, I recall an interview with C. Everett Koop, a former U. S. Surgeon General, in regard to the activities of the elderly. Dr. Koop said that many falls of the aged were simply from moving too fast. One of the most dangerous times for them was upon rising from bed (i.e., stirrin' outta the sack too quick). He described the proper way for the aged to rise. Firstly, the

Cracker Terms, Phrases And Definitions

he or she should put one leg out toward the floor. Rotate the body a little so the other leg could be moved toward the floor. Then, rolling to one's side, one should slowly push his body upright away from the mattress. In this way, the back is protected from stress and strain. When the upper body is upright the older person should sit on the side of the bed for several moments and allow all the systems to adjust to the up-right position. By doing so, the blood pressure increases safely and the balance mechanism is stabilized. Lastly, with feet squarely placed on the floor, one should ease his upper body out over the feet and legs and put his center of gravity over his feet. Then by slowly straightening the body and using the legs to push upright, one should stand for a moment close to the bed to establish good balance before taking a step. He allowed that taking one's time will avoid many accidental falls.

I listened to this whole commentary about rising from bed and commented to my wife, "Shoot, I been doin' it that way since I wuz ten years old." (This sure stirsup a lot of memories for me....)

Stomped: to be pummeled, rolled, stepped on, pinched, thrashed, pounded, walloped, beat, bashed or punched. The term was usually combined: "cow-, bull- or horse-stomped" It could refer to a fist fight that ended in a decided victory of the "stomper." In that case, the "stompee" lost the fight. Some calls to the clinic were relayed to me as, "Clarence said a bull stomped his dog and he's bringin' him in." In that case, there was usually a broken leg. What always amazed me is that these "stomped on" dogs kept trying to work and would often hobble three-legged for the whole day. But most cowboys put them on a trailer or in a pen until the day's work was finished.

Dr. Handley, many years ago, had a small pen behind his hospital with an open lock lying at the door. Cowboys would call and say they had a stomped on cow dog. He'd ask, "When did it happen?" They'd often reply, "Early this morning."

He'd then say, "Take him down to the hospital, stick 'im in the cage out back an' lock it up. I'll check him first thing at daylight and let ya know." It worked like a charm. This practice wouldn't work all that well today, but at that time, in that culture, nobody minded because they knew he was a hard man to "catch" because of his schedule.

I know of a veterinarian out west who went to the same café every morning before daylight. He'd sit at his regular table, have breakfast, read journals, do book work, etc. There would be anywhere from one to four people at the counter. They'd drink coffee and at the stroke of 6:00 am, they'd line up to speak to him. He'd "hold court" with them and schedule a trip to the different ranches or farms. It was commonly understood he had an hour from 5:00 to 6:00 am and was not to be disturbed.

Studyin' on it: to think about, consider, figure, reckon, analyze, ponder, examine or calculate. "Whut are we gonna do about tha yearlings?" "I been studyin' on it an' I think we ought to gather 'um an' move 'em to the north pasture where ther's more grass." If a man was sitting quietly and looking pensive, another might ask, "Whut 'er you studyin' so about?"

Suckback: refers to a cow, bull or calf that stops, changes direction and returns to the herd or pen from which it came. It was sometimes used to identify a group, as in, "There's a whole pen full of suckbacks over there." Or, "She jus' suckback into the swamp whin she saw me." The classic picture of a "suck-back" was in the National Geographic magazine. There is a baboon "sucking back" from a cheetah. Frozen in photographic time, the picture shows a wall-eyed cheetah closing for the kill with a bare toothed baboon facing him and "sucking back," abruptly changing direction. This picture was a true example of "a suckback."

Sull: to show a stubborn or sullen attitude. We used the word mostly with Brahma cattle that would go down in the chute and make no attempt to move. It appeared as if they'd had enough of the confusion and noise and would just lie down on their bellies–right in the middle of the activities. They'd lower their heads and low when approached. They were reluctant to move or to respond to prodding. Sometimes the dogs would intimidate them.

A question from the back of the pens, "Whut's the hold up?"

Answer, "Aw, we got a cow that's sulled in the catch chute. I guess we'll have to build a fire under her sumhow." The best thing we could do was just take a water break and wait for her see the open gate. Eventually, she'd take a notion to try for it and leave. A sick or thin cow wouldn't have any reserve energy and would sull easily from too much stress. Usually, they'd quit prodding her, swing a gate open and say something to attract her attention. In the absence of other distractions she would eventually decide to get up and go.

The term could be used for a description of a man who was upset and acting stubbornly. "Yeah, ol' Henry wuz sulled whin he cum to work. I don't know whut ails him." Or, one could use it referring to his wife, as in, "We was ready to go whin she sulled. I don't know whut I did or said that upset her."

Sumbody send out fer soup an' sandwiches: indicates that there is a problem which will cause a prolonged delay in work. I often used it when the cattle broke out and headed for the woods. Knowing everyone was frustrated at the wreck, I'd say it to lighten up the atmosphere, indicating I would stay til we finished. It usually caused a grin or two. The phrase was similar to, "Since we're gonna be here a while, sumbody start a fire, we need to build a pot of coffee."

Sumtimes I think '"Well…" The complete phrase is best used as a nonsense phrase when one really doesn't know what to say. For example, I used it when things were really slow, while everyone was pondering a breakdown in the routine or in a piece of equipment. It might be very quiet while the men thought about the problem. I would off-handly say,

"Sumtimes I think, 'Well,'" then after a few seconds' pause, I'd finish with, "But then agin, I just don't know."

(See "I don't unnerstan' all I know about it." Same idea.)

Swamp angels: an old time Cracker's synonym for mosquitoes or "skeeters." (See "gallonippers.")

Sweet-faced cows: this term was used when my two nine-year-old nephews were discussing how to tell the difference between cows and bulls. They were riding on the tail gate of the jeep. David, who was visiting, asked Wes, "How do ya tell tha cows frum tha bulls?" Wes replied in an authoritative manner, "Well, the cows hav sweet faces and tha bulls don't… but you gotta watch out 'cause sumtimes tha sweet-faced cows will catch ya."

Sweetheart gate: a type of pasture gate that requires a hugging action to open or close. It consists of two posts strung with barbed wire, like a fence, and, if necessary, a center post to hold up the wire. There is a post at both sides of the gate panel. One side is secured to the anchored end of the fence post. The loose end is held in place by heavy wires attached to the top and base of the other end fence post. To open the gate, you release the top wire by slipping an arm through the wires at the top of the gate, grabbing the fence post and snugging them together, causing slack in the top loop of the gate. This allows you to lift the loop and release the gate post. Then all you have to do is lift the bottom of the gate post out of the bottom holding wire and pull the gate clear for passage.

But, when you put it back together, if you are careless, the top loop will pinch the fire out of the skin on your hugging shoulder. Then, the "sweetheart" name is exchanged for a less kind word.

Sygoggled: in the ancient Gaelic languages: an offset, twisted, nonfunctional or useless article used in construction or it can be used to describe some peculiar or deviated part of a whole functioning piece of equipment, as in, "Well here's the problem, tha thingamabob is sygoggled."

Rare, ancient: as in, "That boy's *attitude* is plum sygoggled," meaning weird or unconventional. "Weird" is often pronounced, "wired' in Cracker, as in: "Son, he's wired."

T

Tail'er up: a method of assisting a cow, bull or horse in rising from a prone position. It is simple in theory: when a weakened downer animal (see term) starts to rise but has a hitch in its "gitalong" (see term) cowboys will get behind the animal and pull its tail up to give it added traction. In general, the larger the animal the more critical it is for them to be standing. For example, a 1500 pound bull or cow lying on a hard surface for any length of time gets muscle damage. Illness, debilitation or injury causing a prolonged recumbence begins to take a toll on the strength of the animal. In other words, the initial problem gets worse due to muscle damage. Elephants, for example, must rise quickly due to their massive body weight. A dairy cow lying on concrete will get into real trouble if allowed to remain there for too long.

The technique of "tailing up" is based on a species characteristic: cattle get up by raising the rear end first, which appears to be a temporary kneeling position, and then they push up the front end. This fostered the old myth that cows pray at night. People would enter the shelters and find some cows in the middle of standing up and got the false idea. It was a middle age fable that cows pray at midnight on Christmas Eve. Sure enough, you go in the stall at midnight on Christmas Eve (or any night) and there she was, praying. Horses, on the other hand, push the front end up first, followed by a controlled lurch of the rear legs to bring up that end.

Speaking of tailin' up, I had a memorable situation happen to me. As a Resident in Dairy Medicine and Surgery at Auburn

University, my job included emergency surgery. We had a huge dairy heifer come into the Large Animal Clinic with a tremendous calf that she could not deliver. She'd been in labor for nearly two hours and this is a critical time for obtaining a live calf. (The calf weighed 114 pounds. I remember 'cause I won the lottery.) We performed a Caesarean section on a hydraulic surgery table, which would rotate from an upright vertical (perpendicular) to a flat horizontal surface. We walked the heifer up beside the table, strapped her to it, and rotated the table to horizontal which allowed us work at her side rather than on the floor.

The surgery room was large with the massive surgery table near one wall. In the corner was a storage room about eight by twelve feet. It stored supplies and had a little ramp into the door so equipment could be rolled out as needed. There were some eight students standing by, one assisting in the surgery, one on anesthesia, and three to attend the 114-pound calf. The surgery was uneventful. When we were ready to release the cow, we rotated the table up so the heifer was in a standing position. With a quick release of the restraints, she was on her feet and looking around at the unfamiliar surroundings. Generally, dairy cows are not haltered but are easily driven by gentle prodding. The heifer walked off, a little weak from the epidural, and went for the first exit she saw—the door to the no-exit storeroom. As she started up the gentle incline ramp, her back feet slipped on the wet concrete and she started to do the splits in her back legs. This is serious in a large cow and causes nerve and hip joint damage. I raced in and grabbed her tail to support her and "tailed'er up." But I, too, slipped on the slick surface, right under her back end and she "sat" on me. My face was directly under the base of her tail and all the associated structures found there. On my chest was a Dolly Partin udder probably weighing about 75 pounds. The students were frozen in shock or fear or fascination. The heifer made an effort to rise by pulling her back legs in to get a new grip in her effort to stand. The students woke up, ran in and tailed her up as I crawled out from under her massive udder. Amid grins and stifled snorts of laughter, I repeated the mantra of the dairyman concerning success in milk production, "Men, always protect the udders." She stood easily and proceeded to the main door.

We marveled at how a million-dollar dairy would hire a high school drop-out to handle the most important structure on the dairy cow; thus our teaching: "Protect those udders."

Despite the laughter and teasing I would have to live with for the next few days, I had the warm feeling that came from knowing I'd just demonstrated that very important principle, however accidental it might have seemed.

Take a deep seat an' ah faraway look: a rodeo phrase where a rider is preparing to be released from the chute for a bucking horse ride. It was used in circumstances where there would be challenging circumstances. It could be used as a warning, as in, "Whin that butt-headed bull gets to tha pens, y'all take a deep seat and a faraway look 'cause he'll butt everythin' in sight." It could be used in other settings. "I wuz sittin' there in tha lawyer's office, an' whin he got started on all tha legal stuff, I just took a deep seat an' ah faraway look."

Take my bidness summers else: obvious reaction to dissatisfaction with tendered services. The first time I understood the phrase was when a story circulated about an old Cracker who used to call Dr. Handley. He would call whin he got in at dark and discovered some problem that occurred earlier that day or even days before. Well, Handley would go tend to the affected horse or cow dog until it was obvious that he'd never get paid for anything. This went on for a year or two–until the accumulated bill for all the night and weekend service was out of sight. Finally Handley just quit going to the man's place at all hours to give free veterinary service. He said he thought the other veterinarians in the area ought to get a taste of the fella and help carry the load. He'd just tell him, "Sorry, Sol, I cain't come." Well, the word spread that when ol' Sol was in the feed store one Saturday morning, he made a big fuss about Handley not coming out to treat his horses at night anymore. He said, "I swear, if Handley don't start comin' out to my place anymore, I'm gonna take my bidness summers else."

This became imbedded somewhere in the dark halls of my mind until one day it slipped out. Dr. Bill Manint of Highlands County was a respected and capable optometrist and cared for me for years. Unlike Sol, I paid him.

But one day a funny thing happened. When Dr. Manint had glasses cases that had not sold for a considerable time, he'd put them in a basket with a sign advertising they were free to anyone who needed them. Well, after my visit, I saw them and selected a fine leather case for my sun glasses. Time went on. A year or so later, the stitching came loose and they became unusable. I happened to be in for my annual exam and I thought I'd have some fun. So I grabbed the old, wore out case and went to the counter. I said, "This free glasses case is fallin' apart–if y'all don't start givin' away a better quality stuff, I'm gonna take my bidness somewheres else." The girls at the desk looked plum disoriented for a solid three seconds before they broke into shrieks of laughter.

Taste outten yer mouth: the phrase, "taste out of your mouth," most often described the extent of an injury, such as hitting, kicking, butting, hooking, slamming or head butting or the potential for this happening. For example, "Watch 'im, boys--he'll kick the taste outten yer mouth." It was often used to describe what happened when a man hit another in a fight, as in, "Son! He jus knocked the taste outten his mouth."

In my parallel universe of Cracker terminology, regarding taste, my grandmother on my mother's side would use this phrase as a handy excuse for taking a second (or third) helping. As the family finished those wonderful home-cooked meals, all nine around the table, she'd take a fork and stab another piece of fried chicken, for example, saying, "I think I'll

Cracker Terms, Phrases And Definitions

have another piece–jus' ta git this taste outtah mah mouth." (She wasn't very deep in reasonings–but she could cook the best fried chicken!) I guess my mother carried on this tradition.

Takin' a Navy shower: Hubert Waldron was a pure-bred Cracker. He served in the Navy during the Second World War aboard a destroyer. He didn't talk about it much other than the description of the first time when he was sleeping in his bunk and the ten-inch guns went off. He said, "That lik' to hav' scared this Cracker boy to death." He also joked one day about the instructions he and his buddies were given by a salty Master Chief. He said the man told them how to take a two-minute shower. Water aboard the old ships was at a premium. Hubert said, "Tha ol' (*expletive deleted*) said, 'Boys, I'm gonna tell you how to take a Navy shower. You have two minutes in the stall. First you wash up as far as possible. Then you wash down as far as possible. Then you wash possible.'"

I am reminded of my cousin's grandson. I might begin by reminding the reader that I feel like "Cracker" is not only a term for Florida cow hunters, but also can be applied to the frontier mentality. It's just there. My cousin described a situation with her grandson during a bathing session. She said she had applied soap and shampoo and while rinsing him off, she said, "All we have left is to wash your *tooter*" (a euphemistic term for "private parts"). He said, "Naw... I'll do it."

"Okay," said Cousin as she handed him a soapy washcloth. He stood up in the tub, cocked a leg up on the side of it and began twirling the washcloth like an airplane propeller, repeatedly "wack-wack-wacking" himself vigorously in the groin. (I have a hard time deciding if this is just "boy." "Cracker," "the frontier mentality" or something else. However, the mental picture of this causes me much amusement. And, also, I couldn't think of any other place to include a famous family story.)

Tear up ah (*fill in the blank with a descriptive noun*): said when someone, especially a child, has broken something. It is common among some families to hear a variation of this phrase after a kid breaks an item, "I swear, Boy, I think you could tear up a hammer." Other words can be substituted: an anvil, ah oak tree, ah rock, ah nail or spike, ah bar ah steel, ah crow-bar, ah magnet, ah piece of wire, etc.

That ain't gonna buff out: a phrase from shade-tree mechanics, referring to the removal of scratches on the finish of a vehicle. Minor damages could often be buffed with polish and remove most of the damage.

But mostly it was said in understatement in these circumstances: describing damage to a truck when a rancorous bull or cow smashed into it or any vehicle, or any wreck where there was obviously severe damage to the exterior of a vehicle.

That ain't nuthin': a preliminary phrase to a "see-if-you-can-top-this" story. I was in a country store one time. The weather was nasty that day so I took advantage of the situation and went down to visit to see just what it was there that I couldn't do without. No other customers were there so I sat on a stool near the owner; we both shifted our hats back and struck up a conversation. I happened to be looking on the shelves and saw a product used for emergency filling of flat tires. The cans were neatly lined up like soldiers on review. I mentioned, "Ya know, that's ah handy thing to have in yer truck–ya never know whin sumbody will need to pump up their tire. I had a flat once and it sure worked good."

He replied, "That ain't nuthin'… we had a fella cum in here, said he used that expandin' urethane foam to fill his flat lawn mower tire. He said the foam oozed out two or three holes. He waited til the stuff dried and cut off the excess with his pocket knife. He told me that it rides real rough, but it's held up two years now."

While attending the Highlands County Fair Beauty Pageant at our county fair one year I overheard a man talking rather

Cracker Terms, Phrases And Definitions

loudly about the expenses his son had incurred in preparing his show steer. Since the fella was less than discreet, many by-standers listened in, as well. He said, "Well, I'll tell ya, he has about $800 to $900 worth of feed in 'im already. We had to re-build a shed for 'im, too. Time we add all the halters and gear, tha boy's gonna have nearly $1100 in that steer."

I couldn't help it. I spoke up three rows behind him and said, "Hey, that ain' nuthin. Look up there on the stage! You see that brunette in the center of the second row and the blond on the end? I'm gonna have $100,000 each in them before they leave home." The whole section laughed.

That's ah lotta money, or $ (*fill in the amount*) isah lotta money: a bargaining statement expressing reluctance to pay the cost of something. The best example that comes to mind was told to me by a preacher after my daddy's funeral. He told of a man and wife at a county fair. They noticed a crop-duster pilot taking people for short rides in his plane around the fair grounds. Being curious, they sat on a bench watching the excitement. Things slowed down as many people went home. The pilot pulled up to the bench, let out his passengers and noticed the man and woman watching the activity.

He asked them, "Y'all want to ride?"

The man said, "How much does it cost?"

The pilot replied, "$10 for the both of you."

The old man said, "Well, $10 is ah lotta money."

The pilot said, "Well, tell you what... I take you both for a ride and if you don't say anything while we're flyin', it won't cost you anything."

The old man looked at his wife and said, "That sounds like ah good deal. Awrite."

They crawled into the back seats of the crop-duster and the pilot took off, knowing he could scare them enough that they would scream. He did some aerobatic tricks that would cause anyone to panic. He did a stall and re-start, a loop-the-loop, a dive at a barn and flew upside-down for a time. No sound from the back seat. He figured he was wasting his fuel since these folks were tough customers. He landed and as he shut off the engine and instruments he said, "Y'all did real good–I didn't hear a sound out of you."

The old man said, "Well, I lik' to have squawled whin my wife fell out."

The pilot was thunder-struck… he said, "Why didn't you say somethin'?!"

The old man replied, "Well, ten dollars isah lotta money."

That'd be lik' pokin' butter up a wildcat's butt withah hot ice pick: a phrase that brings forth a few wrinkled noses and brows, but is an apt description of a procedure on a seriously bad dog or mean horse. "Misterman, if y'all are gonna try to worm that horse, brace yerself cause it'll be lik' pokin' butter up a wildcat's butt withah hot ice pick."

One Christmas morning I tried to treat a bobcat that was brought in with diarrhea. It was not a pretty sight. (I charged them $10 for the exam, $15 for the medicine and $125 for a new shirt, cleaning the exam room, the clinic floors and parking lot….)

A similar synonym phrase is "That'd be like playin' leap frog with ah unicorn."

That's gotta hurt or it's gonna hurt: An emphatic remark during or right after some imminent procedure. I was in the Air Force in Texas and happened to accidently get exposed to a heavy amount of mold spores. The reaction was severe, requiring a trip to the base hospital. My neighbor, Bill, was one of the general medical officers there and took me to the hospital. I entered the emergency clinic in acute respiratory distress. A short but strong-looking TSgT was the assistant on duty (obviously from Texas). Bill ordered him to give the Captain an adrenaline injection, and an injection of Decadron in the butt. (Decadron is cortisone in oil. And the injection does smart considerably.)

After some rummaging around in cabinets and drawers, he walked up beside me, placed a hand on my shoulder, looked up sweetly into my face and said, "Captain? If you'll drop yer britches, I'm gonna give you sum shots." His his face transformed into an evil grin as he continued, "And, Sir? It's gonna hurt." (It did. Every time after that incident when I saw the TSgt in the halls of the hospital, he'd grin and say, "How's yer butt, Sir?")

That jus' ended it up: an emphatic phrase that pronounced that an activity is finished, or sometimes that an activity has been interrupted unexpectedly. "Whin she caught him in tha bed with her cousin, that jus' ended it up rite then and ther'." The phrase often was used as an obviously humorous relating of a funny story about someone's misadventure. "Whin he tried to let the bobcat out of tha sack, it whirled around an' scratched the hide off his arms—that jus' ended it up rite ther'."

I am reminded of the time that a little short woman, accompanied by her 6-feet-6-inch husband, presented her pet raccoon for a rabies vaccination. (Picture a 4-foot-7-in woman with a 6-foot-6-inch man with a raccoon. Memorable ain't it?) Rabies vaccination was legal for wildlife at the time, but Mr. Coon was not too happy about anything and coon-growled at me when she put him on the exam table.

I said, "Ma'am, he's gonna come uncorked when the needle hits him. He'll bite me a dozen times before I can get away." She replied, "Naw, Doc, he's a sweetheart! He is the best pet I ever had—I love him to death. He won't bother you. I can hold him."

We cautiously proceeded to hold the irritated beast still while I inserted the needle and administered the vaccine. That particular vaccine approved for raccoons had a peculiar after effect—it would begin to sting *after* the injection and burned for several seconds before subsiding. Mr. Coon crawled back to her shoulder to perch there as was his custom, and proceeded to give me a resentful look.

She quieted him with assuring baby-talk phrases, "It's ah-wight, Baby. Dat mean old man hurt my Baby, didn't he? Come on, Honey, let's pay our bill and doe home."

While standing near the front desk, the burning began. Mr. Coon evacuated a considerable portion of slimy white and speckled-green mucous from his lower bowel on her shoulder and down her back. She looked like a gull roost. (What in the world had she been feeding him?) "Ou-u-u-u-u!" she said as the receptionist handed her tissues.

Dr. Handley stuck his head around the corner, grinning at me, saying, "Well, Baby ended that up, didden he?"

Speaking of raccoons and rabies vaccinations, I recall a story told by Dr. Walter Gibbons in about 1966. Dr. Gibbons was an outstanding clinical veterinarian–at least one of the first ones in this country. He literally "wrote the book" on Large Animal Medicine and Surgery. Dr. Gibbons told of a rabies outbreak outside of Ithaca, NY. (From his stories we all had the idea that there wasn't much difference in the rural people there and the people around east Alabama; however, they wore more plaid flannel than Alabamians.) There was a town meeting at that time to discuss and endorse the "new rabies vaccine" for all dogs and cats in the little town. Well, the mayor, the health officials and others all tried to convince the townfolks to have their pets vaccinated. The crowd grew hostile at being "forced" to vaccinate their animals. Angry voices were raised at this un-American mandate. In frustration the mayor asked the veterinarian, who hadn't been allowed to speak up to this point, to have a try at convincing the people to vaccinate. He arose, reached behind his chair and picked up a small carrier. He opened the door, reached in and brought out a small mongrel dog. He placed the little dog on the stage floor where everyone could see it. The dog was foaming at the mouth, slinging its head from side to side and pawing at its mouth. The dog was drooling thick stringy saliva–a perfect rendition of what they'd all been warned a rabid dog would do.

The place cleared of people in under a minute. The veterinarian picked up the little dog, reached into its mouth and removed a small rubber band off its tongue. The dog was unhurt, and the next morning at the appointed time, there was standing room only at the vet's office.

An old country doctor from Clearwater, Florida, told a tale of an event that happened many years ago. One Monday morning when he arrived for the day there was a fella waiting at the office. The man told the doctor that he needed a shot "'cause I think I caught somethin' from a gal I know." After a quick exam the doctor determined that there were no signs of disease. Considering his practice time was valuable and the fella looked rather shiftless, he decided to give an antibiotic injection "just in case there was a problem brewing." The man left without paying.

The next morning there were three men at the office when he arrived; this time the fella from the previous morning brought two newcomers. One of the new men said, "Doc, we need a shot, too, 'cause we been with the same gal as Buck." Well, the doctor said he'd had enough of it. He reached for a bottle of vitamin B-12 in oil. (To repeat, for those who don't know about oil emulsion injections, they hurt like all "gitout.") The doctor had the man drop his britches and drawers; he socked the needle to the hub and pushed the irritating injection deep in the muscle. He said the fella screamed, stumbled over his britches which were around his ankles, knocked over a cabinet of instruments and a tray, and proceeded to have a fit on the floor. The other two men looked terrified. They grabbed their buddy, dragged him toward the door as he tried to pull his britches up and quickly departed for anywhere else. (Well, "that jus' ended it up, didden't it?")

Tha thumps: this term was used to describe a horse, cow, dog or man that had exerted itself to the point of heat stress. When you roped from a horse and worked the fire out of him in the heat, he'd get exhausted to the point that he couldn't get his breath–he'd simply be breathing with such force and rapidity that his breaths would be accompanied by an audible "thump" as he contracted his diaphragm. Cow dogs were notorious for getting the "thumps;" they'd simply work themselves near to death. They didn't seem to know when to quit. They lived for the work. They were in their element. The working of cattle was all they knew. Many times a rider would get off his horse and drag a hot, exhausted dog to a water hole or pond and soak him in the cool water. They'd leave him, and after a time, the dog would reappear and go again at the task. A cow or bull with the thumps would be totally fractious. We often left them alone to cool off. We'd have killed some or they would have killed us if we hadn't.

This is where the related term "cold water enema" developed. Yeah, I know you think it's funny, but it saved more than one cow dog's life. The colon is a marvelous water-absorbing organ. Ice water baths and cold-water enemas were just the ticket for a heat-exhausted cow dog. It took a 107+ internal core temperature down almost immediately and corrected severe dehydration. We always kept a bag or two of Ringer's Solution in the refrigerator for the "thumpy" cow dog. This technique worked well for horses and bulls, too, but you had to careful with violent blowbacks. (Rectal temperatures approaching 109 usually meant a cooked brain; these individuals hardly ever survived.) I guess I really understood how they overheated, knowing the environment in which they worked.

Tha whistles: to suffer the usual outcome of over-consuming a bowel-irritating food, such as chili, chipotle and jalapeno peppers, or green guavas. The result is repeated bouts of bowel evacuation and the accompanying irritation thereof. In context, "Ou-u Wee! I wanna tell ya… three plates of chili peppers last nite gave me the whistles this mornin'!" This was followed by some descriptive phrase, such as, "I'm so sore I cain't touch myself with a powder puff." and the sound of a reverse whistle by the cowboy.

That ort to clir yer sinuses: this was used mostly by college graduates when intermingled with Cracker cowboys. A contraction of, "That ought to clear your sinuses," it was reference to an event, unsettling activity, happening, accident or a near wreck where adrenaline was flushed into one's system. It was reserved for use after the cow had caught you out in the open pen, as in, "Boy, that'll jus clir ya sinuses." Usually, others add to this comment with something like, "Now, don't that jus turpentine the tomcat?" or "I wish you'd look at that!"

That ort to mak' tha paper: An exclamation describing the level of significance of some, injury or wild incident or catastrophic event; as an example: if a man was seating himself in the saddle on a cantankerous horse, which went into a wild bucking, throwing him off, someone might say, "Well, that ort to mak' the paper." Speaking of makin' the paper, how about this classified ad? "Starting a retirement home for cow dogs. Must have been injured at least twelve times and over two-years old. So far there are 157 on the waiting list. Send $10 and résumé to: Retired Cow Dogs, General Delivery, Possum Trot, Florida. Attention: Bubba (Don't call us –we'll call you. Deposits not returned.)."

A Florida rancher asked his wife to put a "help wanted" ad in the local paper. As with many local papers, the classifieds editor wanted to be politically correct. After the ad was rewritten, it said: "Cowperson wanted. Applicant must use profanity and share a bunkhouse with four male cowpersons who seldom bathe."

That works real good, don't it? a sarcastic understatement meaning the opposite for the expected outcome. If one of the men spent considerable time fixing a broken tractor part then to have it tear up the moment he starts back to running the machine, he might say, "Well, that works real good, don't it?"

The best example of the use of the phrase comes from a story from a humiliated veterinarian. Back in the days when canine distemper was prevalent it was not unusual for dogs to be brought to veterinarians in the terminal throws of severe encephalitis (viral inflammation of the brain). These dogs had a fixed glassy stare, involuntary muscle jerks and a rectal temperature approaching 106 degrees. They were most often terminal. Well the veterinarian told the people that the case was pretty hopeless and "putting him down" was the best thing to end the dog's suffering. (Truthfully, the dog probably was oblivious to any stimulation.) The clients agreed to have him put to sleep and left the clinic.

The animal was taken by the nervous and newly-hired kennel boy to the back treatment table. The doctor had just started using an injectable sedative and pain reliever called "xylazine." It worked well in causing a patient to completely relax and almost immediately stopped most pain. He mused out loud, "Well, let's use this new stuff; it ought to make him still while I give him the euthanasia injection."

Meanwhile, the new kennel boy didn't want to touch the dog. He was really nervous. The doctor proceeded to administer the recently-approved drug. Nothing happened for a few seconds. Then, as if gathering steam pressure, the dog became highly excited. He said, "Did you know a dog can express, excrete, pass or evacuate from seven body sites? He pooped, peed, expressed his anal glands, salivated, vomited and two or three other things I didn't know a dog could do. Well he did all of them while lying broadside and unconscious on the table! He scattered body fluids all over the walls and the floors. My new kennel boy like to have fainted. After a few seconds of these unconscious activities the dog slumped into pleasant sleep."

Cracker Terms, Phrases And Definitions

He continued, "I didn't let on much. I just put the vial of xylazine on the shelf and commented, 'That stuff works real good, don't it?'" The kennel boy was speechless, but impressed.

Later when reading the fine print on the drug, he found that using on animals with conditions of brain swelling or inflammation, the drug will cause extreme excitement before it becomes effective. He said his only consolation was the fact that the dog was oblivious to it all, saying, "It took thirty minutes to clean up the room. I still don't think we got it all. The kennel boy was never the same after that."

You might say, "Well, that ended that up, didden' it?"

That's anuther bunch of dogs: indicates a surprise proposition during a negotiation, not related at all to the topic at hand. Examples include, "I didn't mind tha divorce but whin she tried to take my rifle, that's anuther bunch of dogs." It also means something is clearly different than first thought. "Well, he wanted to bet me in ah race of our mares, but then he jumps a new horse off the trailer; that's a whole nuther bunch of dogs."

A man named Ronnie Chandler can be mentioned here. Ronnie was the first person arrested under a Federal drug enforcement law commonly called, "the kingpin law," established sometime in the seventies, as best I can recall. Ronnie, who has served his time and cleaned up his act, had several marijuana and moonshine operations which were stationed across a few state lines. After arrest and conviction, in Cracker terminology, Ronnie "worked for the state" several years. (See term) In a documentary program, an ordinary, clean-cut Ronnie explained all the various means he and others used to avoid the "Feds." One local attorney was asked to comment on Ronnie's activities since he was the first prosecuted under the new law. The Georgia attorney, referring to moonshine, said, "Well, it wasn't unusual for several folks to meet at a local house and sip a little moonshine on Saturday nights. First thing ya know, someone brought in some music. People enjoyed a little shine and the music. After a time, they started a little dancing. Well, the whole operation was shut down—drinking a little shine and music is one thing, but dancin'? That's a whole nuther bunch of dogs."

Them yer legs? Though the question has been asked in many contexts and locations, the cow pens seems to be the most appropriate place for a Cracker to ask the following question to one wearing short pants there. The context is especially heightened when the legs are white and/or skinny. When someone showed up to leave supplies or bring a replacement chute part to the pens–wearing shorts–one of the hands would comment, "I don't believe I'd let them things out in public." "How long you been bowlegged?" "Sumbody git my sunglasses out of the truck." "Them yer legs? Or'er you ridin' a chicken?"

Things are jes not tha way they used to be: a classic line from Carl Hurley when he was describing two ladies talking about olden times and shelling peas on the front porch. One said, "Things are jes not the way they used to be." The other replied, "I don't think they ever have been." (Think about it.)

Think I'll farm: One time on a fishing trip, Ron and I were cooking Snook filets and hush-puppies while the other fishermen sat around talking. The group was made of diverse men. Eddie was in construction, Robert was in automobile sales and service, Ron was a farmer from the Plant City area, David was a ranch manager and I was the veterinarian. This was a weekend when the Florida State Lottery was huge, somewhere in the neighborhood of $8 million. As I watched the fish turn golden-brown in the hot oil, the fellas decided that we should each buy a one-dollar lottery ticket, pick our own numbers and split the winnings five ways if anyone of us hit the correct numbers. The next discussion was related to how we'd each spend the winnings. Eddie said he wanted to buy him a new Ford Diesel truck for his business and a new Ranger Bass Boat. Robert was going to invest in his own business and pay off his house. David was going to buy a little ranch and some Purebred cattle, and pay for the new baby that would soon arrive. They asked me what I would do with the money. I said I thought I'd build a new veterinary hospital and pay off loans. Ron didn't say anything for a time. He had a far-away look in his eyes, as if seriously studying the matter. Finally he spoke up, saying, "Well I'll tell ya, boys, I think I'll just farm til it's all gone."

(It reminded me of the adage: How do you make a small fortune in the cattle bidness? Start with a big one.)

Thingamabob, ratchit, kanuter valve, mahatmahand and ratastat: describes technical workings of broken intricate machinery, the names of which we did not know. When we would tear into a tractor's inner parts to make repairs, finding the process was much more complicated than we first thought or that we were totally in over our head and beyond our abilities, one would say, "Her's the problem: the ratastat is hung up on the kanuter valve. It's pushed the thingamabob against the mahatmahand. It looks like tha ratchit is broke." With these code words, I knew the next procedure was to call International Harvester or Caterpillar Technical Services. We even said it when we found a cow down for no apparent reason. He'd say, "It sure looks like her kanuter valve is frozen…" I'd respond with, "Naw, I think her mahatmahandic declamometer is fevered. We need to give a dose of ratastat." (We get bored easily.)

This hir' is mah boy, Cletus: a generally unknown introduction of someone to a group of Crackers, especially when the one introduced is <u>older</u> than the speaker. Cracker cowboys aren't always the friendliest of people when you first approach them, especially in the cow pens. They don't know you, have business on their minds and are a little stand-off-ish at first. I learned to get on with the business at hand. Visiting will come later once they see how well you work. But it never failed to cause a hesitation while the listener processed the information. The best example of the phrase occurred when I went to a ranch with a friend who obviously was older than me.

Nobody there knew him so I said, "Hey, boys. How'er y'all doin'? This hir is mah boy, Cletus."

They looked at one another, finally getting the joke, but one asked, "How do you explain that, Doc?"

I said, "Well, he's by my fourth wife who was considerably older than me... and that's why we are so close in age..." That seemed to satisfy him. (It almost made sense.)

Thought a lot of 'im or 'er or I'da thought a whole lot more of 'im if he'da (*fill in the blank*. There is a story that illustrates this phrase.

A Baptist and an Episcopalian were arguing about the use of alcohol. The Baptist said, "It's ah sin to drink alcohol."

The Episcopalian said, "No, I don't agree; there's nothing wrong with drinking alcohol. Getting drunk and loosing self-control is wrong."

The Baptist said, "Naw, I don't think anyone should drink at all."

The Episcopalian said, "Well, you know that Jesus drank wine."

The Baptist replied, "Yeah, an' I'da thought a whole lot more of 'im if he haddenah."

Three things you don't mess with: In the Cracker culture, it is said that there are three things you don't mess with: a man's wife, his dog and his paycheck – however not necessarily in that order!

Throw yer hat in the door or toss yer hat in tha (*fill in the blank*): means "approach with caution." If, for example, a cowboy and his wife had words before he left for work, and she was really angry, the fella would often share his woes with his buddies. One might suggest, "Well, ya better throw yer hat in the door 'fore you go in the house." It was understood that if the hat came back out the door, don't go in – especially if it was cut or shredded. If, on the other hand, she comes to the door and invites him in, he has a chance to make it

Cracker Terms, Phrases And Definitions

right. The worst condition a man could face was a woman who had eaten ham, was plum venomous, madder than a dirt dauber in a beer can, and had thrown his clothes out on the front porch and stomped on his hat... (He best go on back to the woods.)

Thump yer head: a variation of "knock a knot on your head," meaning nearly the same as "jerk a knot in his tail," "clean his clock," "slap up aside tha head;" etc. (See terms)

Time: used to indicate a period, a measurable interval, a happening or act or historical era. After considerable discussion, I conclude that the meanings are strictly cultural in origins. Using Thomas Aquinas' concept of communication by language, I have come to the conclusion that "time" is best described in at least three parts:

1. **Time is "univocal" or literal**. When a Yankee says, "8:00", he means "8:00 or several minutes earlier." A synonym for this time is "Northern Time."
2. **Time is "equivocal."** When a Cracker or Southerner says, "8:00", he means "Sometime around or after 8:00" or "I will probably start thinking about the actual time agreed upon when it gits here, then I will start moving." I often call this "Southern Time." It is a cultural characteristic of Cracker people from the South. The proof of this time is the statement made by one of my Michigan friends: "That's the reason the South lost the war–they always showed up late for the battle."
3. **Time is "analogical" or "metaphorical."** The concept that actual time is irrelevant. Analogical time is common in the mountains and some other cultures. It can be called "True Cracker Time" or "Mountain Time." As an example, "I'll be there at 8:00" means, "I don't have any idea

whin I'll git there or if I'll come at all. I ain't sure if it'll be tomorrow, in a few days, next week, next month or next year; I ain't even sure I'll ever show up, especially if it's deer season. I have no concept of time since you ain't gonna get nobody else to do what you need done. The only way you can get me there is to keep calling me or my mama and force me to come along or owe me money, but even if you owe me money, strange things can happen to people that don't pay."

A tale circulated that illustrates the concept of Cracker Time. A man from Hardee County took his saddle to Okeechobee to a saddle repair shop. He got a receipt and returned home. Four years later his son was looking at the bills and receipts trying to get some order to them. He found the receipt for the saddle left in Okeechobee. He decided to go get the saddle. He took the receipt in to the saddle maker and apologized for his father's oversight. The saddle maker said, "It ort tah be ready in two weeks."

To reinforce this concept of **"Mountain Time,"** the last two battles of the Civil War were fought in Hendersonville, NC, and Franklin, TN, *two weeks* after the South had surrendered. After considerable thought and discussion, I have concluded that Eastern and Western Kentucky, excepting Louisville, all of Tennessee, excepting Nashville, all of Georgia, Mississippi, Louisiana, southern Alabama and the interior portion of South Florida are on Cracker or Mountain Time, although there are not many mountains in some of those regions.

Western Time: I plan to expand "time" to include "Western Time." Though very similar to "Cracker or Mountain time", Western Time is generally related to the concept that there is "nothing to do since the work is done." I am investigating the incident recorded during the winding down of the Civil War. Near Tucson, Arizona, there is a "river" (about four-inches

Cracker Terms, Phrases And Definitions

deep) that runs out into the desert between two mesas. In early 1865, two opposing Union and Confederate cavalry troops, looking for cattle to feed the Eastern armies of their respective sides, rode out into the open facing each other. Shots were fired and one man was wounded slightly. They stopped the gunfire, tended the slightly wounded man, talked it over. Then both cavalries saddled up and went to town together for a drink. The action was based on "western time" and the fact that no one wanted to be the last man killed in a war that was about to end.

"Western time" can also be demonstrated by the fact that western men will stop doing anything to ride a horse 20-50 miles for coffee and donuts. Another interesting incident possibly involving western time occurred in Florida during the state surveys in the 1800's. There is some academic debate whether the surveyor in this incident was a Westerner or a Cracker. However, the records indicate that the Surveyor's Log described the naming of a particular lake. It read, "We are camped on a large lake, we are out of whiskey, and have named the lake 'Lake Distress'." The lake is named that to this day. Though not sure whether this man was a Cracker or Western man, I will continue my investigations in this area.

Indian time: this concept is somewhat difficult to describe to Europeans and is usually the opposite of their understanding. I cite the reference of my stepfather and his Army friend on a Ten Thousand Islands fishing trip in the 1950's. After several days of fishing, Marcus asked Frank if he knew of a place where they could get some whiskey. Being a Colonel in the Army had expanded Marcus' horizons in the area of appreciating spirit beverages. Frank said he had heard that there was a Seminole Indian who had set up a whiskey still on a mangrove island back in the Everglades. They went searching for the island since it was nearly 5:00 pm. They arrived at the place, finding the Indian sitting near a small fire. He spoke broken English but they were able to communicate their desires to buy whiskey.

The conversation went something like this:

"You got whisky?"

"Uhmm – whiskey."

"Old whiskey?"

"Uhmm...old whiskey."

"How old whiskey?"

"Uhmmm...old whiskey...two, maybe three day."

This is a good example of analogous or metaphorical time as described above and I call it "Indian Time."

Hog farmer time: another area of active research is the classification of "time" as used in a story about a man raising hogs in South Florida. A new county agent was sent out to review the husbandry practices of the farmer who was feeding his animals leftovers and café garbage. To the county agent, the diet was lacking in energy and protein. The hogs were somewhat healthy, but thin. The helpful agent informed him that he could speed up the growth rates of the hogs and lower the time required to get them ready for slaughter by feeding some corn and bean meal. To which the hog farmer replied, "Son, what is time to ah hog?"

I'm not sure how to classify the farmer's definition here but will keep thinking on it, if I have the time. I recall a proverb I once heard: "Never try to teach a hog to sing. It irritates the hog and it's a waste of time." (I don't know which time they're talking about.)

Time for a clinic fire: a phrase I've only heard one time in Florida. The State of Florida requires all professional people practicing in the state to attend annual continuing education courses. These meetings last for a few days and are scheduled at some very nice family-friendly places. The general practitioners were mostly, if not all, large animal veterinarians and many were Crackers or, at least, worked with Cracker cow hunters. During one particular required meeting, we were told of the "new rules" governing the use of controlled substances (such as morphine, phenobarbital, Valium, etc.) The speaker informed the audience that the State enforcement officers would inspect all our detailed records and logs of ordered controlled substances and the case records where these drugs were used and the amounts administered. In other words, we had to keep detailed records of the incoming drugs and where they were used and the inventory must balance. Missing controlled drugs would be a violation and our practice licenses could be suspended or revoked. One veterinarian asked, "If a practitioner has not been keeping all the records going back five years, what is the policy?" The official indicated that this was indeed a violation and would be subject to close scrutiny and penalty. There was a pregnant pause as we all pondered the implications of poor record-keeping. From the back, a man with deep voice, drawled, "I think it's time for a clinic fire...."

Tinker's dam: the origin of the term has lost its meaning; the term refers to traveling "tinkers" whose livelihood was repairing pots and pans. In order to solder a hole, a clay dam was attached to a hole of a cooking pot to "dam up" the molten solder as it hardens in the hole. Once the solder hardened and set, the used dam was wiped away. Thus, something worthless ain't worth a "tinker's dam."

Tite: implying difficult, tenuous, dangerous, frenzied or frantic situation. It is sometimes heard like, "Man, we wer' ina tite whin the bulls broke out." "Go to'um, boys–ol' Junior is inna tite! He'll git tha hide barked off his shins if he don't git help!" Meant make haste to go and relieve a man who had "bitten off more than he could chew."

An example of being in a "tite" occurred when we hired a young man to help out at the hospital. Austin "Austie" Heacock had only been at work for a week or so when strange things began to happen to his otherwise organized and predictable world. He'd settled in to routine activities and, though inexperienced, he did well. He was conscientious and amiable. One day a woman brought in a pet raccoon. The poor thing had an ingrown collar on its neck. He'd been mostly chained outside. They'd forgotten that little coons grow to big coons. He'd grown so big in fact that the metal collar had grown into the skin. Actually, the skin had been cut by the collar and the metal had sunken beneath the surface of the skin. He was, to say the least, ill tempered; I would have complained, too, if I had a tight collar digging into the skin of my neck. You couldn't see it for the over-lapping hair, so they didn't have any idea why Mr. Coon was getting angry.

They brought him in the hospital for examination. I knew immediately what had happened by the smell of infected flesh. Yes indeed, it was a mess. So Austie and I took him to the back table for minor surgery. We placed him on the little exam table. We discovered that you could not hold the regular chain that was attached to the torture device embedded in his neck; it caused severe pain. So we put two small leashes on Mr. Coon, keeping him between us with the leashes held on either side of the table. He seemed to tolerate that well. As I tried to get to one small exposed area of the collar with my handy-dandy wire cutters, Mr. Coon was curious about the surrounding. As I'd get close to grabbing the exposed portion of the collar, he'd squirm a little. I was trying to hold one leash, while Austie held another, keeping him centered in the table. Unconsciously, I handed both leashes to Austie, who took them, one in each hand. I eased the cutters into place, touching the tender area of the coon's neck. Mr. Coon decided he'd had enough of this and proceeded to climb up Austie's chest. Though difficult to describe, the situation is something like this: Austie now has both leashes, one in each of his out-stretched hands. His grip on them allowed considerable slack for the coon, which decided to climb the nearest tall thing, Austie; Mr. Coon was growling at the irritation I'm causing by the wire cutters. Austie is face to face with a growling coon. I am concentrating on the intricate placing of wire cutters while Austie if staring into the eyes of an angry

Cracker Terms, Phrases And Definitions

boar coon. He said, "Dr. Jones... Dr. Jones! Dr. Jones! DR. JONES!! I'm in a tite here!" I instantly realized that he had stretched his arms out and could not get any opportunity to take up slack to keep Mr. Coon from climbing on his head! I grabbed the leash from his left hand and we got the climber under control. With patience and dexterity, we were able to remove the embedded collar. Mr. Coon grumbled but seemed overall appreciative. (Wild-eyed Austie asked me if that's the way we handled all coons.)

"Tite" could refer to one's being "up tight" or nervous. It often referred to excessive frugality. As an example, one Cracker referred to a friend as being so tite that when he blinks "his navel smiles."

Titenup: meaning to grasp tighter, speed up, hurry up, come on in a hurry or get on with the procedure. It was used in sentences like, "Y'all need ta titenup," when some were falling behind in the pace while working cattle. Dr. Handley was about the best at getting a crew to titenup when working cattle. He'd tell one fella to go back and help at a bottleneck where the cattle were slowing the whole activity. He'd tell another to move up closer to the front, saying, "Tha second she clears the chute, you job the next one in—I got to go, I cain't assle around here all day..." Throughout the working he'd make changes until the crew was humming efficiently.

Handley's skill was also manifested in the managing of kids. One story told on him was the time he went to Joe Stiles' barn. Joe was a generous and kind soul, allowing the local 4-H Horse Club to keep several of their horses at his old barn on Sparta Road. Handley showed up one day to look at a snotty-nosed mount. After the horse was treated, Handley and Joe began a tour of sorts around the barn. The place was packed with 4-H kids doing the chores. He stopped one girl, saying, "Sister, why don't you git a shovel and scoop all the horse manure out of yer stall so yer horse don't git thrush?" He told a boy, "Son, pull the weeds from under that electric fence so it keeps the wire hot and that calf doesn't slip under it and git killed on the road." To another, "Sissy, go in the tack room and git all the gear up off the hay bales and the floor and hang it up... sweep it out, too; it'll sure help keep the place neat." It wasn't long before he had everyone on a chore. Joe said, "Then he turns to me and says, 'Joe, come on, let's go to tha house an' drink coffee.'"

Tite-jawed: the act or strong potential of becoming angry, steeling one's self for something, being hostile, frustrated, upset; for example: "Man, ol' Spec shor wuz titejawed this mornin'!"

Like the conversation I overheard one afternoon, when the daddy of two brothers left after giving everyone individual instructions on how to do what they had been doing all day. One said, "Whut you reckon's tha matter with Cap? Whut's he so tite-jawed about?" The other one, never hesitating, responded, "I reckon he's got a burr under his saddle 'bout somethin' 'nuther..."

I have seen cowboys, men and women of all ages, horses, bulls, catch dogs, cats, veterinarians and boys exhibit this condition.

Tookitaway frum me: a phrase used when one of the men was, in effect, saying he had control of something and lost it. The best examples include, "We had two ropes on tha bull an' he still tookitaway frum us." "My horse lik' to hav' killed me... I tried to settle 'im down but he jus' tookitaway from me." "Caught flat-footed" and "having something taken away frum you" have some slight differences in meaning: "flat-footed" connotes not being ready, while "tookitaway frum me" implies lost control or a "things-went-down-hill-frum-then-on" wreck.

Took to tha sale: apart from the literal transportation of an animal (or a piece of equipment, etc.) to a market, usually referring to a livestock auction, it refers, metaphorically, to one who has been cheated, skinned, taken advantage of, made a dumb trade, lost money on a purchase or a card game, paid a higher price than he should have or paid an unreasonable price for something. A synonym is "pulled outta tha shuck." (See "Damshur") You might hear comments like, "Whin her lawyer got through with 'im, he knowed he'd been took to tha sale." Also, "Whut happen to that old mean bull you had?" Followed by the literal reply, "Aw, we took him to tha sale." When used to tease someone about a poor trade or purchase, you might hear, "Boy, they seen you acomin', didden they?"

Tooth docter: a dentist. Many times a particular physician was linked by prefix to the anatomy or specialty, as in, foot, eye, ear, toe, knee, elbow, baby, dog, horse, bull, etc., though I never heard any of the men say, "prostate docter," "testicle docter," or "uterus docter." That seemed a little too much personal information for the men. The cowboys rephrased most medical terms, where "pyelonephritis" or "cystitis" simply was called "bad-" or "locked-up kidneys." A Staphylococcus skin infection was called "tha creepin' crud." It wasn't because they didn't understand; it was just best abbreviated to avoid excessive conversation on a difficult subject. "He give me these pills" meant, "The doctor prescribed antibiotics."

I'll always remember a place called Parker Island, south of Lake Placid, Florida. Parker Island was a hammock where the elevation was some two to four feet higher than the surrounding marsh. During the summer-wet season, water surrounded it, thus it would look like an island. One hot summer day Handley was working cattle there. One of the men returned from a trip to the doctor dressed in a nice, clean western shirt, dress boots and new hat and jeans. When he removed his hat, his hair was neatly combed and slicked back. We observed all this from under the shade tree in the cow pens.

Well, of course, everyone wanted a report about the trip to the doctor. They took a water break to cool off, re-hydrate and get the latest information on his trip. It was as if he had vicariously experienced the appointment for all. He explained in much abbreviated form what it was like, the problem, the cure and other vital facts about who was there and about that ol' gal he usta go with that now worked for the doctor. He concluded by pulling a prescription from his shirt pocket, flashing it around to no one in particular, and commented, "I cain't even read this...."

One of the men said, "Let me see it." He passed the paper over for inspection. It moved around the circle of sweaty men, each taking a turn at the Latin.

One of the old cowboys said, "I know exactly whut it means... It's a note to the druggist... It says, 'I got my money, now you git yers.'"

Toss sum water on tha sack: I bet only a few will know what this means. Back in old timey Florida, while working in the hot humid groves, it was necessary to have an oak water bucket with a dipper close by. A "croker", "hemp", "feed" or "potato" sack was draped over the water barrel. They pulled the coarse hemp sack off the lid, removed it and plunged the dipper into the cool water for a drink. When they finished drinking, the top would be re-secured, the sack re-placed over the little barrel and a little amount of water was tossed from the dipper onto the sack. The water on the wet sack evaporated and cooled the barrel water considerably; the principle of evaporative cooling. It wasn't cold but it sure tasted good and cool in the sweltering groves.

Evaporation cooling helped on work shirts as well. In the groves, down in between the rows where no air seemed to circulate, we'd run "spray rigs" to apply chemicals or citrus oil on the trees. We'd have to re-fill spray tanks every so often. We'd pull up under an overhead boom from an artesian well, which looked similar to the booms from water tanks of the old steam engine trains on the western railroads. After removing the lid from the tank, filling it with cool water and mixing in whatever chemical or oil was needed to treat the diseases or parasites. Every thirty- to forty-five minutes, we'd have

Cracker Terms, Phrases And Definitions

to re-fill and re-charge the tank to continue spraying. We'd get so hot that we'd sometimes walk under the boom—hat and all—as it drained the last bit of water after the well was turned off. It'd take your breath for a moment but it surely served as a natural cooling when the water evaporated on thick work shirts and denim jeans. So, now you know. (I told you early on this book was a wealth of barely essential information.)

Tote: to carry. All kinds of things can be toted: "Boy, tote yer toys over to yer toy box." "Tote me by tha house so I can pick up my boots." "Y'all will hav' tah tote them posts over to tha shed if ther's any left over." Another use refers to children. For example, "Whose gonna tote this youngun?"

Hubert Waldron made an idle comment once about his daughter, Joy. She came to their family late in life when most of the other children were older and responsible. The children, and Hubert, too, "toted" Joy nearly everywhere, especially around the cow pens. Hubert once said about Joy, "She'll be six years old before her feet touch tha ground."

Touchus: a slang word meaning that something is sore or tender, irritated or upset. The word is found in several scenarios. A man with a severe cut or mashed finger might draw a comment from his fellow cowboy, as in, "Son! That danged thing looks plum touchus." In reference to a spat with his wife, a cowboy might say, "I don't know whut set her off; she wuz touchus this morning." Or a cowboy would use it to describe an upset horse.

The classic story where this word was defined for me many years ago occurred at the Okeechobee Livestock Market. During one of the breaks, while waiting for the next load of cattle to be delivered for the sale, the bored cowboys were standing and sitting around the unloading area. As things often happen with bored cowboys the discussions got around to interesting experiences. The discussion stalled on hot shots, better known as cattle prods, those battery-powered shocking devices used to move reluctant cattle. (I will not get into the controversy between the animal rights people and cowboys at this time. All I can say is I have been hit by them on numerous occasions and never got any permanent damage. Stung, yes; damaged, no. Usually the worst thing that could happen was a last minute prod on the nearest body part during the attempt to leave the area. Cracker kids often had little play-fights with hot shots, usually ending in one or more running for cover.)

Each cowboy contributed his "I-can-top-that" story. One described a man that could hold a stinging hot shot to his bare belly. He described his method, "Onct you git past the first jolt, you can keep yer holt on it forever, but that first jolt is bad." Many shook their heads in agreement. One man spoke up, "Shoot, I can hold a hot shot on my bare butt for five seconds! I'll do it for five dollars apiece." This caused renewed interest in the day's lagging activities. Here was something to talk about...

Things began to get serious when several of the men said they'd put up the money if ol' Brave Heart would let them supply the cattle prod. He agreed if he only had to hold firm for five seconds; there was now some potential for big money. They jawed back and forth finally deciding to send one man to the local animal supply to get a new hot shot. He put Alkaline Plus batteries in it. It almost shot fire as he pulled the trigger.

Every man that was not busy came to watch. Brave Heart, gulping a little, got in the corner of a pen, dropped his jeans, put each hand on a board slightly above his head and bent over in preparation for the big "hot-shot-on-the-bare-butt-for-five-seconds" bet. The confident shocker approached the squatting shockee, mashed the trigger and poked Brave Heart on the bare bottom. Brave Heart screamed, "U-H-H-H-H-H-H-H", involuntarily pulled himself straight up and over the corner of the pen, and fell over into the alley way. He rolled around in the dust and dirt, moaning, crying and rubbing

Cracker Terms, Phrases And Definitions

his stinging behind. The assembled crowd watched this show with loud, somewhat hysterical hoots and laughter. Everyone got on the fence, looking over at Brave Heart. A couple men felt sorry for him, jumped to his aid, and helped him pull up his britches. He leaned for several minutes against the fence, wiping tears from his eyes, and said in the usual cowboy understatement, "Boys, I wanna tell ya–that's a touchus place…"

They gave him most of the money anyway. It was worth $5.00 a head for the entertainment. Far as I know that was the last time that event was held. True? I don't know and nobody will admit to the affair.

Toothless as ah rooster: describes an individual without teeth. Interestingly, cattle don't have upper front teeth. They have a coarse dental pad. The grasses are mashed tight against it and the head jerks so the bottom teeth cut it loose. Cowboys, feigning amazement, get a kick out of teasing children and tourists: "Lookie her', boys, none of these cows hav' got upper teeth."

Tougher'n a bus station steak: a phrase I first heard from Carl Hurley, a professor from Eastern Kentucky. The expression, having the potential for multiple usages, means that something was durable, tough, hard, mean, resistant, enduring, or solid. It was based on the facts that Eastern Kentucky bus stations, in particular, and all small town bus stations, in general, use cheap cuts of steak, subsequently overcooked on a flat grill. They are generally thin, charred, and require a good set of teeth and a pocketknife. The phrase packs tremendous potential for evaluating men, women, dogs, cats, cattle and horses–particularly ones that have survived against the odds. Using this saying almost always gets a laugh as it gets the point across. It can be used with other phrases, like, "Reminds me of an ol gal I knew—tougher than a bus station steak."

One man told me his son was so tough when he was a baby they had to tie him in a corner and feed him with a sling-shot.

Trade or traded: Crackers often ask, "Where do y'all trade?" meaning "routinely shop" for such as groceries, vehicles, etc. You can trade money for items or services, for horses, cows, calves, dogs, pocket knives, pistols, rifles, trucks, hats or caps, saddles and other riding gear, spurs, belts or jokes; the list is endless.

Trail 'em up: track something or someone. "Yeah, he trailed me up about dark," means the person (or dog) found me. Another example used during cow hunting, "Whin y'all git in tha hammock, see if you can trail 'um through. We'll wait on the edge of tha marsh 'til we see you come out." Also, the expression could be heard in the context of hunting. "That ol' dog can cold trail 'im… he carried tha mail all tha way through the swamp." (See term) This, of course, refers to the dog's ability to track by his sense of smell.

Speaking of that, I heard about a Cracker that claimed he owned a deer hound that followed a track all the way back to where the buck was born. (Think about it.) My step-father said he had a dog that had such a good nose he could blow the spider webs out of a deer track and catch up with the deer.

My first experience with such concepts was with Walker Hounds. They were fast trailers. Jack Coker of Okeechobee said, "We'll spend more time chasin' these dogs that we will huntin'." While most dogs rejoined the hunters when they lost the trail, some wouldn't quit easily–especially the Walkers. Rather than hunt the dogs all night, they implemented an old Cracker method: they'd build a fire, throw a coat on the ground by it and come back in the morning. The dog would usually be there bedded down on the jacket.

Trap: a word generally referring to a literal animal trap, or a holding pen for cattle beside the cow pens. "Y'all load the trap with enough cattle to work this mornin'," is an example. If used as a verb, it meant to guide or assemble into a group.

Another use was, "We got tha whole herd trapped up." The term was often used as slang for any capture or commitment, as in, "Yeah... Whin he found out jus how purty she is, he wuz trapped." Crackers used the term to express a variety of situations. I know of an old Cracker veterinarian in Arcadia, many, many years ago that used "trap" when he'd come in from working all day in the cow pens. He'd slow down as he approached his clinic. Looking ahead if he saw his parking lot full of small animal clients, he'd say, "Man! The trap is full..." Then he'd shift down into second gear, drive on by the clinic adding, "They'll thin out innah hour or two." It wasn't that he objected to the small animal work, he just didn't like whiney owners. When tha trap thinned out, i.e., the owners left their pets, he'd come back and treat the animals without a lot of conversation or whining.

Dr. Handley used the term often and it has become a fixed term in my vocabulary. To this day when I drive by a veterinarian's office with a dozen cars in his parking lot, I'll mention to any passenger, "Son! He's got 'im loaded in tha trap, don't he? He better titenup if he wants to git done by dark." I think of Dr. Carlton and I can almost hear Handley's voice when I say it.

Tryin' to keep ants in a pile: indicates frustration or futility. "Breakin' up that fight wuz lik' tryin' to keep ants in a pile." Another illustration was a fella helping out with the toddlers at church. He said, "Keepin' them little fellas together wuz lik' keepin' ants in a pile." ("Herding cats" is a synonym.)

Turkey huntin': Turkey hunters are not at all like hog hunters. This type of hunting appeals to an entirely different class. Though this is not to say hog hunters don't turkey hunt, turkey hunting is generally more sedate and less dangerous. Turkey hunters build obscure blinds of cabbage palm fans near a favorable spot where the birds usually walk by. Some even invest money in light-weight portable blinds made with camouflage patterns that make a place to sit unobserved by game. Turkeys have unbelievably acute vision. Some folks have said they can see a hunter blink his eyes. Wild turkeys can run away or will take to the wing if chased. We had a Weimaraner that would run them down if they weren't quick enough to take flight. I've seen him leap and grab a mouthful of tail feathers from a fleeing turkey.

"Roostin' turkeys" is spending time determining where the wild turkeys roost, so you can return before daylight and be ready when they fly down to feed. Turkeys will fly up at twilight, usually in high pines or oaks. One can hear them fly up on cold late afternoons and, if one is able to slip around under the roost; their dark outlines can be seen against the remaining light in the sky. Usually, early in the morning, they'll pull their heads out from under their wings, drop a load of manure, then after looking all around for danger, will alight from the roost and begin feeding. It is difficult to sneak up on feeding turkeys because there's always one scout looking for danger.

"Turkey callin'" is the actual imitation of the turkey's call in order to draw him closer. The "hen call" entices the gobbler to investigate so he can "strut for the ladies." A "pip call" is an alert call, while a "lonesome hen call" says (to turkeys), "I'm oh so lost an' lonely." A "feeding call" is the soft chuckling when they're eating. A "gobbler call" is sometimes used, as well. This art form is highly desired among serious hunters. There are "in-the-mouth" calls, wooden box calls worked with a striker against wood or stone, and there are electronic calls for a range of creatures: turkeys, quail, coyotes, hogs, wildcats, etc. I have no experience with the new electronic callers. There's a whole lot more to turkey huntin' than I have written here. Turkeys are marvelous birds and fun to "hunt." I emphasize "hunt" since more often than not, that's all you do and come home empty-handed.

I'll never forget the first time I took my wife turkey huntin'. We were courtin' then. She had flown in from New Orleans and was awestruck by the cattle country of Central Florida. We went out mid-afternoon. It was cold but sunny. We sat back-to-back in the woods at an area frequented by a flock. I guess we had been there for thirty minutes when she very softly spoke, "Howard... what does a wild turkey look like?" I figured that hunt was over before it started and it was cold anyway, so we left that shaded spot and moved to a dike where three oaks had grown out at nearly the same place. It was a good spot to see a long ways off and it was in the warm sun. Finally getting warm, in the quiet of the woods and soft afternoon rustles of little creatures making a living, we both fell asleep... until we heard the motor of a truck coming down the dike. Sonny drove up and stopped and looked. He said, "Whut in tha world are you all doin'?" I said, "We're turkey huntin'." He grinned, "Is that what they call it now?"

Twiced: in dialect: two times, as in, "Has she been married onced or twiced?"

Twist 'er (or his) tail: to literally twist the tail of a fractious cow to get her out of a chute. The twisting caused some minor pain (kinda like pulling a hair in your nose), but encouraged them to move on. It also meant to hurry one along, as in, "Sumbody twist Buddy's tail and git him in the truck." Also, "Don't git yer tail in a twist" meant "don't get all hot an' bothered" about something. "He's a real tail twister" means the fella (or animal) is mean, insistent, aggressive or pushy. "Don't git yer shorts in a twist" is a variation of the old standby, "Don't get your panties in a wad."

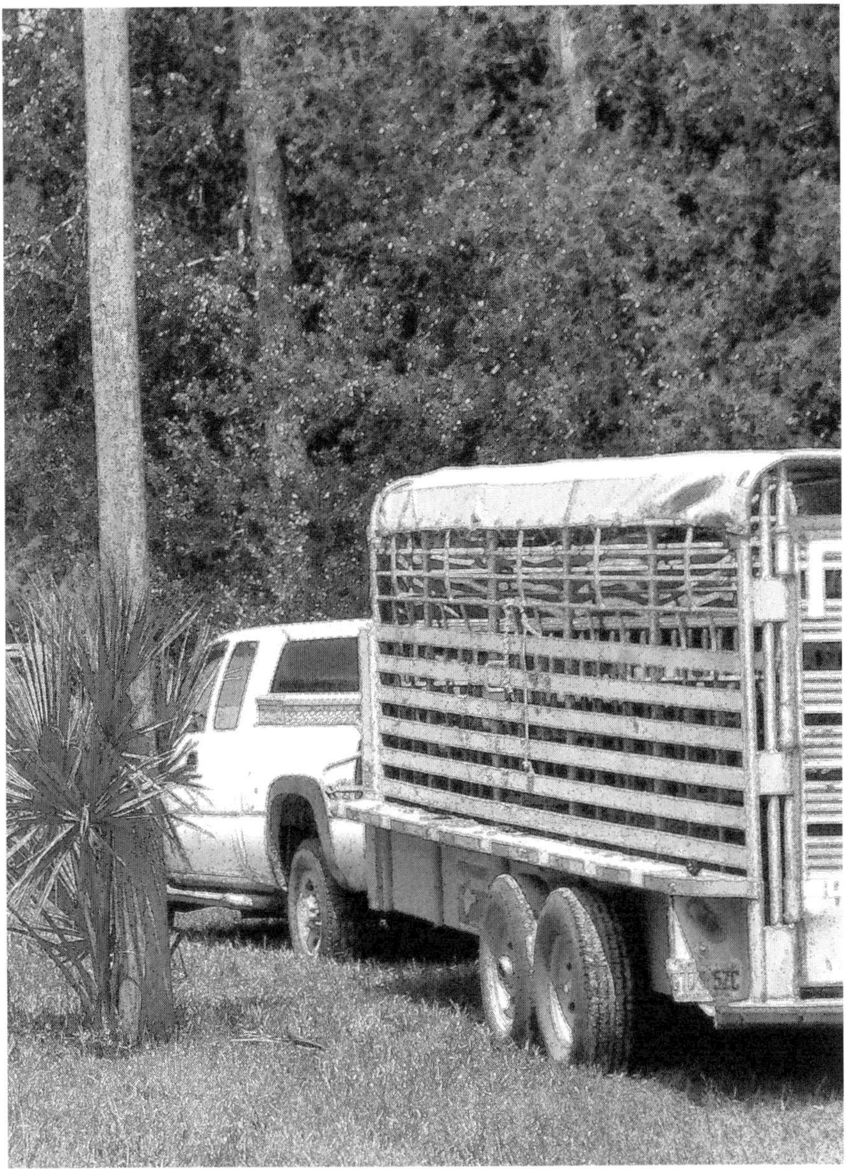

Cracker Terms, Phrases And Definitions

U

Unbelievable number of horses in Highlands County: a phrase spoken about our practice in the headquarters of Syntex Laboratories. The story has nothing directly to do with Crackers, but has a basis which finds foundation in our Cracker culture. In the early eighties I returned to Highlands County after my foray into academia. At the time, prices for cattle were low and the cost of medicine and biologicals were climbing. Since fluctuation in cattle prices affected cattlemen greatly, they naturally had to control expenses. As prices fell, so did the activities in the cow pens. At the time, deworming cattle costs were anywhere from $2.50 to $4.00 per head, depending on the product. Fresh from the hallowed halls of higher learning, I just happened to have been researching some new, yet unreleased, anthelmintics (drugs for the elimination of intestinal parasites in cattle and horses). The particular product I had researched was approved for horses but had not been released for cattle. Dr. Handley and I had a conference. I showed him all the technical data relating to the drug. It was effective on most of the main cattle intestinal parasites and, for some yet to be determined reason, seemed to "boost" the immune systems of cattle causing a "bloom" in body condition. At double-dosage rates it also affected adult liver flukes. It was a perfect de-wormer for our area. There were no deleterious effects whatsoever. But the key to the product was we could use the horse product in cattle. We researched everything about it and came to the conclusion we could buy the product and deliver it to our big ranch clients and their cost would be $1.00 per head to de-worm adult cattle. We contacted one of our big clients and outlined our plan. He readily said he would like to try the product. Cases and cases of the product were delivered to our door. We'd put a dispensing label on each jug without name, address, instructions, etc. Well, the first thing you know we had an excellent response to the product.

The rest of the story happened about one year later. We were, by this time, ordering fifty- to seventy-five cases of the stuff per month and using it at our client's ranches. The drug company representative came by one day and said I had an invitation to attend a company meeting in Scottsdale, Arizona—all expenses included. It sounded like fun so I told them I'd go. I thought it would be a dry, technical meeting so I decided to go alone. But come to find out, it was at an exclusive golf resort with $500-a-day room, all meals, entertainment and lots of free golf. (I was caught "flat-footed" by not taking my wife... but don't mention it to her.)

The final revelation was about a month later when I saw the drug representative. I told him I was surprised by the extreme generosity of the company. He said, "Doc, when they saw how many cases of horse wormer you'd purchased, the vice-president of the company said 'There must be an unbelievable number of horses in Highlands County!'"

(I suppose 40,000 head of horses is a lot. At the time, we were legally dispensing the product, but later the rules changed.)

Uncorked: to lose control, get crazy mad, as in, "Things wuz alrite 'til ol' Ring decided he'd catch 'im—that's whin tha bull come uncorked."

Up front–wher' the action is: means, "get to work where the critical work is," "where there is additional help needed," or "don't stand idle in the middle of the work." It brings us thoughts of the battlefield "Front Line." A classic tale about the use of this expression occurred when a foreman was harassing and cursing a young greenhorn crew because he didn't know how to work with people in any other way. He was running the head catch, while the crew was still in shake-down mode and not a finely tuned machine at that point in time. Each member was to learn how to coordinate efforts and speed the work up. Every time there was even a slight slow-down or hesitation of someone, this crew boss would yell, "(*Expletive deleted*) it! Y'all git up frunt wher;'

tha action is!" The men became a little tite-jawed (See term), sullenly working and wishing the man would find another line of work. But as work proceeded, Boss continued his persecution. He was busy running his profane mouth when a cow hit the head catch at wide-open speed, knocking the handle out of his hands and slamming it upward under his jaw. He was knocked out, colder'n kraut. The boys hesitated momentarily, grinned back and forth at each other, then dragged him over to a pile of roofing tin, laid him in the sun and went back to work. The fella slowly regained consciousness, groaned and sat up holding his jaw. When he began to get his senses, the boy on the head-catch at the front of the chute, to the utter delight of the crew, yelled, "Hey, Buck! Up front wher' tha action is!"

Upta now, ever'thing wuz awrite: the best illustration is as follows: A little boy was born into a fine Cracker family. He was a good lad and showed no development abnormalities until he reached the age when he should have started saying words. He didn't talk or even make any effort. The family doted over him and finally took him to a doctor for evaluation. They poked and prodded the lad and ran all kinds of tests, but concluded, "He's normal. We can't find any reason for his not speaking. He'll talk when he's ready." So the puzzled family took him back home.

The years flew by. The mother, the lad's aunts and grandmothers fussed over him since they all felt he was a special child. They met every need with affection. Then in his eleventh year at a family Thanksgiving gathering, everyone was enjoying the dinner, food was passed, plates and dishes rattled, forks clinked, iced-tea glasses tingled and everyone was talking and enjoying the fellowship. Then out of the clear blue sky, the boy sullenly said, "Would sumbody please pass tha mashed potatoes?"

Gasps and then a stunned silence broke through the conversation and lasted for a full 10 seconds. Finally Grand-daddy quietly spoke up, "Son, why have you waited so long to talk?"

The miffed boy replied, "Well, upta now ever'thing wuz goin' awrite."

V

Vascilate: to vaccinate or give injections. How it got so contorted I do not know. At first, one might think it refers to applying Vaseline or petroleum jelly.

The first time I heard it was when a man brought a dog into the hospital. Our receptionist asked, "What can we do for you today?" He replied, "I need my dog *vascilated* for rabies." She, by the hardest, contained her mirth. We also had one individual say, "I need my dog *suggested* for rabies." (I assumed this was a synonym for "vascilated.")

Many years ago, when money was not inflated as badly as it is today, we charged $3.00 for a rabies vaccination. This was a time when gasoline cost about 32 cents per gallon. Fruit-pickers were often paid in cash at the end of each day's work. Occasionally a man who'd just been been paid would want to have his dog vaccinated for the county-mandated rabies vaccination. We'd step out to the truck, vaccinate the dog and tell the client to step into the office for the vaccination certificate and tag. Some of these men would fork over a $100 bill. If the girls were low on change, they'd tell him they couldn't make change. These men would often say, "Send me a bill." But Doc Handley was always prepared. He kept $97 in his wallet at all times. He'd been "stung" so many times on billing fruit-pickers, he solved the problem with readily available exact change for a hundred-dollar bill.

One of the colorful Cracker cowboys I know once asked Handley, "Frank, do you give this vascilation in tha muscles, I.B.M. or under tha skin?" Frank was confused by the term, "I.B.M.", asking what that meant. Boy McGowan said, "You know…, in Between the Muscles."

Cracker Terms, Phrases And Definitions

Venomus: indicates meanness, vindictiveness, anger, wrath, or cantankerousness. My stepfather used it in reference to my mother on occasion—especially when she was upset or out of sorts about something one of us did (or didn't do). He was never angry when he said it—he enjoyed teasing her. In front of her he would say, "Boy, you better throw yer hat in the door before you go in—yer mama's been eatin' ham again—she's plum venomus."

Vomick in mah purse: There is only one documented case of the usage of this phrase. My wife tells of an incident related to her by a friend she's known since high school. The fella was in the textile business in the seventies (before the industry was forced out of business in this country). His family owned a few textile mills in various locations in the southeastern states. In order to keep the complicated weaving machines in good condition or repair, Mark's job was to fly the repair expert to and from the various mills. A machine broke down and stalled the production line, so Mark called the woman who knew how to repair the monster. The repair woman or expert is not what one would think: she was one-hundred percent pure, unadulterated Cracker. She'd learned all the technical skill over the years by on-the-job training.

Mark said she appeared to be a little uneasy as he taxied the plane toward the far end of the runway. He casually commented, "Miz Jane, if you get to feeling sick, there's some little white air sick bags in the seat pocket in front of your seat." In absolute seriousness, she replied, "Awe, that's awrite, Mr. D, if I git sick I'll jus vomick in mah purse."

Vetinary: obviously a colloquial pronunciation of "veterinarian." There is a sub-category of words and phrases used by the Crackers. I learned what they meant by association (and usage). Many of the descriptive terms are already listed in the main text but here in no particular order are some of the examples. (You may want to skip this part...)

A funny thing happened to me one time. While I was looking at a lame horse, the owner said, "It's funny, Doc... sometimes he's walkin' normal; other times he has a bad limp. Whut do you think I should do?" I scratched my head thinking of all the possibilities. One of the Cracker cowboys leaned over and said, "I know whut I'd do... next time he's walkin' good, sell 'im."

VETERINARY TERMS
APPETITE, INDIGESTION, BODY OR DENTAL CONDITION

Drawed down or up: in poor body condition or thin, "Slack-bellied."

Eyes lik' two holes in a blanket or hollow-eyed, **gaunt, puzzle-gutted' (see terms), sunk-eyed, gut shot (see terms), knotty, dried-up, wormy-lookin'**: words used for clinical signs of dehydration and/or starvation.

Foundered: a sore-footed horse (see terms).

Colicked: an intestinal condition resulting from over-eating or rapid changes in diet, or having a painful abdomen, indigestion, an intestinal or colon impaction.

Locked up: stiff, sore or unable to move a joint.

Locked bowels: constipated.

Off feed: not eating.

On his feed or full feed: eating well. (See "bellied-up.")

Bloated: see terms.

Blocked gullet: choked or having something lodged in the esophagus.

Lampers: an old time expression that meant the roof of a horse's mouth was swollen to the point of making it painful for the horse to eat, causing it to lose weight. I have no idea where it comes from, but I de-wormed them and they got better. In the older days, some "horse docters" cut the roofs of lampered horses' mouths.

Undershot: a genetic or hereditary abnormality where the bottom teeth protrude beyond the front teeth.

Wolf teeth: refers to the residual premolar teeth which erupt in front of the major molar teeth. Many horse people feel that these teeth, about the size of a pencil, cause the horse to fight or throw the bit. There are equine dental instruments called "elevators" designed to extract these small teeth but a $1.00 screw driver works just as well in the right hands.

I had a lady pass out on me one time while we were extracting some wolf teeth. I managed, but it was interesting. It was: hold the horse, step over Joy, catch the horse, open his mouth, pry a little, step back over Joy, stop, drag Joy away, re-catch the horse, remove teeth...

Wormy: to be infected with intestinal parasites, or to be small in stature.

Parrot-mouthed horse: to have the front teeth over-shot or protruding over the bottom front teeth.

Float his teeth or file off his points: to remove the sharp edges of the outside edges of the upper molars and the inside edges of the lower molars. This was done with a manual dental rasp or a mechanized rasp. Floating the molars of the horse allowed them to eat better and not waste grain.

LAMENESS OF THE FOOT OR MUSCLES

Corns: the soft, tender growths that are found between the two hooves (claws) of the front feet, usually in the heavy bulls.

Foundered; road-, grass- or grain-foundered: see terms. "Road founder" refers to the trauma sustained when horses are walked or run on concrete or a similar hard surface for an extended time.

Every year during the annual Cracker Trail Ride, some "soft" horses would get road founder. We'd meet the folks on this annual event commemorating the old Cracker cattle drives. They'd start in Bradenton and travel to Ft. Pierce. We'd meet the riders somewhere near the Highlands and Hardee County line. They usually "dinnered" in a hammock about five miles west of the junction of US highways 98 and 27. Mules seemed to have fewer problems than horses.

Foot rot or foot canker: infection of the foot, possibly including the soft tissues, the hoof wall, the sole of the hoof or the bone of the foot in cattle; sometimes it was found in horses, as well.

Scissor-billed or scissor-toed: a reference to the over-growth of the hooves in cattle where the toes are too long and over-lap forming a "scissor-like" appearance to the hooves.

Gravel: an abscess that develops under the sole of the horse's foot and eventually erupts at the top of the hoof. A "gravel" is often associated with a stone or literd knot bruise or a nail puncture since abscesses don't generally go out the hardened hoof; the abscess "seeks" a path of least resistance. Any sore foot on a cow horse was often expressed as, "You reckon he stepped onah nail?" "Stone-bruised" is an area of tenderness in a localized spot on the sole of the horse's or cow's foot. It can be from the animal's stepping on a sharp object which injures the sensitive tissues underneath the sole and it may or may not become infected.

Hamstrung: a condition in which the major tendon on the horse's hock is severed. This is similar to the rupture or severing of the Achilles tendon in the human heel. There are records from western pioneer journals where settlers would take an axe or similar cutting tool, "whack" their horse behind and above the hock at the onset of fall, and turn it loose. The horse would be lame, could not be ridden and, therefore,

Cracker Terms, Phrases And Definitions

the Native Americans wouldn't steal them. The horses were reportedly sound by spring. (Of course, in those bad winters, horse meat was often the only food source available.) How many times this anti-theft method could be used was not recorded.

Thrush: an infection from a foul-smelling bacteria found in the "frog" of the horse's foot. The "frog" is the V-shaped crevice on the sole of the hoof.

Fevered: a term describing swelling, increased heat or sensitivity from infection. For example, a broken bone or bone chip fracture in the early stages is not inflamed but it becomes "fevered" as swelling advances.

Stifled: used to describe a horse that has a knee problem. One of the three major ligaments that hold the knee and patella (knee cap) in place traps the patella under it and causes the horse's knee to lock in place; the horse then cannot flex its knee joint. The cowboys remedied this condition by backing the horse up until the patella was released. This problem develops in certain types of conformation, i.e., straight legged horses; and Shetland Ponies seem to have a higher incidence. Surgery can be done to prevent the trapping and temporary crippling of such a horse. But "stifled" could be used for any unusual back-leg lameness.

Stove up or knotted up: to be stiff, sore, slow or in pain.

Kidney colic or locked kidneys: a local term which misleadingly denotes abdominal pain not related to the kidneys. The "kidney-colicked" horse stretches his abdomen and, apparently, tries to urinate. Many Cracker cowboys were convinced that this was a real disease. The veterinarian would examine the horse for signs of colic (abdominal pain) and determine the cause(s) of it. (It's the same principle as the painful left arm in a heart attack, called "referred pain.") The old Crackers wanted a "shot to unlock his kidneys." I would give an injection for pain and a diuretic. The pain injection worked, alleviating the horse's discomfort. And the diuretic worked at the same time, causing the urine to flow freely, thus satisfying the owner. (Sometimes, on a midnight call, it was easier to give an injection for pain than to get into a long discussion about "kidney colic.")

Tied up or Monday mornin' tie-up: refers to a horse with acute muscle inflammation. It would make the horse sore in the major muscles of the back and thighs. It was a complicated metabolic problem related to nutrition and work stress. A fat horse, one regularly over-fed, was more likely to develop this "myositis" from the excessive lactic acid generated by activity after several days or weeks of not working. It might develop after the horse leaves the barn and/or after a strenuous bout of work early in the day. Occasionally, horses "tied-up" during extreme stress when the rider is roping rank bulls. The horse would begin to sweat, slow and/or stop handling well. Usually with a little adjustment of diet and conditioning the problem could be avoided. Pain medication and anti-inflammatories helped, but prevention was by adjusting the nutrition of the horse during times of reduced activity. More than once I heard, "Doc, I need a shot for *Homer*. He's tied up agin."

Hitch in 'er getalong: a problem of locomotion from lameness or injury.

Poultice: a pasty powder under a bandage placed on a swollen or fevered lag of a horse to "draw down" the swelling.

SKIN DISEASES

Cancer or cancered: any growth on the skin or eye.

Cankered: moist and foul-smelling infections. "Ear (or eye) canker" referred to the location.

Crud: any skin infectection.

Scratches: any dermatitis, but usually, the intense itching and hair loss around the ears, chest, face, thighs or tail of the horse. The synonym for "scratches" is "fly-bite dermatitis." It was seasonal and occurred during the peak of the fly season. Most horses would rub their affected areas on fences, posts, or anything to relieve the discomfort. The area at the base of a horse's tail and the surrounding area could become hairless. Often, the cowboys would ask if I thought the horse had pinworms, a parasite of the lower bowel. Most of the time, in our area, it was fly-bite allergy reactions.

Pinkeye: any eye infection where there was redness, excessive tear formation, painful lid spasm, ulcers on the cornea, or infection of the inside of the eyelids (the "conjunctiva"). Crackers might call cancer (squamous cell carcinoma of the eye), "pinkeye."

Ringworm: true fungal ringworm, "scratches" or any skin problem.

Sloughed or rotted: referred to any area of gangrene or necrosis (i.e., "dead tissue").

Fistula, fistulous withers, saddle canker, saddle sores, saddle galls or galled: "Fistula" and "fistulous withers" refer to abcesses at the withers (the top of the shoulders in front of the area where the saddle is cinched). The deep ligaments in the area abcess and cause a nasty draining tract of pus. It is due to injury or infection. A saddle, if improperly padded, can cause "saddle sores" or "galls" which are areas of pressure necrosis (dead skin tissue like "bed sores" in people). If a horse was tender when a saddle was thrown on him, sometimes he was called "saddle sore" or "touchus" (See term). (In veterinary school, we had an Equine Clinician we called, "Ol' Saddle Sores" because he had worked on Cavalry horses.)

Mange: any skin disease.

REPRODUCTIVE ORGANS
OF THE COW, BULL, MARE OR STALLION

About to pop, springin' or springer or all swolled up and tighter'n a drum: a cow near calving when the abdomen is huge and all the pelvic ligaments are loose. "All swolled up" and "tighter'n a drum" refered to the size of the abdomen right before calving.

Found calf: to find a cow with her newborn calf, meaning the cow had delivered.

Drawed down (or up): usually meaning they suspected she'd already calved when discovered; it could mean the cow was a good milker and the poor body condition was due to poor nutrition or nursing a hearty calf.

Walkin' straddle-legged or staggerin': a description of a cow which has a calf hung in the pelvis. This partially paralyzes the back legs of the cow by putting pressure on the nerves on the inside of the back legs. "Hitch in 'er getalong" meant she was having trouble walking with the calf lodged in the pelvis, or anyone who had a limp.

Patootie: (see terms)

Cast 'er withers: a cow or mare with a uterine prolapse where the uterus has turned inside-out exposing the organ outside of the birth canal. (Speaking of that, a ranch manager and I witnessed a freak happening: Bob was taking me out to a cow with a prolapsed uterus. She was in a trap and we thought we could walk her into the pens to a catch chute. Well, she bowed up at us, attacking the truck and darting away. While we sat in the truck, as she whirled sideways so she could keep an eye on us, her pendulous uterus fell off! I couldn't believe what I'd seen. I told Bob, "She's dead and didden know it." I figured we ought to get her into the chute and tie-off the pencil-sized blood vessels–thinking we could at least save her life for future sale. We did succeed

Cracker Terms, Phrases And Definitions

in getting her into the chute. Upon examination, she was fine; the fist-sized cervix had contracted so tightly that there was no bleeding. We marked her ear to designate she was destined for slaughter and turned her out. Weird? I thank... (See terms)

Fevered: any swelling in an area.

Pizzle-sprung: see term in text.

Cods: colloquial term for testicles.

Dew poisoning or prolapsed prepuce: a swelling and eversion of the interior of the prepuce of the bull. It looked like a pink donut hanging out of the prepuce. The Brahma bulls were especially susceptible to "dew poisoning" due to their pendulous reproductive structures. Dew had nothing to do with the malady – it was the constant damage done by roots, rough grasses and bushes.

Sprung: a general term for the hematoma of the penis of the bull. During mating which is a vigorous event, sometimes the cow moves as the bull thrusts. He subsequently bends the penis to the point of rupture of ligaments and blood vessels. This results in a massive blood clot which looks like a subcutaneous Italian sausage. From a practical standpoint, the bull is then unusable (See **pizzle-sprung**).

Rig: a horse with a retained testicle in the abdomen. Some horses don't "drop" both testicles during development; i.e., one remains inside the abdomen and does not descend outside the inguinal ring (a natural slit in the abdominal muscles in the area of the "groin" of males). The technical term for this is cryptorchidism. Horses are "gelded" or castrated to eliminate the bad behavior of the stallion. Castration of male stock is one of the oldest surgical procedures known. Only males with desirable breeding characteristics are kept as breeding stock. The problem arises when the "dropped" (descended) testicle is surgically removed and the retained testicle is left inside the abdomen. The abnormally positioned testicle continues to produce the hormones that make a stallion difficult to handle. This kind of horse is called a "rig." He may look like he has been castrated, but acts like a stallion, even breeding at times. Many a "rig" has been sold to unwary buyers who find out later that they have a "tough" horse to handle.

Freak calf: a deformed calf

Hung up: the explanation of a lodged or blocked calf inside the uterus or pelvis of the cow. In difficult labor sometimes a cesarean section was the only way to deliver a live calf. "You think we need to cut on 'er?" meant was a C-section needed.

Fevered: usually meant that the cow was sick after calving or from infection.

Full-bagged or slack bagged: referred to the size of the cow's udder: full, because the calf had not suckled, or empty, from the calf having suckled or the cow did not make any milk for some reason.

Makin' a nest: meant the cow, mare, bitch or sow was preparing for labor by showing signs of restlessness and discomfort.

Dry cow: a cow that has no milk in the udder, is not near calving time or is not even pregnant.

THE NERVOUS SYSTEM OR COORDINATION

Blind staggers, boogered or boogery: see terms. "Blind staggers" was often substituted for "sleeping sickness," both referring to encephalitis in the horse. Cattle can have "circling disease," which is Listeriosis. Lead poisoning can cause blindness, staggering and incoordination.

Circlin': an animal that continually walks in aimless circles; usually associated with brain disease or brain inflammation.

Head bobber, head weaver and stump sucker: refers to the vices of the stalled horse. The term is probably related to a behavioral problem from boredom or when "first cousins keep marryin'." (See term) A **stump sucker** will place the front upper teeth on any available place in the stall, mash its head down and suck in air. (See **stall sour**)

Readin' or studyin' tha ground' or far-away look: refers to an animal of diminished mental state or severe depression of mental abilities. This type of animal is reluctant to move away, is listless and seems to be staring at the dirt–much like those who've just received their income tax bills.

Limber-tailed: tail paralysis.

Staggery: uncoordinated.

Goose-steppin': a peculiar gait or means of walking; often associated with blindness, brain injury or brain disease.

THE RESPIRATORY SYSTEM

Tha snots: reference to the runny noses of animals with respiratory disease.

Ah cold or tha flu: same as above.

Heaves, heevie, wind broke: describes symptoms of emphysema due to inflammation of the lung from allergies or exertional damage from severe over-work. A "heave line" refers to the abdominal muscles that enlarge from the affected horse forcing expiration. (See **Tha thumps** in the terms above.)

SITUATION, STATUS, CLASSIFICATION OR DISPOSITION

Eater, sale cow (or bull), slaughter, cull, cutter, freezer-cow: denotes cattle that would be unprofitable or unsuitable to keep in the herd. All the terms indicate the destination of the cow, either to the home freezer, the sale barn or to a local butcher for custom butchering for home use. Most ranches had a pen or pasture where a cull could be kept until ready for sale to slaughter. Some ranches butchered their own beeves for the cowboys to share. (Of course, when a cow was injured a few of the cowboys would kiddingly ask, "Reckon we ought to put'er in the freezer?")

In summary, familiarity with these terms helps one to understand what the cowboy is seeing. Even then, it "didden always work."

W

Wad or wadded: a term for a tangle or jumble, or an excessive amount of anything. This is a versatile term and can be used in several contexts: "Ther wuz a plum wad of quail flew up." "He-ah! Take that wad of dogs an' put 'em in the horse trailer." "Look how tha rope is wadded up." "Hey, get me a wad of grease for tha door hinge." And, "Boy, he sure had a wad of foldin' money; it'd choke a mule." ("Wad" and "gob" are pretty much interchangeable.)

Wall-eyed: I never fully understood what this meant. It could be used to describe bulls, dogs, men and sick individuals, as in, "He come runnin up--all wall-eyed" or "That dog went plumb wall-eyed whin he caught that hog." I suspect it means to become excited and aggressive. Hubert, one of my best Cracker cowboy friends, used it with fellas that came to work on Monday mornings after a wild and riotous weekend. From the context, I think he meant that they were fatigued. Apparently, the word has multiple uses and meanings, as in "I git plum wall-eyed thinkin' about it."

War bridle: the name may have come from the Native Americans when they first started riding the Spanish horses. The difference is they often put the rope in the mouth and not always on the sensitive gum under the upper lip. This is the use of a make-shift soft rope for applying pressure under the upper lip and behind the ears of uncooperative horses.

Though difficult to explain, I'll do my best. The first aspect of a "war bridle" was placing a soft rope (or, in emergency, a lariat) on the upper neck. Care must be taken to ensure the rope will not be a slip knot that could choke the horse. I used a non-tightening "bowline knot" on the end of the ten-foot rope, placing it over the horse's neck and running the rope through the end loop. One then has to make another loop by turning the rope and placing it behind the ears and into the mouth seating it under the upper lip of the horse.

A modern war bridle is a type of bitless bridle made by applying a thin cord run over the poll (the area on top of the head and sort of between the ears of the horse) and then either through the mouth or under the upper lip, against the gumline of the upper incisors. In some cases, the lower loop goes around the horse's muzzle rather than under the upper lip. A loop is used so that it tightens on the horse's head when the end of the line is pulled. Sometimes a pulley is used to provide mechanical advantage. All designs tighten on both the poll and the lip or jaw. The war bridle is not intended for riding; it is used on the ground for management of an animal. The use of a war bridle is usually considered by most horse people as a *last resort for handling an uncontrollable animal.* I don't totally agree that it is a last resort if applied with common "horse sense."

Some consider use of a war bridle as animal cruelty. I have been around some horse owners who have little understanding of horses. They often expressed their concerns about any devices used for restraint or re-training. And, more often than not, their horses were "nuts." (Yes, we all would love to see innumerable equine herds running free on countless acres of prairie, but the real world is not that way. And yes, there's nothing worse than ill-informed people using devices to apply what they think is "discipline", which in reality is impatiently and ignorantly used, causing unnecessary difficulty for the horse.) The limited, careful and patient use of a war bridle did the same thing as a chain lead on the end of a long cotton rope, but the same fundamental principle applies. When the horse flares back and away, pressure is applied to the sensitive upper gums and at the poll; the result being the horse thinks he is causing the pain by his bad behavior. Fractious horses "discovered" that after three or four times of pulling back and feeling the tightening of the war bridle, it is much better to cooperate than fight. It worked in my hands almost every time after a few blow-back attempts–and these horses remembered me and how my handling wasn't so bad after all.

Many Crackers and almost all backyard horse people were impressed at how well their horses cooperated with me. I always used these occasions to teach them patience and understanding the horse's mind.

Speaking of patience and understanding, my step-father once said, "A fella cain't pee over a three-rail fence 'til he's forty" (i.e., *years of age*). Horse men and women must learn patience and understanding of horses, which comes with age and experience.

Water break: in the cow pens, it was announced as "Water Break!" as the foreman told the worker to shut off the chute. Men would come toward the chute, especially if it was under a shady shed, which most were. Horse play and "jawin'" was common. These breaks were gladly welcomed in the heat of the day. Cows and calves would bawl back and forth across fences loudly expressing their dissatisfaction at being separated and most of the men just relaxed and sat awhile. Then, after a ten- or fifteen-minute interval, the chute would "fire up," men way back in the back of the pens would "load the hopper pen" and the whole waltz started all over. Some foremen were restless at these times and acted as if the cattle would spoil in the sun. Thunder and lightning storms often force welcomed water breaks, but the rains cooled the cattle.

Cracker Terms, Phrases And Definitions

Welcome back: Ordinarily this would not be included in a Cracker Handbook; however, since the story behind it is unique, I feel it should be recorded. It occurred in an upper South Florida doctor's office. A doctor, whose name has been changed, had a serious bout with cancer. He was a prominent general practitioner, giving care to a multitude of patients over many years. After the chemotherapy for the cancer was completed he was able to return to work. He started seeing a backlog of patients who wanted only him as their personal physician. Shortly after he resumed practice, one of his long-time female patients appeared for her annual gynecological appointment. He and the assisting nurse went into the exam room where the patient had assumed the standard examination position in the stirrups. After the initial greetings, the doctor removed the drapes. On the inside of her legs written in lipstick was, "Welcome back, Dr. Olsen." After the outbursts of hysterical laughter, she explained how difficult it was to write the message on the inside of her legs, with lipstick, upside down and in a mirror. (And, yes, she was a refined Cracker.)

Welcome to Hardee County: a phrase I said to myself when crossing the Highlands-Hardee County line. Early one morning as I was heading to Wayne Collier's ranch, I looked ahead and saw a cur dog get up and stand in front of a little shack of a house. The old yellow dog wagged his tail and was looking up at something hidden by the bushes next to the porch. As I got closer, I could see a man standing on the porch in baggy white boxer shorts and a "Marlon Brando" tank-top undershirt, yawning and rubbing his huge belly. The old dog looked like he was grinning. This struck me as funny. Out loud I said to myself, "Welcome to Hardee County!"

Well I swan or Well I swanee: phrases used by my mother when she wished to express mild astonishment. I have no idea what it means--only that originally it came from Western Kentucky. She'd hear something that was outlandish, but interesting and unconsciously say, "Well I swanee." Sometimes she'd say, "Well, I declare." Both seemed to fit in Cracker culture. No one ever questioned what it meant in all the many times she used the expressions. "Well I swan," could have been euphemistic for, "Well, I swear." (Obviously an anathematic phrase for a Baptist–you weren't supposed to swear.)

When tha fruit is ripe, it'll fall: a standard answer from a Cracker veterinarian (or country doctor) when asked when a pregnant female should go into labor and have her baby (or litter, as the case may be). I have heard there was an old country doctor who was reportedly one-hundred percent accurate in his predictions of the gender of unborn babies. Being a prominent physician in the area, the reports of this uncanny skill spread rapidly among the folk. He'd visit with the various patients after their examinations and sometimes casually mention something like, "Well, I see you're going to have a fine baby boy." "How do you know?" would be the usual the curious reply from the expectant mother. He'd say, "I just know. In fact, I am so sure, I'm going to write it down in my memo book." When the baby did arrive, if it was a boy, he had hit the mark. If a girl, the mother and family would remind him he had missed. He'd say they were wrong and get his memo book. He'd look up the name of the women, the date and the sex of the unborn baby he'd written and read aloud: "Sarah Jane Baggerly; office visit May 12, 1979; girl." Then he'd show them the book... with a sweet smile. (Yes, everyone eventually caught on to his method but he had a lot of fun with his patients.)

I used a modified version of this technique. When some young people (or gullible adults) were around as I examined a pregnant mare, I'd say something like, "Boy! This colt is going to have some long legs!" (They all do.) Or, "I bet this foal will hold his head high when he gallops." (Ditto) But the most fun was when I was examining a show heifer for the 4-H members. The kids were enthusiastic and generally excited that their show heifer was pregnant. I'd say something like,

Cracker Terms, Phrases And Definitions

"Yep. Good news: she's pregnant. She was bred just before sunrise, 41 and ½ days ago, by a black bull, and it was cloudy that morning." Many a jaw has dropped at this kind of remark... until I grinned.

Whin you run with tha bulls yer gonna git horned: an all-inclusive warning that there are consequences for certain dangerous actions. For example, when you tried to date a bad fella's girl, he could beat the stuffings out of you at the local juke. (See "juke") A reckless driving citation and subsequent revoked driver's license would be an example. Adultery was the perfect example of runnin' with tha bull. (The horn was the divorce.)

Wher' are tha signs? a question referring to the position of the moon as it relates to: (1) a particular part of anatomy on a ranch or farm animal; or (2) in seed planting, etc.

As a young man in Cracker Florida a new concept crept into my experience: "The Signs." Now, I'd heard of tales of people doing things by the mystical signs. It was right up there with water witches, planting by the moon, astaphidity bags, etc. Any Farmer's Almanac can tell you when the signs are right for planting, working hogs, horses, cattle, etc. There is something to it–I just don't know what.

After surgical wrecks, I was always afraid to look and see where the signs were. I didn't want to know I'd chosen a wrong time. The Crackers would ask my friend and first mentor in veterinary practice, Dr. Frank Handley, "Are the signs right to cut a colt." He'd always say, "The signs are in the feet now; it ought to be a good time." If he knew them well, he'd say, "If you have $25–the signs are right."

We once had a man ask if the signs were right. Handley replied, "Yes."

The fella then asked, "How much do you charge?"

Frank replied, "$25." (That is about $150 in today's dollars)

The man asked, "How much will you charge to cut two colts?"

Frank said, "$20 each - $40."

The man studied a while, then questioned, "How many will I have to bring in to get them done for nuthin'?" (This fella was always thinking.)

I heard him tell a man once, "If you cut (i.e., castrate) tha colt now, he'll prance to the barn with his ears forward." (Of course, they all do that going to the barn.)

You may think this "signs" business is fantasy or myth. It probably came over with the mystics from the Celtic lands of Ireland and Scotland. I learned that there are insensitive things that affect animals and people. "Lunatics" are said to be affected by periodic behavior related to moon phases. There was more going on than met the eye it seemed. Maybe there is something to the "signs." But I took up Dr. Handley's word: If they had the money for the surgery, the signs were right!

Wher' dozzah fella git one of them things? Though I've not documented many instances where this phrase was used, the best example was given to me by Dr. Charles Payton. He told me of a veterinarian who had a broken portable X-ray unit. Under the law in the state in which he practiced, there was a "grandfather clause" where old-time laymen or "lay-veterinarians" could continue their "practice" without a license. Well, a particular lay-veterinarian would travel throughout the area, castrating people's stallions. The procedure was crude and without anesthesia. But when it came to the "lay-doctor's" stallions, he called the local licensed graduate veterinary practitioner to do the castration.

On one of these days, the practitioner had the broken X-ray unit lying in the back of his vehicle. The lay-doctor presented a fine colt for the surgery. He eagerly watched everything the doctor did, in hopes, no doubt, of up-dating his technique. Well, the doctor was using a drug for immobilization and administered a local anesthetic as well. The immobilizing drug is called "Sucostrin." It is used in people under anesthesia to relax muscles, allowing the surgeon to more easily do the surgery without tense muscles. In the horse, we'd give a small dose; a ten- to twenty-second delay would occur before the horse would become recumbent. We'd have a halter on the horse to keep him from hurting his head as he went to the earth. In the story, the veterinarian knew he was being closely watched by the layman for "pointers" on castrating colts. He administered the Sucostrin, turned quickly, set the timer on the broken X-ray unit for five seconds and pointed the machine-head at the colt's head. Five seconds clicked off the timer and the colt hit the ground right on cue. Much impressed the layman watched the whole procedure; then he turned to inspect the X-ray machine. He asked, "Wher' dozzah fella git one of them things?"

Wher's ah way outta this place? a phrase which originated from a story told years ago in Okeechobee. The story went something like: In the middle of a fight, a fella runs into the back room of the juke joint (see term) and says, "Wher's a way outta this place?" The bartender stopped re-stocking shelves and said, "Ther' ain't none." The fella said, "Wher' do you want one?"

Whinnin' an' moanin': an expression for the lack of pity for someone's excuses (for failure, reluctance to do something, or for complaining), as in, "Boy, don't you come in her' whinin' an' moanin'—I know you caroused around an' laid out all nite… we don't wanna hear it."

Whippin' ah dead horse: a useless act; indicating that one is wasting his time in whatever effort is being expended, as in, "Yer truck ain't gonna start. Yer whippin' a dead horse, Buddy." To tell the truth I think this is an old phrase used in many cultures. I recall a veterinarian from New Mexico who spoke Spanish. During his presentation on Management in Large Dairy Herds, he was asked a question on how he handled a particurlarly complicated herd infection in his practice. He responded in Spanish and was met by silence He then interpreted for us and said, "It is an old Spanish expression meaning, 'When one encounters a dead donkey in the middle of the road, drive around him; everyone else does.'" By his response we were sure he meant that tackling the particular problem was "whippin' ah dead horse."

Whut'd tha folks at tha feed store say? a question I'd ask Crackers who were wanting free information. I'd get calls from men and women folks occasionally who'd want information about a problem with a dog, cow or horse. It was obvious to me by the way they talked they really weren't interested in spending any money for professional services and, after a month or two, I was their last resort. To confirm this, I'd ask, "Whut'd Johnny (or 'the folks') at tha feed store say?" After a very brief pause, the answers could range from, "Well, the medicine they give me didn't do any good" to "They said if tha (*animal*) ain't doin' right, I should call you." The worst case scenario was when they called late at night to "consult" on a case after exhausting the experience and knowledge of the people at the feed store. In some cases the animal was worse from the "feed store recommended treatment." I would say something like, "You better call Johnny at home and ask him what to do with what he sold you. Call me back after he answers your questions. I really don't know what he gave you." (Johnny didn't particularly like being called at home but I figured if I had to get up and answer the phone, no need to be the only one.) Generally though, we had excellent relations since we had the same goals. (If we'd been lawyers we'd have given away a fortune in advice.)

Whut tha (*expletive for 'place of the departed doomed' deleted*) are y'all gonna do? I know this question has been used in many contexts and circumstances. The most memorable time for me was in Montana. On an elk hunting trip, we heard the big Florida-Georgia game was scheduled to play on a Saturday on the ESPN channel. Wes, my nephew, told the guide we really needed to watch this game. He said there was no satellite access back in the mountains where we were headquartered. We were concerned. The guide suggested we try the local motel in Ennis. We decided to go rent a room, split the cost between the eight of us, go by a "Sack-and-Go" for drinks and snacks and watch the game in comfort. Well, everyone wanted to go, including the guide. We loaded all nine of us into the big Suburban and pulled out for town. Since it was early winter in Montana we were dressed in cowboy hats, quilted jackets and boots. Wes went in to broker the room. I happened to be watching the office as Wes talked with the elderly clerk. The man snapped his head toward the Suburban, then, he looked back at Wes with an expression that looked like confusion and anxiety. Wes said something and the clerk smiled and went about collecting the money.

When Wes returned to the vehicle he told what happened at the desk. He said he asked for a room for three hours. The clerk looked out at the Suburban. All he could see were eight burly, un-shaven men with cowboy hats. That's when he asked Wes, "Whu tha h - - - are y'all gonna do?" Wes then told him we wanted to watch a football game on ESPN. Wes said the fella relaxed upon hearing the reason for a three-hour room rental. I wonder what he was thinking...

That trip was memorable for me since my horse stumbled on ice on a snow-covered trail and we slid down the slope together. It happened on the second day so I was out of business for the rest of the trip and hobbled around for the next several weeks. After a couple of days of icing my knee down and the boys bringing me some crutches, I hobbled down to the dinner table. At that time the head guide's wife was Mexican. Her Spanish-speaking sister brought food and water to me in the bunkhouse. She was a very healthy (heavy-set) girl and had a quiet countenance. Since she only spoke Spanish and I only spoke Spanglish, a mixture of the two languages, somehow we communicated on how much I really appreciated her tender care. When I was able to return for meals with the men, I mentioned to the table how kind she'd been to bring me meals. I commented, "Ya know, that ol' gal would begin to look pretty good if we wuz trapped up here durin' one of them three-month snows." One of the young fellas said, "I don't think it'd take more'n a couplea days!" (Oh, to be young again!)

Whut happened to yer teeth? a question asked by Wes Williamson to a hired hand in Alabama. After many days of coming to work, the man appeared without his teeth. No one knew he had false teeth. Wes said it was a shock to see the man abruptly missing all teeth. He asked, "Whut happened to yer teeth?" The toothless fella replied, "Aw, my wife had to go to town so she's usin'em today."

Whut wer' you thinkin'? a slang for, "What were you thinking *at the time of the incident*?" This phrase was used to understand the logic of one's action when things didn't turn out as planned. I was at a dairy once when a man decided to tie a plastic gallon milk jug to a dairy cow's tail. (I don't know why either–bored maybe?) The cow was boogered by the jug; she proceeded to run down the lane, jump the fence and run out into the woods. The manager came up and asked, "Billy? Whut wer' you thinkin'?" The fella drawled, "I ort not do this." (See "boogered", and "ortinah dun that.")

Whut you call'im? or Whut you call'er? asking what an individual's name is. I once overheard a group of men talking about a cow dog; it went something like this:

"Whut you call yer dog?"

"He ain't gotta name... he won't come anyway."

"Why's zat?"

"He ain't got no legs."

"Well, I'll be.... How does he do his bidness?"

"I have to take him out fer it inah wheelbarrow. He run a rabbit tha other day an' like to hav' killed me! So now I take

Cracker Terms, Phrases And Definitions

'im in the truck ever mornin' an' slide 'im off a ramp. But he reely is ah smart dog."

"How's that?"

"Tha neighbor said tha ol' dog crawled up to a sign on his fresh-painted porch. It said, 'WET PAINT'—an' he did."

"Ain't you tired of totin' that dog ever'wher'?"

"Yeah, so I fixed 'im sum wooden legs. He was able tah get around for ah while."

'Whut happened?"

"He run into ah grass fire and burnt to tha ground…"

"Sounds lik' he's more trouble'n he's worth."

"Nah… I cut a hole in a feed sack, stuck his head out and tied 'im to tha saddle horn, sos he kin cow hunt with us."

"How'd that work out?"

"Not reel good. Ever' time he wants to catch a cow, I hav' to get off my horse, untie the sack an' carry him up close to 'er sos he can grab ah ear. Feedin' 'im wuz ah problem, too."

"How's zat?"

"Well you know how ornery dogs can be whin you feed 'um together. I'd have to tote him over to fight tha other dogs for food. It got to be a chore, but he wuz ah good hog dog."

"Yeah? How so?"

"I'd jus' toss him over in tha palmettos and he'd scare tha hogs reel bad—they'd think he wuz ah barkin' snake an' they'd pull out. We'd catch 'um as they made a run fer it. But the other thing he was good at wuz for cleanin' out armadillo holes in tha yard. I'd put him down and he's wiggle down in tha hole an' spook out anything in it. He got trapped in one once. It musta been thirty-feet long. Sum how he got wedged inah tite place or got lost. I had tah dig him out. He'd bark an' by the time I'd dug down, he'd moved down the hole. I guess I tore up a half an acre of yard tryin' to locate 'im."

"You still got tha dog?"

"Yeah, but he's retired now; just lays around, like me, but I'll tell ya, that dog wadn't near as special as the one Orville Hicks had up in Boone, North Carolina. He told a tale on him that I thought wuz plum funny. He said his daddy wuz cuttin' hay with ah scythe one day. Mama hollered for him to come to dinner. So he laid the scythe down next to tha fence with the blade up–so he could find it when he come back to finish. Orville said they had a dog that loved to run rabbits an' he wuz hot on tha trail of one runnin' right down tha fence line. He said tha dog ran into the scythe and it cut 'im right down the middle.... His daddy ran out and put him back together agin with some sheets and tape. They laid 'im in tha barn an' fed an' watered him for ten days. His mama an' daddy went out an' took the tape and bandages off an' tha dog had mended! Only problem wuz, he had two legs up and two legs down! His daddy had put tha halves back together wrong."

"Whut happened?"

"Well, he said tha ol' dog would still hunt on two legs. Said when he got tired, he'd just flip over to the other legs and keep ahuntin'. But tha thing that got me wuz Orville said he wuz tha only dog in the mountains that could bark outta both ends."

(On and on and on this went... no one laughed out loud but there were chuckles and amused smirks on the circle of faces.)

A young man from Avon Park came in the hospital one night with a female dog he called "Judy." I looked for her record under "Judy" but couldn't find it. Thinking this might be a new dog, I asked, "Is this a new gyp?" He said, "Naw, her first name was Susie." I asked, "Why'd you re-name 'er?" He

Cracker Terms, Phrases And Definitions

said, "We re-named 'er after my ex-wife, Doc, 'cause they got ah lot in common."

Names of cur dogs and hog dogs are common but others are unique. Some were named for friends, ex-wives, color, some for ability, some for temperament traits, and some just for fun. Some of the names I remember are: Buck, Jack, Gator, Bull, Frank, Snap, Snapper, Whimpy, Pencil, Roy, Butch, Cookie, Belle, Otto, Rowdy, Bingo, Brindy, Ring, Lady, Laddie, Lad, Otis, Odes (See term for meaning), Boss, Bertha, Grit, Hammer, Storm, Spike, Midnight, Suzie, Gyp, Killer, Fang, Banjo, Jim, Rip, Ratchet, Cruiser, Cooter, Rat, Hazer, Blackie, Brownie, Blue, Whitey, Yeller (for color or voice), Joyce, Judy, Beulah, Spot, Tiger, Tobie, Tige, George, Fat Boy, Boots, Tippy, Junior, Vice-grip (or Vice, for short), Billy, Cletus, Phylo, Wally, Tom, Sugar, Smokey, Whiplash (or Whip, for short), Freda, Joe, Pig, Raider, Rambler, Hatchet, etc.

Many, many others I've forgotten, although some mean ones were called, "That (*fill in the color*) sonofah b - - - - ."

Whut'er you doin' here? or Whut'er we doin' here? a question often asked in a humorous mocking or teasing manner. The first phrase was said to someone who appeared unexpectedly, perhaps because he should be doing some other chore or activity. If a tractor broke down, drivers were often told to join another crew. If a man came back to work when he had the day off for some reason, it was asked to find out why he came back to work. If the second phrase was asked by the newcomer it was often tongue-in-cheek because it would be perfectly obvious. When a cowboy walked into the pens where there was heated activity, like working calves at a rate of one per minute, he might ask "Whut'er we doin' here?" or "Whut'er y'all doing to that puny thing?" when it was obvious. In sarcasm, its use would follow to underline difficulties, as while working a particularly rank set of yearlings. One might say, "Whut'er y'all doin' to these sweet calves?"

"Whut'er we doin' here?" was not an existential question of man's role in the universe—it was mostly something to say as a greeting. The best example was when a Sheriff's Deputy came to the pens one time to visit. He was in the area, used to work cattle as a kid and just wanted to smell the air and visit the crew. One of the men smiled at him and said, "Whut'er you doin' here—we ain't got no donuts...."

Whut'n tha hamfat: a less offensive substitutionary expletive that was often used at moments of astonishment, as in "Whut'n tha hamfat's goin' on here?" Apparently, ham fat had some mystical meaning at one time that has been lost in subsequent generations. I have heard it said in South Texas, Alabama, Eastern Kentucky and Southern Florida. It may well have been derived from the expression, "That's when the fat hit the fire." But in the evolution of the word phrase, "ham fat" has elevated this term to a more honored position.

I cite the significance of "ham" in Cracker lore with the story about the woman who went to get her husband out of jail, doing thirty-days for stealing a ham.

She asked the sheriff if he would let her husband out a little early.

He said, "Well, I guess you miss him."

She said, "No."

He said, "Well, I guess he's good to the kids."

She replied, "No, he ain't."

The sheriff said, "Well, if you all don't miss him and he ain't good to you or the kids, why do you want him out early.

She said, "We're out of ham."

(I heard this one from a man at our veterinary clinic who had told me that the $10 professional service fee seemed reasonable for the quality of jokes I was telling. He was from Tennessee, but the story sounds a lot like a Carl Hurley story. Dr. Hurley used to come to Okeechobee, visiting a friend of ours.)

Whut's good fer (*fill in the blank*)? the beginning of a question to a veterinarian, always ending with a subject of some sort. For example, "Doc? Whut's good fer ah snotty-nosed calf?" "Whut's good fer ah bad case of the scratches?" ("Scratches" generally is a term used for fly bite- or allergic dermatitis in the horse.)

Two examples stand out in my mind: Carlos Falla, my Cuban Cracker friend, once asked me, "Oward (Cuban for "Howard"), whut's good for keepin' a fella frum getting drunk? I need to do sumthing to drink Victor under the table—he always seems to out-do me at the parties."

I suggested he drink iced tea in a Scotch glass but that didn't suit him. I then said, "Well, why don't you try a big dose of some mineral oil? That might coat yer stomach and gut some and slow down the absorption of the alcohol. Not too much now—it'll give you the whistles." (See term)

A few days later, Carlos called to tell me it didn't work well. He said, "I drank a cup of olive oil before I went to Victor's house, jus' like you said. It dent seem to make any difference...."

"Carlos", I said, "I told you mineral oil!"

"Oh," he said. He then asked me, "Whut's good for diarrhea?"

I told him Nyquil, figurin' he'd use Pepto Bismol.

Dr. Handley had a Cracker fella ask him, "Doc? Whut's good fer stoppin' a cough? My chest is plum sore frum coughin'."

Handley immediately replied, "Drink a cup of mineral oil."

The cowboy responded, "Will that stop tha cough?"

Handley replied, "No—but you won't."

Whut happened? Man, that was quick! a rare question when one is confused and/or missed the action. Although I only remember one incidence where this was said by a Cracker; it was memorable. Let me start by saying people have some psychological resistance to medical things sometimes. We watch television and cinemas where people and animals are being violently decapitated, shot, knifed or sliced up with chain saws but somehow many are able to compartmentalize it, never associating it with real life trauma. I've seen children that have watched hours upon hours of bloody horror movies get really sick in the real world when their pet has been injured. If a veterinarian will tell the truth, many, if not all, have had queasiness or outright nausea at times–especially when they first started out in medicine. It is a natural reaction that has to be overcome in most people.

I recall a time when I had to remove an eye with a squamous cell carcinoma from a cow in Avon Park, Florida. Eye removals in cows were good surgeries if the cancer was not established in the bone around the diseased eye. The affected cow does very well after one cancerous eye is removed, whereas bulls get a little timid because they can't see well enough to fight other bulls.

So as the tale opens, I had two Crackers helping me one day in an eye removal on a fine mama cow. I made the initial incision and heard a soft "ka-flop" on the ground. The younger of the two men had passed out cold. We drug him to the shade, propped his feet up on a five-gallon bucket, crossed his legs at the ankles, laid his hat over his eyes, folded his hands on his belly, making it look like he was taking a nap. We then went back to the surgery. He came around as we finished and wasn't sure if he hadn't taken one fat nap. He said, "Whut happened? Man that wuz quick!" (Yeah, right. It was a good fifteen minutes off his meter.)

I got used to all kinds of unsavory and repulsive things. I could turn my repulsion switch "off" as I handled some pretty bad situations. I learned to use this tolerance for my purposes. Frank Handley told me once, "Sling stuff around so tha people won't crowd you while you're workin'."

Cracker Terms, Phrases And Definitions

I first tried this "scattering-nasty-substances-to-get-room-to-work" technique at a ranch where I had to open an abscess on a bull. All five of the owner's kids, the owner and two other men crowded over the fence to get a close-up look. I could hardly breathe for the enclosing crowd of on-lookers. I opened the abscess, which was under considerable pressure, and let it spray. The odor was noxious, almost knocking us over. After several audible "Ou-u-u-s" from the audience, I had a good ten-foot circle in which to work. In fact, that was the last time I was crowded by the kids. (I had another incident with a foul smelling situation. The cowboy helping me said, "Whew! Tha smell ain't too bad, Doc. It jus' burns' my eyes.")

Whutta you think? a typical Cracker question of a superior, the boss, or a knowledgeable or experienced person. In the pens one might hear, "That ol' cow looks bad. I guess we ought'a cut her out of tha herd and sell 'er. Whut do you think?" My experience with this question occurred with my step-father. I was nearly forty-years old when I began to think ahead for my family. I knew he had been very successful in managing money and investments. The conversation went something like this:

"Ya know, I'm near forty-years old now. I need to start thinkin' about savin' some money for Hunter and the kids. Maybe forty is too late to start. Whut do ya think?"

My step-father replied, "Boy, a fella cain't pee over a three-rail fence 'til he's forty...."

I continued, "Well, I know you've invested some over the years and have done okay. I was thinkin' about putting some money in some stock market mutual fund. Whutta you think?" (I was thinking he'd say General Motors, AT&T or Texas Instruments.)

He pondered the question, smiled a little and said, "I know how you could make 1000% on yer money."

My ears perked up. I said, "How?"

"Buy an' plant a dime's worth of turnip seed."

A similar phrase, "whut 'er your thoughts about (*fill in the blank*)," can be illustrated by the following: the son of a friend of mine asked his dad for advice about getting an engagement ring for his girl. He inquired, "Daddy, you know I'm gonna ask Josephine to marry me and I need to know what kind of diamond ring I should get her."

His Daddy thought a moment, and then said, "Well, Buddy, I'll tell ya. I'd go down to a reputable jeweler and buy the gaudiest fake diamond I could get–you know, one of them zirconiums. I'd pay a good bit to have it mounted in a nice setting. Make sure they put in one of their store's boxes. Now, that'll work."

The son asked, "Daddy? Whutter you thinkin' to get such a cheap diamond?"

Daddy replied, "Well, if she's happy, she'll be pleased as punch all 'er life. Her mama and daddy will like it and she'll show it to everyone. That'll be the end of it. If the marriage don't work, and y'all git a divorce, who cares? Yer only out a couple of hundred bucks..." (The names have been left out to protect the identity of the conspirators from the two mothers and the wife.)

Whut you reckon got into'im? said when an ordinarily quiet animal did a "dido" or "cut" or "pulled a shine" (see terms), usually early in the morning. While I was working at a ranch one day, Bill Murphy told me about an incident where the father-owner asked one of his sons if he could borrow the son's brand new truck, stating he wanted to go check some pasture. The boy said, "Sure. Gotoit."

Forty-five minutes later, he reappeared. The trim on the new truck, on both sides, stuck out like some kind of insect antennae, flapping in the sun as the truck bumped to a stop. Then, out loud to no one in particular, brother asked, "Whut you reckon go into'im?" meaning, "I wonder how he managed to tear up my new truck." (Daddy had misjudged the width of the pasture gates on the way out and snagged the truck's left trim. On the way back, he swung wide to make plenty room and raked off the right trim.) The funny thing to me was Bill said the crew just kept on working, not even slowing down to observe the situation. The incident didn't ruffle anyone's feathers. It was just another day in paradise.

Wooden take a million dollars for that man: the phrase comes from two incidents in my life: in a causal discussion with an Arkansas Cracker (who is now a cardiologist), he told about his childhood on the family farm. They also had an apple orchard. He talked about their neighbors–one couple in particular. The wife was the ramrod of their farm as the husband was slightly retarded. (As a friend once said, "He doesn't do deep.")

The outspoken wife directed the farm activities while the husband did the heavy work under her direct supervision. Bill said they came to the farm to pick up a few boxes of apples one fall. Their truck had a flatbed on it that was especially high. Well, Bertha told Jim to pick up those boxes and load 'em on the truck. So Jim obediently picks up the huge boxes full of apples and heaves them up on the flat bed with apparently no strain or effort. Bertha, with a proud smile on her face, looked over at the family. "I wooden take ah millyun dollers for that man."

I have used that phrase when someone performed an unexpected feat. It has lightened the atmosphere considerably and humorously catches people off guard. It has become ingrained in my comments, always lurking in the back hallways of my mind. I have repeated it to the point that my wife says it to on-lookers when I do some significant (or insignificant) feat (like take out the garbage or paint the porch). In fact, my wife recently used it in an incident. The story goes something like this:

We often buy fresh produce at a nursery near our home. On one occasion we purchased several items, including two huge watermelons. I was loading the car while my wife chatted with the owner's wife, Mrs. Henderson. She commented to my wife that I was pretty handy.

Hunter replied, "Yes, and he cooks, too."

I thought I'd be smart and hollered over my shoulder, "Yeah, an' I do my own laundry."

Mrs. Henderson looked at Hunter and said, "Whut'll you take for 'im?"

Hunter replied, "I wooden take a million dollars for that man." (Neither one of them laughed—but they both smirked. Did she mean I was a little slow? She won't say.)

Work-an-patch pens: referred to a set of cow pens where the crew worked awhile and then had to stop to repair the fences, boards or chutes. "Work-an-rebuild" pens is a synonymous phrase. I have worked at many such places. Out west they call them "rawhide outfits" or "pens," which means the boards, oil-well sucker rods or mesquite limbs were tied together with rawhide strips.

One of the longest days in my life occurred at Lemon Grove in Hardee County. There was a set of pens on a leased pasture where the two sons of a prominent Florida pioneer ran cattle. Wayne and Charles Bass were as tough as nails and didn't think it was a big deal, but these horned cattle were rank, wild Brahma crossbreds. (I doubt the Bass brothers even remember it.) There were only about eighty head in the rough pasture and the pens looked like they'd been abandoned for years. Polk weed and wild bushes were growing in the alleyways and traps. The first thing we had to do was stomp down the weeds to find the gates. Inside the fences some poor soul had nailed hog-wire fencing along the inside of the boards. One area had some old plywood nailed to the posts. The gates had raggedy cotton clothesline ropes for

Cracker Terms, Phrases And Definitions

tying them shut. The second thing we had to do was repair broken boards and cover-up the holes. One of the boys cut some cabbage fans and stuffed them in these places to hide the holes. (Cabbage Palm fans can be used for a variety of needs with varying degrees of success.)

When we finally did get around to working the cattle it was a real "site" (See term). The cows didn't go for it. Every one of them had to be man-handled into an alley-way toward an old chute we called a "man-killer." It took three men to run it. Heavy levers and side panels could sure ruin your day if you were hit by them. The catches didn't work well so a few of the cows got out and had to be roped and returned to the pens a second and third time. Wayne worked up front with me while Charles would bring'um in from the back. There were a couple of other fellas helping, too. Charles would get one cow started in the right direction, turn his back to the cow, hold onto the fence and literally push them in–one at a time. The cows' rumps would sometimes be a foot or so off the earth as they were pushed a gruntin' step-at-a-time. About half-way through, we ate lunch and rested. It must have been 90% humidity. I didn't complain but my jaw was getting tighter because I knew things were backing up on me at the hospital. I sure messed up on the scheduling; I'd told everyone at the office I'd be back in a couple of hours. It was a long day. But in retrospect, Wayne and Charles considered it just another day at the office. They fussed a little but not much; however, I did learn some new cuss words that day. Instead of the usual rate of 80 to 100 head an hour, I figured we ran them through the chute at an average of one every twenty-two minutes. Repairs were at a rate of one repair every other cow. But I sure did like Wayne and Charles. (See "Move ta Hardee County.")

Work: generally, activity with an organized approach; to expend effort in accomplishing something; to exert some motion toward restoration or refurbishing something and any associated activity toward achieving a finished product involving sweat. The Cracker definition is anything occurring after daylight until about nine o'clock in the evening, especially when it involves leaving the house above 75 degrees or below 55 degrees on the Fahrenheit scale of temperature determination.

One young fella told me once, "Me and my brother is drivin' our daddy nuts."

Of course, I was intrigued and asked what he meant.

He replied, "We hid his unemployment check under his work boots."

Workin' extra: to work additional hours. Though rarely used, the term was first utilized by a cook in the Arcadia area who had worked at the same café for years. Suddenly one day she quit her job there. When asked why she quit, she responded, "Well, I wuz workin' frum 6 am 'til 6 pm and they changed my hours to 8 'til 8 an' I wadden gonna be workin' no extra two hours for the same money!" (I think I know this woman.)

Workin' fer tha state: serving prison time. Speaking of workin' for the state, I recall a returned bill for emergency veterinary service. At the time, the statements were printed on an old copy system called a "thermofax copier." The actual client record of charges was copied and sent with the balance due. Well, this young cowboy never made any effort to pay on his account. Month after month we sent the same bill with the old "PAYMENT OVERDUE" stamp on it. Finally, the return envelope came in. We opened it and found the original thremofax with a hand-written note that said: "Mr. Sellers will not be paying this bill as he is in prison." Signed, "His Mama."

A tale that always inhabited a warm place in my heart was told to me many years ago by a close friend. It seems a man took his wife out to a fine restaurant for dinner on their twenty-fifth anniversary. Toward the end of the meal, during the after-dinner wine, he started blubbering like a devastated man of despair. His wife asked, "Honey, what's wrong? Are you okay?"

He said, "You remember the night I proposed to you on yer front porch?"

"Yes…" she cooed.

"Well, do you remember yer daddy came out to have a talk with me that night? Remember, when he was the Sheriff?"

"Yes, l do." Now her curiosity was piqued.

He continued amid sobs and nose-blowing, "I never told you what he said. (Pause) Your daddy said, 'Boy, I'm giving you a choice: either ya marry my daughter or I'll arrest ya and send ya to prison for twenty-five years or I'll shoot you down right her' on the porch an' say you attacked me. Whut'll it be?'"

His wife was moved by his admission and said, "Aw, Honey, he was kiddin' you. Why are you so upset?"

He blubbered and among the sobs replied, "I'da bin gettin' outta prison tomorrow."

Workin'on'um or workin'onme: means something has or will cause some action, reaction or a good, bad or serious outcome, such as, "Man! We got to git these cattle out of tha skeeters (mosquitoes)… ther' reely workin'on'um." Or, "When tha docter got through workin'onme I felt purty good." Another example, "Once I got tha first bowl of his chili down it started workin'onme." It can be used in past tense, as in, "Once he thought about how he lied to her, it got ta workin'on'im."

"Did a number on 'im," is similar in meaning.

Worried sic: a term used when properly prefaced, to indicate relief, express pleasure at someone or something when it is finished, over or completed; as my mother often said, "Where hav' y'all been! I wuz worried sic!" Her use of this phrase was idiosyncratic, never achieving a cult status among her sayings; it expressed her concern, anticipation, fears, relief, and contentment. The context was always related to our being late in arriving from an extended trip or as short an interval as being only 30 minutes late for a meal. Tardiness for important appointments could elicit her saying this as well. If Paw had an appointment, got stuck in the Jeep or had some little ranch crisis, arriving late for departure, she'd meet him at the door, saying it as he eased out of the Jeep.

My wife and I were living in Texas when Madeleine was born and we drove to Florida for Christmas that year. On the way we ran out of diapers and stopped to get some, but all we could find were Curity Medicated Diapers, to which (we found out on that thirteen-hour trip) she was severely allergic. Its being holiday time, we couldn't find a room anywhere OR a store that sold cloth diapers. It took us a couple of hours to discover her problem; by then we were all suffering the effects of that red bottom. Even the diaper rash cream was ineffective.

I admit to pure desperation. I remembered the old "sugar-teat" Kentuckians told about for colicked babies. So we opened our gift bottle of "Dry Sack", added a teaspoon to Madeleine's formula to calm her–and us.

Have you ever tried to get good whiskey in the dry county of Eufaula, Alabama, at nine o'clock on a Thursday night? What do you ask for? "Sir, do y'all have any good Kentucky Bourbon... I need a teaspoonful to make a sugar-teat." (Forget it.) But I knew that half of all Kentuckian's would have died in infancy if sugar teats hurt babies. Madeleine slept well, bare-bottomed, for a blessedly quiet few hours, while I drove, staring at the road through bloodshot eyes.

Upon our 4:00 a.m. arrival, Mama came down to the garage to let us in. Hunter handed Madeleine to her and burst into tears. Reeda, accepting her, said, "Wher' have y'all bin–I wuz worried sic." (We weren't expected until the next afternoon, but she said it nonetheless.) My stepfather, whom we called "Paw", cracked the upstairs bedroom window, "Y'all're gonna hav' to pay for a full night!" Those blessedly familiar phrases woke us up from our nightmare. It's amazing how just the sound of Mom and Dad's voices brings everything into focus.

In practice, I used this phrase when my partner, John Young, came in late from a large animal call. He came in with indescribable substances on his coveralls, haggard, dehydrated and exhausted from some ordeal. It got so that, when I'd say, "Wher' hav' you bin?" he'd retort, "Hav' you bin worried sick about me?"

Y

Ya sounded lik' a sow makin' a nest: This phrase has no meaning for those who have never watched a sow very close to her "due date." They exhibit some pre-labor signs where they are restless and focused on preparing for birth. Sows instinctively exhibit this behavior. Piglets are extremely susceptible to cold and it is a major cause of neonatal death. In Cracker culture, any rustling, banging around, rearranging, rooting or shuffling out of the speaker's sight could elicit this comment: "Boy, whut are you doin? You sound lik' a sow makin' a nest."

Yaunt to? This is a simple phrase that can be used either as a question or a suggestion. For example, "Les go... yaunt to?" when translated means, "We are leaving for (*a particular destination or event*). Do you want to go, as well?" The other use was a very relaxed order. I was first exposed to it when I was working as a big-footed boy (see term) in Okeechobee. Sonny would often preface plans or orders to us, as in, "If y'all want to, we need the cows in the south marsh brought to tha pens..." He has been known to say variations, as in, "I'm flyin' up to Kissimmee, you can go if yaunt to..." or "I'm goin' to town, yaunt tah go?" The last time I heard the phrase was at a neurologist's office in Bristol, Tennessee. Dr. Jimmy Brasfield asked a patient, "Let's go look at yer x-rays... yaunt to?" (Jeff Foxworthy was the first I've heard say, "Who said Southern doctors cain't communicate good?" (Can't you picture his description of a brain operation?) "Well, let's see here... the first thing we gotta do is open up yer punkin and takeah look around. If we find sumthin' that don't look rite, we'll take 'er out and put in sum new parts. Then we'll put ever' thing back together. We'll be gathered up an' ready to roll the furst thing in tha mornin'. Be here at 7:00... if yaunt to....")

Yawl laff, yah krathie hun-thah-hithees: As far as I know there is only one documented use of the phrase. The best way to pronounce it is to take a dry paper towel or tissue, grab the tip of your tongue and say, "Y'all laugh, you crazy sonsah (*expletive deleted*). The context is from my being injured in the cow pens.

The worst I ever got hurt was by a puny little one or two day-old Brahman calf. She couldn't have weighed more than forty-five pounds, still wet behind the ears. Her navel had just dried. We had run the calves through the main chute to sort them from their mamas. The little, long-eared whelp kinda' stumbled through, but was soon left behind. All the rank ones had already left the area. She walked into the chute, half confused by the activity. The man behind the catch chute spooked her but she didn't respond. So, being a brazen young lad, I walked into the chute to grab her long ears to pull her out. As I leaned over to go into the chute, something spooked her; she bolted forward like a load of buckshot and butted me in the chin. It was not a killing blow, but it was precise. My tongue was between my right side jaw teeth (Don't ask how that happened—I don't know) and I bit the whole right side of my tongue–nearly all the way through. All I think the crew saw was my wallowing around in front of the chute. I was knocked silly, i.e., silly-butted, at 4:00 in the afternoon, with no juke joint in sight.

Now if that wasn't bad enough, the next few days were utter misery. I couldn't sleep, eat, chew, move my mouth or talk.

Cracker Terms, Phrases And Definitions

I managed to get some soup and water down but it hurt like all get out–couldn't even swallow an aspirin.

My stepbrother, Sonny, didn't comment for a few days and then, in front of several men, remarked, "I been thinkin'. It has been such a pleasure to work with you while you can't talk. I suggested to Daddy that we have all the men bite their tongues so we could git more work an' less talkin' done around here, but he didn't think the men would go for it."

I looked at him with sunken, haggard eyes, miserably trying to mouth the proper curse words back to him and the laughing audience. It came out as, "Yawl laff, yah krathie hun-thah-hithees!" As far as I can determine this is the first recorded use of the phrase in that tongue-sore approach—not to say that it hasn't been said frequently in a clear strong manner.

Y'all: (I will waste no time on this one – y'all know what it means.)

Y'all go on and hav' fun, I'll be here: an unconscious phrase used by my partner, Frank Handley. Sometimes we'd work non-stop for weeks at a time with little break. I remember the first time I heard Frank respond to my request for a Friday off from work to take the family to the beach for the weekend. He automatically replied, "Y'all go on... have fun... I'll be here... I handled it (i.e., the practice) seventeen years before you got here... I can handle without you... have fun.... " (I remember feeling my esteem deflating—especially since I had hung in there keeping the same pace. He didn't mean anything by it. It was the Frank who'd worked seven days a week for seventeen years before I got there. One could say it was "Ah-Handley.")

Y'all wanna go crank up sum fish? a question that has long ago lost its significance to people under seventy-years old. It is related to the old crank up phone in the early decades of the 1900's. You may have read of the old party lines where nothing was private. Your phone had a special number of rings in some cases. For example, one party could be the assigned four rings as their phone in one's residence. The party line certainly cramped the life of young love. It is said that nothing was private when the neighbors listened in. Soft clicks could occasionally be heard as the listeners lost interest in your conversations. I remember party lines and I am not that old, but the crank up phones were before my time. One would crank the handle to run a current down the line for an operator who would dutifully connect you to "Evergreen-4-3473" or some such designation. The first two letters of the word were corresponding to the number on the dial; i.e., "E" was the "3" on the dial and "V" corresponded with the "8." So, "Evergreen" meant the first two numbers were "38."

But the original question is based on the use of an old crank phone in fishing. If someone had access to a disconnected crank phone, they could run a wire off the generator, drop it into the water, crank and stunned fish would float to the top of the water. Fish biologists and others associated with surveying fish populations or the elimination of invasive alien species of fish still use electrical current to stun fish to the surface. If left alone, the fish will recover. In Cracker culture, when it was used, the fish ended up in a fry pan. Therefore, "crankin' up fish" was an unfair and illegal (albeit effective) means of fishing for supper.

Yeah: Affirmative. Sometimes it almost sounds like "yowh." The classic example was one time when a trooper stopped a Cracker and asked to see his license and registration. Then he asked the Cracker, "Sir, do you have any weapons in your vehicle?" The man replied, "Yeah, whut do ya need?"

Yer makin' ah big mistake: a phrase used by Sonny, my step-brother, upon leaving a taxidermist's shop in Canada. We were located on the eastern slope of the Canadian Rockies at the end of an elk and deer hunt. A few of us had been fotunate enough to shoot an elk. And we'd taken the meat in for processing and shipment back to Florida. We visited the taxidermist to make arrangements for mounting our trophies.

Cracker Terms, Phrases And Definitions

The man explained what he would do and suggested that the horns be fixed for removal for shipping, thus needing a smaller shipping crate. I liked the idea so I said that's what I wanted. We decided to have all crates shipped to Emory Walker's business address in Okeechobee, since it was central to us all. As we left the building, Sonny said, "Howard, I think yer makin' a big mistake. You know they could send the wrong horns on yer elk." I said, "I'm not worried about it." Well, sure enough, about six weeks later, Emory's office worker called and said I could pick up the crate anytime. I went by his shop and loaded the crate in a truck. When I got the crate home, I opened it with anticipation. As Sonny had warned me, there was a beautiful shoulder-mounted elk with the knottiest, most unsightly, genetically abnormal, under-sized set of horns wrapped around the neck inside the crate. They were prepared to perfectly insert on the elk, but they were horrible. I laughed out loud when I saw them. I knew I'd been had. The remarkable thing was the taxidermist had spent time in making them so they would fit on the elk. Well, not to be undone by Emory and cohorts, I asked Gail, my secretary, to call Emory's office and raise sand.

She called, as I listened in, and said, "This is Wanda at Kennesaw Taxidermy in Canada. We have just had a call from a Doctor Jones in Florida. He claims we sent the wrong horns for his elk mount and he's demanding his money back."

"Uh-h-h-h," replied Emory's office manager.

Gail continued,"I personally packed the crate and I know we did not make a mistake. Do you know anything about this matter? He's quite upset. We have never…"

The man interrupted and hurriedly replied, "Look, Ma'am, it's a joke—we switched horns when it arrived; we're jus havin' a little fun."

I laughed on the phone and they then knew they had been caught flat-footed (See term). We had a good time reliving this "mistake." (In retrospect, I thought Sonny was correct as the crew did stay a little longer than necessary in the shop. They were laying plans… and the taxidermist was culpable.)

Yow-yowin': a "yow-yow" is a call, loud disturbance, a vocalization, a holler, shout, bark or cry. The manner in which it could be used is, "I heard y'all yow-yowin' over ther';" meaning the speaker heard some people talking. "Whut's all tha yow-yow about?" means "What are you arguing or disagreeing about?" "The dogs went to yow-yowin' right after we got ther'." Another use could be, "Well, the lawyers got to yow-yowin' about this an' that an' we just left 'um to it."

Z

Zoo-zoos: gnats, midges or "no-see-ums." At times the gnats would swarm so bad that you had to keep your mouth shut or breathe through your teeth for fear of swallowing some, much the same way you'd have to use your teeth as a strainer when drinking pond water with debris or mosquito larvae in it. One might hear, "Them zoo-zoos lik' to hav' eat us up in the marsh."

Partner Sills would often vividly describe, with graphic swallowing demonstrations, how it felt to swallow gnats and mosquitoes and how they would try to crawl back up his "gullet." He allowed that he was tempted to try to "swaller" a green tree frog or a gold fish to see what it felt like, but said he couldn't work up the notion. (See "gullet" and "galla-nippers")

The only one I know of that admitted swallowing green tree frogs said, "If yu'll drop him intah ice water first, he'll stiffen up enuff so you can git 'im down. I won $15 one nite 'til the boys figured out how I wuz doin' it."

(Technically, I think this was "DFUI", Drinking Frogs Under the Influence, and I suppose it would be likely to have a citation for DUI and DFUI.)

Afterthought

By no means is this an exhaustive study; I know someone will think of some terms or phrases I've forgotten. I will have to tightenup an' take a holt to improve these definitions a mite, when I have the time, git arountuit and feel like runninitdown. Rite now, I feel a little wall-eyed puny–like an older'n dirt nightcrawler with his guts slung out. Rite this minute, I 'spect I'll go cut a cabbage. If I do a good job at it, someone will say, "Well, I wish y'all'd look at that!" Well, dodge the Yankees. I bin ta two county fairs an' a goat ropin' and I ain't never wrote nothin' like this before, but I hope itsah ahgoodun... Shaugh, y'all ain't nuthin!' See ya....

Instead of "The End," I prefer what my smiling friend Partner Sills occasionally said when we completed a tedious job:

"Well, that's been did away with...."

About the Author

Howard Selby Jones, Jr was born in Henderson, Kentucky, and moved to south Florida during his teen years. He was introduced to the Cracker culture on the Williamson Ranch in Okeechobee, Florida. After two years at the University of Florida, he was accepted at Auburn University School of Veterinary Medicine where he gained his Doctorate of Veterinary Medicine. Following a stint in the Veterinary Corps in the United States Air Force and five years in a large/small animal partnership in Sebring, Florida, his teacher's heart brought him back to Auburn where he completed a two-year Dairy Medicine and Surgery Residency while earning his PhD in Ruminant Nutrition in the Department of Animal Sciences. After one year as the Dairy Extension Specialist for the Alabama Cooperative Extension Service, he returned to Sebring and purchased his former practice. For a total of more than twenty-four years, he covered over a fifty mile practice radius including Highlands, Polk, Hardee and Okeechobee Counties in the heart of his beloved Cracker cattle country. Now retired, Dr. Jones lives in the Blue Ridge Mountains of Western North Carolina with his wife of forty-five years.

Made in the USA
San Bernardino, CA
08 December 2013